Contributions to Economics

The series *Contributions to Economics* provides an outlet for innovative research in all areas of economics. Books published in the series are primarily monographs and multiple author works that present new research results on a clearly defined topic, but contributed volumes and conference proceedings are also considered. All books are published in print and ebook and disseminated and promoted globally. The series and the volumes published in it are indexed by Scopus and ISI (selected volumes).

Carlos Larrinaga • Donatella Strangio
Editors

Tourism Destinations and Policies in Europe During the 20th Century

Evolution, Strategies and Markets

Springer

Editors
Carlos Larrinaga
Department of Economic Theory and
Economic History
University of Granada
Granada, Spain

Donatella Strangio
Department Methods and Models for
Economics Territory Finance (MEMOTEF)
Sapienza University of Rome
Rome, Italy

ISSN 1431-1933 ISSN 2197-7178 (electronic)
Contributions to Economics
ISBN 978-3-031-88446-7 ISBN 978-3-031-88447-4 (eBook)
https://doi.org/10.1007/978-3-031-88447-4

This Springer imprint is published by the registered company Springer Nature Switzerland AG
The registered company address is: Gewerbestrasse 11, 6330 Cham, Switzerland

Contents

Contributors

Annunziata Berrino University of Naples Federico II, Naples, Italy

Aleksandra Brezovec Faculty of Tourism Studies, University of Primorska, Koper, Slovenia

Tomi Brezovec Faculty of Tourism Studies, University of Primorska, Koper, Slovenia

Yves-Marie Evanno Catholic University of the Western, South Brittany, UCO-BS, Arradon, France

Steve Hagimont Laboratoire des sciences sociales du politique (LaSSP), Institut d'études politiques de Toulouse, Toulouse, France

Víctor M. Heredia-Flores Department of Economic Theory and Economic History, University of Malaga, Málaga, Spain

Petra Kavrečič Boževlav University of Primorska, Koper/Capodistria, Slovenia

Carlos Larrinaga Department of Economic Theory and Economic History, University of Granada, Granada, Spain

Marta Luque-Aranda Department of Economic Theory and Economic History, University of Malaga, Málaga, Spain

Donatella Strangio Department Methods and Models for Economics Territory Finance (MEMOTEF), Sapienza University of Rome, Rome, Italy

Metod Šuligoj University of Primorska, Koper/Capodistria, Slovenia

Laurent Tissot University of Neuchâtel, Neuenburg, Switzerland

Neuchâtel, Switzerland

Johan Vincent ESTHUA, University of Angers, Angers, France

List of Figures

List of Tables

Chapter 1
Introduction

Carlos Larrinaga and Donatella Strangio

Abstract This book analyzes key aspects of European tourism development in the twentieth century, focusing for this on the development of tourist destinations, as well as tourism policies that were created to shape these destinations. The book also examines the private sector, which has traditionally played a determining role in European tourism development. While doing so, this volume presents case studies of Western European and Eastern European countries, such as Switzerland, Italy, France, Spain and Yugoslavia.

The aim of the book is to analyze, from a comparative perspective, important aspects of European tourism development in the twentieth century, focusing on the configuration of certain tourist destinations, especially before the emergence of mass tourism, and on the policies implemented by the administration to shape those destinations, while also taking into account the impact of the private sector, which has traditionally played a decisive role in the development of European tourism.

The red thread running through the individual contents, organized chronologically and from the general to the particular of the cases examined, is the way in which the state, localities, or regions have dealt with moments of crisis or break at an economic and social level, such as wars, financial shortages, and how these have been a turning point for strengthening, improving, or changing or "inventing a tourist destination" through tourism destination policies, adapting, or being resilient to the transformations of the time.

PID2021-122476NB-I00 research project, financed by MICIU/AEI /10.13039/501100011033/ and by ERDF UE.

C. Larrinaga
Department of Economic Theory and Economic History, University of Granada, Granada, Spain

D. Strangio (✉)
Department Methods and Models for Economics Territory Finance (MEMOTEF), Sapienza University of Rome, Rome, Italy
e-mail: donatella.strangio@uniroma1.it

C. Larrinaga, D. Strangio (eds.), *Tourism Destinations and Policies in Europe During the 20th Century*, Contributions to Economics,
https://doi.org/10.1007/978-3-031-88447-4_1

This perspective has not been the subject of specific books, so this book differs from the previous publications on Europe as Battilani (2001), *Vacanze di pochi, vacanze di tutti* or Segreto et al. *Europe at the seaside* (2009), or Battilani and Larrinaga, *Coastal Tourism in Southern Europe in the XXth century* (2021) and from others that dealt with comparative cases between Italy and Spain such as the pioneering Barciela et al. (2011), *La evolución de la industria turística en España e Italia* or Larrinaga and Strangio (2022) or Battilani and Strangio (2007) on tourism and cities.

It also stands out from the series of volumes that have delved into certain aspects of tourism but at a global level such as the *Handbook on Tourism*, edited by Robin Nunkoo et al. (2022), or *Tourism Economics* (2015) edited by Metin Kozak together with Nazmi Kozak that examines the economics of tourism in detail, providing a series of specific case studies of tourism operations in various countries around the world. The contributions in this volume come from a variety of locations, with ten countries represented on four continents: Canada, China, Greece, India, Iran, Poland, Portugal, South Africa, Spain, and the United States. It differs from *Tourist Behaviour* (2016b), also edited by Metin Kozak together with Nazmi Kozak, which provides a collection of arguments from both theoretical and practical approaches to construct and examine the theory of how consumers think and act in the context of tourism consumption. And it is different from Tissot's (2003) *Construction of a Tourism industry,* or the one on *Destination Marketing* (2016a) edited by Metin Kozak together with Nazmi Kozak that advances the current literature on destination marketing using innovative and up-to-date case studies from a wide geographical representation. The contributions examine the new marketing methods and approaches used in the sector through a combination of theoretical and practical approaches and not from an economic point of view and above all as a response to economic crises and the inevitable long-term transformations of the economic system in general with particular reference to Europe.

One of the main original features of this volume is to analyze some of the most representative cases from Western Europe, such as Switzerland, Italy, France and Spain, and from Eastern Europe, such as the former Yugoslavia, a country that played a key role in the development of tourism in the central Mediterranean.

In this regard, the book delves into the qualitative aspects of the connections existing between private agents, state administration and the policies implemented by the latter when it comes to shaping a tourist destination. At the same time, the book's main contributions would remain in the chronology, having opted for the long term; in the variety of case studies, all undoubtedly representative of the tourist expansion experienced by Europe in the twentieth century; and the inclusion of Eastern Europe, when it is often left out in this type of book.

This is why we have managed to bring together some internationally renowned tourism historians and specialists in the volume. Moreover, we think that, first and foremost, tourism historians, but also economic and business historians, will appreciate the book's originality and the intellectual contribution that underpins it.

Even today, based on the lessons learnt from these case studies, with the right policies, the tourism sector can play an important role in the global economic recovery, as the post-COVID-19 has shown us, provided that a sustainable business environment is created and the jobs created are decent and support social and economic progress.

Tourism is one of the most important aspects of the world economy right now. With distant antecedents in the eighteenth and nineteenth centuries, modern tourism, born in the transition from the nineteenth to the twentieth century, became an industry that eventually not only played a decisive role in the modernization of the societies concerned, but also in its own economic growth, with an increasing impact on its GDP. Before the COVID-19 crisis, of which we are almost losing track, the sector accounted for one in ten jobs worldwide and around 10% of global GDP, figures that have been restored after the pandemic emergency.

From an activity initially limited to minority elites, with the passage of time, and especially after the Second World War, ever wider strata of society began to participate in tourism. So we can speak of two very clear dimensions, namely: on the one hand, the social one, due to the changes it brought with it, and on the other, in economic. Precisely, in this book we want to insist on the economic aspect of tourism; specifically, its evolution in Europe throughout the twentieth century, focusing on such outstanding aspects as the creation of companies linked to tourism, the territorial policies set by the administration, the consolidation of international tourist markets, the rise of coastal tourism, or the environmental problems derived from tourism in fragile environments, for example.

Specifically, we have taken these studies from the general to the particular: starting with four contributions highlighting the role of the administration's policies in strengthening the tourism sector by adapting it to the transformations and necessary evolutions of tourist destinations in the face of changes resulting from critical or otherwise "breaking" events such as the Second World War, the collapse of the Berlin Wall, the Golden Age, the Euro. The objective is to present the different strategies implemented by the tourism authorities of these countries during the different periods of the twentieth century, and it seemed interesting to highlight the different attitudes of the administration in the long term by examining in comparative terms four cases that examine particular aspects but relating to the country as a whole: thus France, as a first mover in this sector, Switzerland, in the heart of Europe, Spain, as a fast mover, and Yugoslavia as an emblematic case of Eastern Europe. We then examine these cases from a micro perspective to appreciate the transformations of the "destination" in the face of crises or changes brought about by important caesuras such as the First World War (the case of France and Italy) or the creation of destinations such as Spain on the Costa del Sol, and a second case, after the war, devoted to a destination in the former Yugoslavia, Piran-Pirano, transformed into a major Eastern European tourist destination.

Through the very case studies in this volume, it is interesting to note the transformations taking place in first-mover countries in this field, such as France, examined over the long term by Steve Hagimont in the chapter *Tourism and Nature Conservation in the French Mountains: A Tumultuous Arranged Marriage (1890–1980)*. We wanted to start from this study in order to define this red thread that also connects with the contemporary in a sort of web that links two temporal extremes, in this case determined by the environment, the great challenge of recent years, which however finds its roots precisely in the twentieth century, and in one of the countries considered to be prime movers in the tourism sector. Hagimont asks why tourism and nature conservation came together in the twentieth century. He shows that shared concerns about the rise of tourism can be observed from the beginning of the century, but that at the same time tourism appears as a bulwark against hydroelectric development, seen as predatory. Tourism was theorized as a way of remunerating the protection of nature, which became an economic resource. Tourism can protect and develop, but always threatens to destroy. It is a kind of pharmakon. Hagimont also shows that tourism was a response to the feeling of dispossession engendered by protection. He invites us to retrace the chronology of the social, economic, and ecological reflections that gave rise to sustainable tourism. According to Laurent Tissot (*Switzerland: A New Playground for Tourism in the Twentieth Century?*), Switzerland was a pioneer in the development of tourism in the nineteenth century, but its development in the following century is mixed. Forced to abandon certain strategies that made it successful due to changes in the economy (crises) and in the political situation (wars), faced with an increasingly competitive international market, it adopts new institutional, technical, and financial tools that gradually transform all aspects of the tourism sector. While the winter season is becoming predominant in the tourist calendar, more attention is also being paid to the cultural and historical diversity of the country. This has led to a change in the hotel stock, with new buildings attracting a socially and internationally diverse clientele. But more importantly, the intervention of the central government not only makes it possible to find ways of reducing the burden of debt, but also to solicit new financial resources to renovate infrastructures, many of which have become outdated. Carlos Larrinaga analyzes the case of Spain (*Public Policies and Tourism Development in Spain in the First Third of the 20th Century*), as pointed out, a case of a fast mover. According to the author, in the configuration of tourism systems, the Administration constitutes an agent of special importance, together with the private actors themselves. For this reason, this chapter intends to analyze which were the official national agencies of Spanish tourism, studying the tourism policies they carried out, as well as the degree of satisfaction that these policies generated in the aforementioned private actors. To do so, the authors start from the hypothesis that these policies were not really satisfactory and that, at the time when Spain was engulfed in the birth of modern tourism, with the birth of the first Spanish tourism system, private actors had fewer opportunities than the State could provide. On the other hand, Tomi Brezovec and Aleksandra Brezovec (*Tourism policies in post-WWII Yugoslavia*) highlight how the central planning of economic activity was characteristic of the socialist states that emerged in Eastern Europe after the Second World War. The nationalization of enterprises and state ownership of the means of industrial production and agriculture were accompanied by a series of 5-year plans with which the socialist governments in Eastern Europe directed the economic development of their countries. Yugoslavia, which is neither a free market economy nor a member of the Soviet-controlled Eastern bloc, has developed its own economic model. Although the state followed the socialist model of nationalization of industry and central planning, the Yugoslav economic system was less rigid than in other Eastern European countries. Although the country maintained economic relations with the countries of the Eastern Bloc, the Yugoslav economy was heavily dependent on Western markets. In the 5-year plans introduced in 1947, tourism was always addressed in some way. However, the importance given to tourism has changed over time. In the first 5-year plan, tourism was viewed primarily from the perspective of the Yugoslav working class as a tool for the regeneration and recreation of workers, who were considered the cornerstone of society. This view changed when tourism was recognized as a potential foreign exchange earner. In the 1960s and early 1970s, 5-year plans allocated large funds for investment in new tourism infrastructure, mainly built on the Adriatic coast. These investments were targeting the growing tourist demand from Western European markets. Within a few years, the share of foreign visitors in the Yugoslavian tourism market doubled. Tourism soon became a key contributor to country's balance of payments. In the 1980s, the consolidation of the country's stagnating economy required large sums of foreign currency. This put pressure on tourism, which continued to rely on mass tourism without making new investments. With the emergence of new competition on the global tourism markets (e.g., Southeast Asia and southern Mediterranean countries), Yugoslavia's tourism offer began to lose its attractiveness. In the last years of the decade, tourism demand began to decline and collapsed completely in 1991 with the break-up of Yugoslavia.

In the fifth chapter, Annunziata Barrino (*The First World War and the Crisis of International Investment in Tourism in Italy*), studies the Italian case. In her opinion, in the history of tourism in Italy, the First World War represented a moment of profound transformations in the structure of investments in tourist services and accommodation. After the national unification and the proclamation of the Kingdom of Italy (1861), the Italian peninsula, already very attractive for European and American tourists, had also become more accessible and interesting for foreign investors, who actively participated in the expansive and liberal phase of the early twentieth century. The outbreak of the First World War interrupted many economic circuits and cultural and professional relationships. So, this chapter seeks to analyze two important phenomena. The first is the interruption of the flow of foreign capital—Swiss, French and Belgian—invested in the grand hotels of the cities of art and spa towns in Italy. And the second is the political effects generated from disorder and difficult to manage hotel sector during the postwar economic crisis.

Yves-Marie Evanno and Johan Vincent (*French perspectives of the genesis of a new international tourism in the interwar period*) also address the subject of the tourism sector by looking at the First World War and the financial crisis that devastated national public finances in Europe. Even before the end of the conflict, the belligerent states realize that tourism is one of the few economic activities capable of quickly repatriate the gold spent for almost 5 years. In France, to attract international tourists, the government thus decides to promote memorial tourism of the Great War while continuing to promote the picturesque sites which had forged its fame in the past. But the success of such an enterprise was impossible without a favorable context. Tourism, which had benefited from nationalist perspectives to organize itself during the nineteenth century, became a national economic actor. In the 1920s, the country took advantage of the weakness of the franc against other foreign currencies (in particular the pound sterling and the US dollar) to attract foreign customers. While continuing to develop its national clientele (with the progressive diffusion of paid vacation), France was becoming tourist. If the economic crisis of 1929 suddenly changed the outlook by favoring a nationalist withdrawal, including in the field of tourism, the development of international tourism did not stop entirely. In fact, it is encouraged by international structures. The conditions are now ripe for the emergence of a new international tourism which will not materialize after the Second World War.

In the case referred to Spain, the fast follower in this field, Marta Luque and Víctor M. Heredia (*Costa del Sol. Tourism and business in the configuration of a touristic area in Spain*) analyze the emergence of a tourist destination that, over time, has become very popular, the Costa del Sol. In fact, during the first third of the twentieth century, before the Spanish Civil War, the Mediterranean coast of Andalusia specialized in tourism. The area around the city of Malaga, known as Costa del Sol, in Spain, evolved from an initial vocation of receiving minority tourism of Anglo-Saxon origin, which sought warm weather, to a clear specialization in mass tourism from Europe and based on the sun and beach segment, which occupied a large part of the active population. This chapter analyzes the stages of this process and the creation of specific infrastructures such as hotels, golf courses, airport and other services.

The chapter of Metod Šuligoj and Petra Kavrečič (*Implementation of the Yugoslav socialist accommodation sector model in the Municipality of Piran—Pirano*) is interesting and original compared to the more established European cases. They have formulated an innovative model of the accommodation sector, modeled and implemented by the socialist Yugoslavia in the Municipality of Piran-Pirano in the Upper Adriatic. The model illuminates the internal incongruities within the Yugoslav socialist framework. Accommodations were provided to the privileged political and economic elite as well as less price-sensitive, discerning international tourists (e.g., good hotels, private second homes, campsites in the Adriatic/Mediterranean environment). Simultaneously, accommodation was offered to the domestic working class, offering holiday options despite their lower economic status and disadvantages (e.g., holiday homes, cheap campsites). Employing a modeling technique often overlooked in tourism history studies, the research illustrates a unique amalgamation of Western and socialist holidaying (accommodating) practices and provides a narrative elucidation of this phenomenon.

The variety of cases studied in this book clearly reflects the different types of tourism that developed during the twentieth century in Europe, contributing not only to economic progress, but also as a response to the social transformation of those societies.

References

Barciela C, Manera C, Molina R, Di Vittorio A (eds) (2011) La evolución de la industria turística en España e Italia. Institut Balear d'Economía, Palma de Mallorca

Battilani P (2001) Vacanze di pochi, vacanze di tutti. L'evoluzione del turismo europeo. Il Mulino, Bologna

Battilani P, Larrinaga C (eds) (2021) Coastal Tourism in Southern Europe in the XXth century. New economy and material culture. Peter Lang, Berlin

Battilani P, Strangio D (eds) (2007) Il turismo e le città tra XVIII e XXI secolo. Italia e Spagna a confront. FrancoAngeli, Milano

Kozak M, Kozak N (2015) Tourism economics: A practical perspective. Cambridge Scholars Publishing, London

Kozak M, Kozak N (2016a) Destination marketing: An international perspective. Routledge, London

Kozak M, Kozak N (2016b) Tourist behaviour: An international perspective. CABI, Wallingford

Larrinaga C, Strangio D (eds) (2022) El Turismo en España antes del boom turístico. Sílex, Madrid

Nunkoo R, Wen J, Kozak M (2022) Handbook on tourism, public health and wellbeing. Research handbooks in tourism series. Edward Elgar, Northampton, MA

Segreto L, Manera C, Pohl M (eds) (2009) Europe at the seaside. The economic history of mass tourism in the Mediterranean. Berghahn Books, Oxford

Tissot L (ed) (2003) Construction of a Tourism industry in the 19th and 20th century. International perspective. Alphil, Neuchatel

Carlos Larrinaga is Full Professor of Economic History at the University of Granada (Andalusia, Spain). He is the Main Researcher of the project "Tourism in Spain in the first third of the twentieth century. Characteristics and evolution of an economic activity and a social practice in comparative perspective", funded by the Government of Spain and ERDF.

Donatella Strangio is Full professor of Economic History and Director Department of methods and models for economics territory finance, Sapienza University of Rome. She has published several books and among them for Springer: (2020), Italy and China Trade Relations. A Historical perspective, Studies in Economic History, Springer Palgrave; (2012) The Reasons for Underdevelopment. The Case of Decolonisation in Somaliland, Physica-Verlag, A Springer Company, Contributions to Economics. For Palgrave: with Carlos Larrinaga (2023).The Development of the Hotel and Tourism Industry in the Twentieth Century Comparative Perspectives from Western Europe, 1900–1970. London: Palgrave Studies in Economic History.

Chapter 2
Tourism and Nature Conservation in the French Mountains: A Tumultuous Arranged Marriage (1890–1980)

Steve Hagimont

Abstract Hagimont asks why tourism and nature conservation came together in the twentieth century. He shows that shared concerns about the rise of tourism can be observed from the beginning of the century, but that at the same time tourism appears as a bulwark against hydroelectric development, seen as predatory. Tourism was theorized as a way of remunerating the protection of nature, which became an economic resource. Tourism can protect and develop, but it always threatens to destroy. It is a kind of pharmakon. Hagimont also shows that tourism was a response to the feeling of dispossession engendered by protection. He invites us to retrace the chronology of the social, economic and ecological reflections that gave rise to sustainable tourism.

Introduction

With global warming and the biodiversity crisis, the tourism economy, which today accounts for over 8% of greenhouse gas emissions, 11% in France (Lenzen et al. 2018; Ademe 2021), is facing radical criticism. Calls for public policies committed to more sustainable tourism are in fact reminiscent of older discussions, which this chapter intends to explore in the long twentieth century in the French mountains.

Tourism has long been criticized. The tourist is a figure disparaged as soon as it appears explicitly in the early nineteenth century (Urbain 2002). Tourism is also criticized for its cultural and social effects: it is said to distort the mores of host communities, and to give them the lure of gain, which falsify encounters (Anderson 2016). The question of the effects of tourism on nature has yet to be fully explored

S. Hagimont (✉)
Laboratoire des sciences sociales du politique (LaSSP), Institut d'études politiques de Toulouse, Toulouse, France
e-mail: steve.hagimont@sciencespo-toulouse.fr

C. Larrinaga, D. Strangio (eds.), *Tourism Destinations and Policies in Europe During the 20th Century*, Contributions to Economics,
https://doi.org/10.1007/978-3-031-88447-4_2

by historiography. This denunciation was spotted in literature at the heart of the nineteenth century: the writer William Wordsworth writing around 1840 against the arrival of the railroad in the British Lake District (Mathis 2012), the art critic John Ruskin lamenting in 1865 the commercial assault on the mountains by the railroads (Nifosi 2021), the geographer Elisée Reclus, who in 1866 produced a comprehensive critique of the effects on landscapes of the urban quest for nature (Reclus 1866), and the historian Jules Michelet, who in 1868 denounced the effects of hunting tourism and excursions on Alpine fauna (Plas 2020). At the same time, the development of tourism, particularly in the mountains, was based on a quest to escape the evils of progress. The rise of tourism in the nineteenth century results in fact in the multiplication of places of refuge from the tumult of societies in turmoil. These artificial places exploit a need for nature that was more or less primitive and wild, in complete safety. They bear witness to the ambiguities of contemporary relationships with nature (Cronon 1996). This tourism also reflects one of the most pressing environmental concerns of the nineteenth century: the effects of mountain deforestation, which was blamed for eroding slopes and upsetting the climate (Fressoz et al. 2020). The stories and guidebooks also bear witness to an attention to all forms of life that populate the landscapes: local customs, habits and histories, as well as flora and fauna. A whole scientific culture in full movement is in fact disseminated by tourism to the social elites of the time. The singular nature that visitors come to find in the mountains contributes to the formation of an emotional community and the transformation of the mountains into a common heritage (Debarbieux et al. 2010: 124–126).

As the contemporary economy takes hold, tourism finds itself at the heart of environmental conflicts, which raise the question of the compatibility between improving the exploitation of nature and protecting it. This compatibility has often been questioned, and has been coupled with the idea that tourism contributes to the destruction of what it offers to admire, although no site has declined because it has been over-visited (Butler 1980; Deprest 1997). This chapter looks at how tourism has achieved that very special status in public policy which makes it its own antidote: accused of degrading nature, it would at the same time safeguard it. It begins with the rising tensions between tourism and hydroelectricity at the turn of the nineteenth and twentieth centuries, and ends with the law on mountain development and protection of January 9, 1985.

This study is part of the environmental history of tourism, which is a little more than a history of nature tourism (Moranda 2015). It's a history of all the interactions between tourist economy and desires and the rest of the environment (Denning 2014; Hagimont 2022; Tizzoni 2022). In this chapter, however, we will focus on the cultural, political, ecological and social reasons and manifestations of the critics of tourist environmental impact (after Childers 2012; Marc Gigase 2014: 454–487; Humair et al. 2018; Vonnard 2024). We will also address the contribution of tourism actors to nature protection, in line with the pioneering works of environmental history in the United States (Nash 1982; Young 2009).

Tourism and Industry in the Face of Environmental Criticism

From the 1970s onward, tourism projects in France became the main focus of environmentalist struggles to protect nature (Charlier 1999; Franqueville et al. 2022). The sense of threat posed by the "monstrous errors" (SPPF 1909) of industrial and tourist progress seems to have reached its first peak around 1900. Local conflicts multiplied to prevent certain developments, and the mountains were no exception.[1] Less urbanized, they are in fact a unique heritage, coveted and therefore threatened—among other things, by tourism.

In the wake of Switzerland, where the first rack railroad was established as early as 1871 between Vitznau and Mount Rigi, and where 40 funicular railways and 13 rack railways were born between 1888 and 1914 (Gigase 2014: 100, 370), in the wake also of seaside resorts in full urban and hotel boom (Walton 2011), the French mountains saw an increase in private investment, in railways, hotels, spas and casinos; traveler flows increased; tourism experienced a clear economic boom in France (Hagimont 2022). This investment was stimulated by the propaganda efforts of tourism associations: Club alpin français (CAF) founded in 1874 and Touring-club de France (TCF) in 1890. They shared the idea that France needed to catch up with Switzerland.[2]

Tourism associations are also heavily involved in landscape protection in France. They denounced the agropastoral economy as economically inefficient and environmentally dangerous: sheep grazing was said to ruin slopes, promote erosion and, due to the absence of trees, affect rainfall, with repercussions as far down as the plains (Ferrand 1907; Nussac 1910: 18–20; Cardot 1909). Anxious to preserve France's picturesque character, the CAF and TCF took part in the major congresses organized from 1909 onward for the protection of landscapes (1909), forests (1913) and nature in general (1923 and 1930). As in other European countries (Mathis 2012; Piccioni 2020: 55–76), tourism and nature protection generally went hand in hand, even if there were excesses to combat.

The Desecration of Nature by the Industrialization of Tourism

In 1889, just as the first "French Rigi" was about to be launched, a cogwheel railway that would run from Luchon, a major world-class resort in the French Pyrenees, to the Entécade summit on the Spanish border, the popular daily *Le Petit Journal* reported on an imaginary debate that revealed a preservationist concern. It features "old Luchonnais, lovers of the mountain for the mountain's sake," who believe that the mountain should "be respected in all its imposing majesty, with its mossy rocks, its tortuous trees, its *gaves* [torrents] carved out by melting snow.... Man is but an

[1] See for examples Nussac 1910: 16–18.

[2] « À M. Floréal, revuiste à Luchon », *Luchon-Thermal*, october, 1899.

atom in the immensity of the Pyrenees." The article ironizes on "endless discussions, during which the more practical Swiss made their mountains accessible to all."[3] We don't know if the journalist made it all up, or if the mountain protection argument was actually used, but a police report reveals that the hostility of the guides is real. The hostility stemmed more from the fact that the railroad would deprive them of income from one of the resort's main excursions, while shopkeepers feared the opening of a new resort at the terminus of the line, which would displace the heart of tourist life.[4] Around 1905, a tramway project to another popular site aroused more structured opposition from the guides, this time supported by the municipality. The tramway, they claimed in the public inquiry, would deprive them of one of their main excursions, to the benefit of "foreign business people," while visitors to Luchon were "in the majority hostile to mechanical transport." They opposed, among others, the local TCF delegate, hotelier William H. Riggs, for whom it was necessary to catch up with Switzerland or risk withering away.[5] In Chamonix, since 1892, the guides have also been firmly opposed to the creation of a railroad to the Mer de Glace, backed by Swiss capital. With the support of the municipality and landowners refusing to cede their land, the guides succeeded in delaying the project, which finally saw the light of day in 1909, thanks to the backing of the State and certain elected officials in the Haute-Savoie department.[6]

Opposition to mechanical developments was in fact multifaceted and varied, depending on the commune, the actor and the time. At the beginning of the twentieth century, the economic difficulties of many valleys facilitated acceptance of projects by municipalities hoping to capture tourist revenues. Some, however, regretted their credulity and became blocking forces, as in the case of Superbagnères. A plateau at an altitude of 1800 m, connected to Luchon by a cogwheel railway in 1911, which was to be the site of a summer and winter sports resort supported by a powerful limited company, the CHM, its development was in fact largely slowed down by the opposition of the municipality in which—the project is located Saint-Aventin, which realized that its forest and pastures were affected by a concession that was far too favorable to the CHM (Hagimont 2018). Resistance arises when new forms of tourism threaten established ways of exploiting the mountains.

For mountaineers, grouped within the CAF, if access to the mountains is to be facilitated, it seems necessary to educate the crowds in proper mountaineering practices to avoid excesses (Hoibian 2000: 75–76). As far as development was concerned, they were ambivalent: they wanted to facilitate access to the mountains with hut-hotels and high-altitude railroads, but feared the destruction of landscapes, peace and solitude. In 1905, the CAF magazine urged the opening of high-altitude roads and hotels in the Alps, and called on France to adopt aerial cables for

---

[3] Thomas Grimm, « Righi français », *Le Petit Journal*, march 7, 1889.

[4] Archives départementales de Haute-Garonne (ADHG) 4 M 12: Correspondence between the Special Commissioner of Police and the Prefect of Haute-Garonne, 1889–1890.

[5] ADHG 1 818W3.

[6] Archives nationales de France (ANF) 19800028/17: AGM of the Compagnie des chemins de fer Chamonix-Montenvers, June 20, 1906. Debarbieux (2001: 71–79).

transporting tourists in the mountains.[7] But in the same issue, CAF President Ernest Caron is able to tell the railroad company presidents gathered for the CAF banquet that their projects in the mountains "frighten him a little." He sees it as a "danger" and even a "desecration by the railways," even if the problem is more of a moral than a landscape nature: the trains are going to take away from mountaineers their distinction through effort.[8] In 1907, Pierre Puiseux, astronomer and founding member of the CAF, mingled nostalgia and disgust at the sight of the Jungfrau railroad. He described the trains as "gnawing worms whose voracity can be satisfied by nothing," and feared that the Jungfrau, Matterhorn and Mont Blanc would become "pedestals for restaurateurs and postcard dealers" (Puiseux 1907). In 1913, caving pioneer and mountaineer Edouard-Alfred Martel described tourism as "perhaps a more dangerous enemy than industry," due to its "feverish drive to penetrate excessively, its unfortunate tendency to build roads everywhere, even in unapproachable places, whose wildness and difficulty of access considerably enhanced their beauty; a fever and a tendency which, if we look at things calmly, have come to ruin France." These protests, voiced by important figures in tourism and science in the early twentieth century, are not exactly of the same order as those found at the same time in Switzerland, where the movement was even more vigorous, but where, under the aegis of the League for the Conservation of Picturesque Switzerland, *Heimatschutz*, it sometimes flirted with xenophobia, at the Matterhorn, Les Diablerets or Sonchaux (Gigase 2014: 472–477; Humair et al. 2018).

The destruction of landscapes is the main complaint against tourism, but not the only one. It contributes to the growing pressure on plants, which has been a cause for concern in the Alps since the late nineteenth century. The proliferation of high-altitude roads and automobiles heightened fears, as they greatly facilitated access to floristically rich spots, such as around the Galibier and Lautaret routes, where botanist Le Brun noted in 1923 the disappearance of *Daphne striata* and *Potentilla delphinensis* (Clermont 1926: 190). Warnings of the disappearance of alpine fauna, from birds of prey to bears, ibex and chamois, were also heard among mountaineers (Spont 1914: 140–151; Bouchet 1990: 215). In 1923, entomologist E. Barthe lamented, in a highly original way, that the development of the Pyrenean caves at Bétharram and Sare had led to the disappearance of "extremely rare blind insects" (Clermont 1926: 185).

From the interwar period onward, the modernization drive in the mountains was embodied by hydroelectricity, roads and winter sports that gradually became the focus of most criticism. Articles criticized the lack of architectural integration of new resorts (Gaussen 1939: 313), the humiliation of the mountains by lifts that dispensed with effort and standardized the experience, as Arnold Lunn, a pioneer of downhill skiing, lamented in 1941 (Denning 2014: 8). After 1945, the winter sports craze turned some mountain ranges upside down: French mountains went from having a few dozen (sometimes rudimentary) ski lifts in 1939, to 302 (ski lifts,

---

[7] *La Montagne* 1, 1905: 586–587.

[8] *La Montagne* 1, 1905: p. 263–264.

chairlifts, cable cars, funicular railways, etc.) in 1956, and 2611 in 1974, while the number of beds increased by a factor of 20 or 30 (Hagimont 2022: 255). The survey remains to be carried out for France, but in Switzerland or the USA, clashes multiplied as early as before 1970 (Childers 2012; Quin 2023; Vonnard 2024). In France, struggles multiplied from the 1970s onward.

Tourism Versus Hydroelectricity

Tourism, though criticized, became an instrument of struggle against industry. In the mountains, it was the rise of hydroelectricity and the concomitant investment in tourism that catalyzed the alliance between the tourism industry and conservationists in the early twentieth century. Yet there was a strong synergy between tourism and hydroelectricity, first used in the 1880s to light resorts (Argelès-Gazost and Ax in the Pyrenees), then to electrify railway lines, thanks to a player like the Compagnie des chemins de fer du Midi, which was active in both sectors with its subsidiaries SHEM (hydroelectricity) and CHM (tourism). We also find someone like Ludovic Dardenne, from Luchon, who was a member of the TCF, a promoter of winter sports (Superbagnères, with CHM in 1910) and an investor in the electricity industry at the beginning of the twentieth century (CEI in 1917). Installations useful for hydroelectricity were also converted to tourism, such as the Artouste cable car in 1932 (Bouneau 2008: 201–202; Hagimont 2022: 279–293). Conflicts were nevertheless fierce.

The Société pour la protection des paysages de France (SPPF) was founded in 1901 by elected officials, artists and tourism representatives, in reaction to the proposed hydroelectric harnessing of the Lison waterfall (Jura) (SPPF 1909). It also motivated the active legislative campaign led by Charles Beauquier, MP for the Jura region, which resulted in the law of April 21, 1906, organizing the protection of artistic sites and natural monuments—largely without means. The question of national parks was also revived in France as a result of hydroelectric expansion: the CAF commissioned Martel to write a report on the subject in view of the deterioration caused by the "development of white coal companies in France" (Martel 1913: 401). Such was the mobilization that the industrialists' magazine *La Houille Blanche* in turn denounced a "war waged by tourism against the white coal industry" (Heaulmé 2014). Let's take a closer look at some of the conflicts in the Pyrenees.

In 1909, the Cauterets town council protested against a project to harness the torrent downstream from the town to supply a future factory. The resort derives part of its success from its lakes and torrents: "whatever the engineers may say [...] it is certain that at low water, the bed of the watercourse will be completely dry," which will cause, from an aesthetic point of view, an "inappreciable prejudice [...]" (quoted by Heaulmé 2014). The commune therefore requested that its territory be classified under the 1906 law. In 1913, in Luchon, the town council rallied against the construction of an electrometallurgical plant upstream from the spa. The elected officials focused their arguments on the aesthetic aspect, as the tourist idyll was threatened:

> The creation of a metallurgical plant, however salubrious it may be, in the immediate vicinity of a health resort, is [...] likely to alienate customers who might fear that the purity of the valley's atmosphere would be tainted by noxious fumes, and that the calm and rest that visitors are entitled to find in a health resort would be disturbed by the possibility of workers' strikes and the daily and repeated passage of automobile trucks.[9]

Luchon therefore requested that the site be classified under the 1906 law, "the only practical and truly effective means of preventing the creation of a metallurgical industry." But the war proved the industrialists right, in Luchon as in Cauterets. In Luchon, despite 230 unfavorable opinions from the local population against the factory project (compared to 23 in favor, who emphasized the jobs created to alleviate seasonal unemployment), the prefect approved the request for industrial installation in 1915, to contribute to the war effort.[10] From then on, Luchon continued to oppose industry, obtaining classification under the 1906 law for part of the high tourist mountains (in 1927, as did Cauterets), but largely in vain: industrial development transformed the whole of its mountains. A mecca for French tourism in the nineteenth century, Luchon also became a mecca for hydroelectric power in the twentieth.

Cauterets, for its part, managed to resist, thanks in particular to the interpersonal skills of Louis Le Bondidier, who was an influential member of the CAF and TCF, president of the Fédération des Syndicats d'initiatives des Pyrénées occidentales, and defender of the tourist landscape in the Lourdes region. Le Bondidier also spearheaded efforts to save the Cirque de Gavarnie, another mountain tourist mecca threatened by hydroelectric development in 1912. The concession for the hydroelectric development of this world-famous glacial cirque had this time been accepted, but for a fragile project. The affair was revealed in the press on January 27, 1913, by an article by writer Pierre Loti published in one of France's leading daily newspapers, *Le Figaro*. The project was withdrawn. When a project reemerged at the end of the war, mobilization resumed, this time by the commune of Gavarnie itself, supported by the SPPF, the CAF, or Prince Albert 1st of Monaco, mobilized for the protection of the Pyrenees, and penetrated the senior administration. In 1921, this mobilization led to the classification of the cirque under the 1906 law. Until its actual classification as a national park in 1967, the site remained under threat but, like Cauterets, escaped industry, despite the creation in 1946 of the superpowerful national electricity company EDF. In Cauterets, Luchon and Gavarnie, a conflict of power is at play when it comes to defining the future of these mountains, pitting industrial, tourist and pastoral interest groups against each other, who in part use nature protection to steer the territory towards the economic and aesthetic option that seems preferable to them, for political, cultural and economic reasons (Heaulmé 2014; Briffaud Heaulmé 2016; Hagimont 2022).

[9] Archives muncipales de Luchon (AML), 3O10 : City council deliberation, February 27, 1914.
[10] ADHG 4U4/194.

Around the initial criticisms of hydroelectricity and related industries, however, a repertoire of environmental criticisms emerged, concerning the industry's effects on landscapes (disfigured by penstocks, power lines and factories), hydrology, aquatic fauna and vegetation. Trees are visibly affected by hydrofluoric fumes from aluminum plants, chemical discharges into torrents or their detour destroy fish, the creation of dams floods certain wetlands or raises water levels, instantly destroying the fauna and flora of rare habitats—peaty lawns, alluvial deposits, wet sands, as at Lac du Mont-Cenis (Clermont 1926: 190). Not to mention the loss of grazing land and sometimes even the displacement of villages.

Laws, on the other hand, encourage the reconciliation of interests. Beauquier himself says that the aim of the protectors of landscapes "is not to stop the march of the railroads [...] or automobiles, but to bring about a wise agreement between the needs of progress" and the need for nature (SPPF 1909: 12). The Departemental Sites Commission (DSC) created by the 1906 law had to weigh up the "just material necessities, as well as the indispensable safeguarding of the natural beauties which [are] a true national heritage" (SPPF 1909: 13). This conciliatory approach is clearly evident in the composition of the committee, which includes seats not only for foresters, elected representatives and "prominent figures from the arts, sciences and literature" who are the guardians of nature, but also for the prefect, the chief engineer of the Ponts et Chaussées and the chief road agent, all three of whom are rather pro-industry.

Various laws sought to mitigate the impact of the industry, in order to make it more acceptable. The law of March 13, 1913, again spurred on by Beauquier, theoretically imposes reserved flows during the tourist season (the minimum volume of water guaranteed for the section of river between the water intake and the factory outlet). In a circular dated July 26, 1913, the Ministry of Public Works drew attention to the "unattractive appearance of most electrical distribution lines [...] which, in certain regions, destroy the harmony of the landscape." The law of October 18, 1919, which made the State the main authorizer of hydroelectric concessions, incorporated the landscape issue: concession specifications had to provide for "landscape protection" and the "development of tourism." In theory, this strengthens the power of DSC (Heaulmé 2014). A circular dated July 13, 1922, states that for tourism, "one of France's riches," it is necessary to "protect the picturesque sites and historic monuments that are its raison d'être." To achieve this, development projects had to be submitted to site commissions (an unenforced legal obligation), and penstocks had to be painted in a suitably chosen color. On March 15, 1928, a decree issued by the Ministry of Public Works required evergreen trees to be planted around penstocks to enhance their integration into the landscape. The law of May 2, 1930, which reformed the law of 1906, required that the DSC be systematically consulted on hydroelectric development projects. However, it had no blocking power and now included a representative of the hydroelectric industry itself (Gorsse 1949).

In most cases, the tourism industry was powerless to intervene. In 1929, after battling against the "formidable industrial transformation" of the Vicdessos by Alais, Froges and Camargue (aluminium), the Union thermale et touristique d'Ariège congratulated itself on having succeeded in preserving:

> … the tourist beauty of a pretty Ariège valley, and also of not hindering the industrial development of our region. [...] The pre-war attitude of moaning about the ugliness of sites caused by the creations of modern finance is no longer appropriate today. [...] Far from it, the mountains have not been spoiled by the changes brought about by the science of engineering; this is a completely new attraction [...] which should also charm the tourist.[11]

Luchon, unable to prevent the creation of a plant, negotiated compensation: in 1917, the hydroelectric company (CEI) financed the doubling of the town's drinking water network; in 1937, it closed its electrometallurgical plant during the tourist season.[12] In 1931, the decree regulating the harnessing of water from the Lys at Luchon, for example, set the reserved flow for the Cascade d'Enfer, depending on the season and the time of day—Le Bondidier ironized about "this landscape comedy" aimed at tourists (quoted in Gorsse 1949: 53). Fish ladders and regular stocking of managed rivers are also carried out at the companies' expense, in case of destruction—and accidents are frequent. In the absence of ecosystems, fish tourism is the guarantor (Larrieu 1944; Chimits 1952). These marginal adjustments keep up appearances. On a case-by-case basis, industrialists also pay monetary compensation to ensure acceptance of the degradation—a formidable tool, since if communes refuse, they run the risk of having the development imposed on them, and thus losing everything. These compensations can also be used for tourism and pastoralism: after 1945, subsidies paid by EDF enabled certain communes to invest: Bonneval-sur-Arc (1956), Saint-Lary (1956) and Gèdres (1965) were thus able to launch their ski lifts, while Aragnouet went so far as to drill a cross-border tunnel (1967–1976) (Milian 2004: 393–396). These accommodations did not prevent conservationists from expressing regret. Few valleys have succeeded in rolling back the hydroelectric industry.

Tourism to Enhance Our Natural Heritage

Tourism, a tool in the fight against industry, criticized for its effects on nature, is a kind of *pharmakon* curing the harm it can itself cause if misused. Tourism may also have served to compensate for the territorial dispossession induced by nature conservation.

Tourism Promotes Nature Conservation

In a socio-cultural context marked by utilitarianism, nature conservationists are often obliged to defend the economic utility of protection: protected nature is an economic resource in itself. As early as 1904, the Ministry of Agriculture urged its

[11] Archives départementales de l'Ariège (ADA) 7M60: AGM of the Union thermale et touristique d'Ariège, September 22, 1929.

[12] AML 3O10.

departments to prevent "the destruction of picturesque beauties which are [...] sometimes the wealth of our departments" (SPPF 1909, 6). In 1909, the SPPF reminded us that "natural beauties are almost always a source of wealth for the regions which [...] benefit from the affluence of their admirers" (SPPF 1909: 20). In 1923, the Swiss delegate to the International Congress for the Protection of Nature felt that the development of hydroelectricity was beginning to "damage our heritage of natural beauty" and that it was necessary to "mitigate this uglification, which risked, moreover, leading to economic impoverishment" (Clermont 1926: 280–281). At the same congress, the TCF delegate, concerned about the rarefaction of certain birds of prey, adopted a vow that "the bird should henceforth be considered an essential element of tourist propaganda" (Clermont 1926: 329). The curator of the Fontainebleau forest, for his part, believes that conserving forests without exploitation "obviously [...] results in a loss of wood products, but this loss is compensated a hundredfold by the resources created by a tourist movement that is developing more and more each day" (Clermont 1926: 277). In 1935, to justify the creation of the Néouvielle nature reserve in the Pyrenees, its director pointed out that at its heart were "protected sites offered to tourism" (Chouard 1936: 48). This is hardly surprising: in the United States, the decree creating Yellowstone National Park in 1872 stipulated that it would be developed for tourism.[13] Protected natural heritage is perceived as a resource.

Defending the economic interest of protection in the face of hydroelectricity leads us to reflect on the price of tourist services rendered by nature. The task remains relatively unfinished, as the irreplaceable beauty of a landscape "escapes estimation" (Clermont 1926: 248). For the mayor of Ax-les-Thermes, in 1927, tourism brings in "infinitely greater sums than any industry would."[14] Cauterets said the same thing in 1942: "the beauty of these valleys and the prestige of the title of national park would bring in, through tourism, wealth at least equivalent to that produced by electricity."[15] The calculation was double-edged: in 1932, faced with opponents to the hydroelectric development of the Aude gorges, the industrialists and government departments estimated that if the facility was not built, the community would lose nearly a million francs in taxes, in a deprived region.[16] Le Bondidier sees this as a major weakness: it's easy to estimate what the hydroelectric scheme will bring in, but not what will be lost in terms of tourism (Le Bondidier 1944).

After 1945, it seems that the competing conceptions of national parks (tourists, hunters, scientists, local councillors, etc.), which culminated in the law of July 22, 1960, agreed on the economic interest of such creations. The parks are instruments of regional planning, offering a place to recharge the batteries of city-dwellers deprived of "nature," while at the same time preserving a natural environment

[13] *Statutes at Large and Proclamations of the United States* 17, Boston, Little, Brown & Cy, 1873: 32–33.

[14] ADA, 4T22: Mayor of Ax to the Prefect of Ariège, July 7, 1927.

[15] « Congrès de 1942 à Cauterets », *Annales de la fédération pyrénéenne d'économie montagnarde* 10: 333.

[16] ADA, 4T22: « Classification of the banks of the Aude. »

devastated everywhere else by accelerated modernization. At the same time, they are intended to promote the economic development of areas that have fallen into complete decline, thanks to tourism (Préau 1964). The future director of the Pyrenees National Park, forester Pierre Chimits, sums it up: the creation of a park can only be applied:

> … in a few rare cases of sparsely populated mountain areas, in the process of economic regression, where any purely agricultural program is illusory, but where the beauty of the sites makes them suitable for tourist development. Modern civilization is giving city-dwellers a growing and acute need for quiet, restful havens in remarkable regions where the landscapes, fauna and flora are respected…[17]

Finally, for legislators, national parks seem to be an ideal instrument for alleviating some of the problems caused by modernization, while at the same time optimizing the use of the national territory, right down to its margins, thanks to tourism.

In Search of Good Tourism

Franz Schrader, an eminent geographer and president of the CAF from 1901 to 1904, was one of the first to attempt to define the right place for tourism, at a conference in 1897. Mountains, he argued, were precious temples in a world undergoing brutal transformation, so they had to be both preserved and accessible to all—"poor and rich, sick or infirm, children or old." To achieve this, facilities could reach some peaks, like the Brevent in Chamonix, in an attempt to conceal the infrastructure, while all others should be religiously preserved (Schrader 1898). Martel takes up this idea: facilitating access to France's "grandiose beauties" makes them "more loved," while bringing "very happily prosperity to many districts deprived of other sources of wealth," provided that "any development is discreet and does not forever disgrace a natural masterpiece." To this end, he proposed the creation of a national commission made up of painters, engineers, geographers and geologists, who could advise the administration and government "not to grant regrettable authorizations, or to carefully determine the conditions for the construction of a factory, a road, or the financial monopolization of a landscape." The national parks he then called for would be another way of ensuring "convenience of access and stay" by avoiding "untoward modifications" such as hydroelectric installations, but also roads, "large hotels, casinos, racecourses, velodromes, automobile garages, tramways, funiculars, etc., for the use of tourists." Above all, says Martel, "there are sites that must not be accommodated" (Martel 1913).

The first International Congress for the Protection of Nature in 1923 took up these discussions. The measures adopted in the protected forest of Fontainebleau (since 1861) serve as a benchmark for striking the right balance between protection and development through tourism. Sinturel, the forest's curator, reports on the

[17] AN 19960018/80: Pierre Chimits' presentation to DATAR, Tarbes, March 31, 1964.

debate over the right layout, between those who want "tourist traffic to be kept as low as possible," and those who believe that the public should be attracted and educated, which "naturally calls for a complete tourist layout: installation of plaques, signposts and signs, warning signs, orientation tables, benches, shelters, etc., creation of new roads and paths." Sinturel calls for an "average formula" that reserves "a few discreet corners [...] for daydreams" and develops "trails" and "an important network of roads" for the rest, according to a balance to be discussed between foresters, scientists and artists (Clermont 1926: 268–278).

After the WWII, the right balance between tourism and protection, in a context of very strong economic growth and a boom in winter sports, was discussed on a national scale. In France, the Vanoise National Park, created in 1963, was targeted in 1969 by a project to extend nearby winter sports resorts onto a glacier, enabling summer skiing. This necessitated a partial declassification of the park, triggering one of the first massive, and victorious, mobilizations for the defense of the environment in France, with the CAF playing an important role (Charvolin 2012). The many conflicts that ensued around tourism developments continued to raise questions about the possibility of balanced tourism development. In 1978, the CAF announced that it would take into account "the ecological capacity of the environment"[18] for all new refuge projects. In 1980, in a famous article, Butler applied the concept of carrying capacity, derived from ecology, to designate a level of frequentation beyond which tourist sites must not go, on pain of decline. In 1995, the World Tourism Organization's Sustainable Tourism Charter highlighted the ecological and economic risks and opportunities of tourism in a growing world. It seems to us that all this is a continuation of discussions that began at least a century ago.

Tourism and Nature Conservation: A Schizophrenic Couple Exemplifying Modernity?

Tourism as Compensation for the Loss of Territorial Sovereignty?

Let's make a hypothesis here: tourism would have been one of the only ways to make nature protection acceptable to the territories concerned. Let's go back to a strange debate that arose within the CAF during the WWI. At the time, tourism circles were buzzing about the creation of the first "national park" in France, at Saint-Christophe-en-Oisans (Alps). Heir to the forest fears of the nineteenth century, the perimeter acquired by the CAF and TCF totally excluded grazing. Observing the conditions under which this park was built, a certain L. A. Fabre vehemently denounced the risk that this type of park would accentuate the

[18] *La Montagne et alpinisme* 134, 1983: 166.

demographic collapse by depriving communities of the means to survive. Fabre argues that, while grazing abuses must be combated, protectors must also take into account the mechanisms that drive overgrazing, in particular communal indebtedness, which leads to a desire to increase the number of animals allowed to graze in order to bring in revenue. The park was created thanks to this indebtedness, which forced the commune to sell its land because it could no longer meet its obligations. While the sale of the land relieved the municipality of its debts, the inhabitants were deprived of their means of subsistence. This raises a question of social justice immediately after the debate on national parks began in France. The editor-in-chief of the CAF magazine describes the article as "highly curious," but concedes that "instead of evicting its inhabitants," it will be necessary "to try again and again, by all possible means, to retain the mountain dweller there."[19] The discussion continues in the next issue, with Gaston Bergé defending the national park projects, using the famous argument that protected nature creates income through tourism. The valleys are in a desperate demographic situation, the abuse of grazing land is degrading nature; parks are a solution for the future, as they set an example:

> When we see grass growing again, cows producing milk, butter and cheese, a profitable product, gradually replacing the sheep that spoil the soil, tourists coming in much greater numbers, attracted by the beauty of the landscapes and the freshness of the reborn forests, I believe that we will envy the prosperity of villages bordering such parks, and that others will be eager to apply similar methods at home. (Bergé 1916: 25)

Tourism acts as a counterbalance to the hardships caused by nature conservation. At the heart of the conflict between tourism and hydroelectricity, the case of Aulus-les-Bains (Pyrenees) illustrates this form of bargaining. In 1923, two picturesque but little-visited sites (Cascade d'Ars and Cirque de Cagateille) were threatened by hydroelectric projects. The TCF lobbied the prefect to have these sites classified, countering the industrial interest with the protection that would bring in tourist revenue. The commune of Aulus was in favor of classification, but only on condition of a subsidy enabling it to build paths to the sites, which would otherwise remain a hypothetical resource. Faced with the refusal of the subsidy, Aulus rejected the request for classification so as not to jeopardize its industrial future.[20]

Protecting nature means sacrificing resources and therefore economic activity: this has long been obvious. This is why protection has always been confined to restricted areas, and has been tempered by the possibility of developing tourism, which appears to be the lesser evil. For the General Secretary of the 1923 Congress, Charles Valois, there's no doubt about it, prohibiting:

> The exploitation of the soil, flora and waters [would be a] sacrifice which would make the creation of a Park singularly onerous, and by the loss of revenue it would entail, would narrowly limit the number of enterprises of this kind, or else relegate them to desolate regions, at excessive altitudes.

---

[19] « Les Parcs nationaux en France », *La Montagne* 11, 1915: 215–218.

[20] ADA 4T22.

On the contrary, the park must allow for the exploitation of wildlife and landscapes. This is indispensable, all the more so "in very democratic countries" where the various limitations on use (for hunting, grazing, forestry, certain forms of tourism) will represent a strong deprivation of freedoms and income (Clermont 1926: 278–280). This undoubtedly distinguishes the metropolis from colonized areas, where coercion can be applied with far fewer qualms to protect nature supposedly threatened by the natives (Blanc et al. 2022).

The question of territorial dispossession was raised when the French national parks were created. In Bonneval-sur-Arc and Cauterets, local councillors initially defended the creation of parks, seeing them as an instrument to arbitrate ongoing development conflicts in favor of their projects. Except that the parks created by the 1960 law are indeed state instruments, targeting a national interest. Cauterets, which had been calling for the creation of a national park in the commune since 1942, did an about-face when the project was presented in 1962. The park interfered with local planning decisions—in particular the development of ski lifts for winter sports. It threatens the local ability to define legitimate landscape enhancement (Heaulmé 2014). After bitter negotiations, the park's boundaries were revised and its regulations relaxed. The National Parks created in the Vanoise (1963) the Pyrenees (1967), and the Oisans (1973) finally came closer to what Valois had feared: narrow territories that excluded all areas where future ski areas could expand.[21]

Despite the many concessions, nature protection is becoming a symbol of internal colonization (Basset 2013), allegedly orchestrated from Paris. In the face of this, economic development took precedence over protection in the administrative argument. In 1975, when the French government proposed the creation of the second Pyrenean National Park in Ariège, a department marked by extreme poverty, the aim was no longer to protect a mountain under threat, but to create a new resource through the national park label. Rejection is massive in the valleys. In addition to political strategies aimed at exacerbating divisions in a local and national game, opposition is based on a rejection of the central state and of parkland as an "Indian reserve" for the needs of urban society. The social injustice is also pointed out: this park would add constraints, however modest, to poor populations who would have no choice but to accept becoming the receptacle of rich city-dwellers' desires for nature (Hagimont 2022).

In these various conflicts, there are contradictions, as the CAF later points out, in the discourse of "mountain dwellers" who, using "formulas such as 'the mountain for mountain dwellers,'" contest the "foreign 'invasion,'" even though they expect "a not inconsiderable part of [their] income" from it.[22] Tourism is not universally rejected, but what it is fundamentally based on—a view from the outside that assigns the territory a form and a future (a wilderness tourist area)—is. For local residents, this protected nature bears the hallmarks of the socio-economic regression that has

[21] AN 19960018/80; Préau (1964), Selmi (2006).

[22] « Une contribution CAF à la loi montagne », *La Montagne et Alpinisme* 133, 1983: 98.

been underway since the mid-nineteenth century, and the fact that it has been placed under glass is a sign of political, social and memorial abdication.

Development and Protection, Control and Liberalization: Public Policy in a Time of Contradictory Injunctions

In any case, starting in the 1970s, based on the principle that (tourist) development and protection are both necessary and reconcilable, the State attempted to reconcile two imperatives whose hierarchy posed a problem: on the one hand, to ensure (at lower cost) the development of territories globally marginalized by economic development; on the other, to ensure the preservation of a national natural heritage against the deleterious effects of growth. In any case, the idea is gaining ground that protecting nature represents a resource, a competitive advantage to be exploited by regions that are being called upon to move away from a handout approach. The hoped-for happy reconciliation of development and protection, with a well-thought-out dose of tourism, was based on a collection of singular experiences: certain Swiss valleys, Aubrac, Queyras, Cauterets and Bonneval-sur-Arc (DATAR 1974, 1978; Etchélécou 1981; Besson 1982). Their replicability is not guaranteed, however, as they are based on specific configurations of actors, state interventions, budgetary possibilities (such as the taxes paid by EDF at Bonneval-sur-Arc), and unique topographical arrangements. There's no magic formula.

In 1977, a directive was issued centralizing control of urban development and sports facilities in the mountains. This measure, judged by local elected representatives to be too authoritarian and a handicap to regional competitiveness, led to further discussions, culminating in the law of January 9, 1985, on the development and protection of mountain areas. The law was based on a scoping report submitted by elected mountain officials in April 1982 (Besson 1982), which began by depicting a mountain region that had been subjected to "colonial" tourism development and nature protection in the twentieth century. He denounced the 1977 Mountain Directive, "dictated from on high," as "protecting the mountains from themselves." Protection policies have fostered a feeling among mountain dwellers of being "dispossessed" of their territory, "invaded by city dwellers" and transformed into an "Indian reserve." The mountain is also losing its inhabitants, and risks becoming a "desert." The report concludes, in an antinomic manner, that "the policy of protecting the mountain environment must therefore give priority to maintaining or increasing activities." The final version of the law therefore contains enough exceptions to ensure that any constraints can be circumvented. This law pursues the idea that protection could only be accepted on condition that locals could develop tourism, but it also clearly sets out the antagonism between the two, ultimately favoring the former (Hagimont 2024).

Conclusion

This history of the relationship between tourism and nature conservation adds historical depth to the debate on sustainable tourism. In the mountains, nature conservation is partly a product of tourism. Since the early twentieth century, the possibility of preserving the integrity of nature (first landscapes, then ecosystems) has been associated with that of developing the tourism economy. Protection was conceived as a resource (a heritage) that could be economically enhanced. After fighting the evils of the agropastoral economy at the end of the nineteenth century, various players in the tourism industry (mountaineers, tourist boards, elected representatives) took up the cause of protecting nature against the expansion of hydroelectricity in the twentieth century. At the same time, tourism was becoming increasingly important, first through roads and railroads in the mountains, then through winter sports resorts. Certain forms of tourism were therefore combated, but tourism remained essential to protection, because it could provide income to compensate for the losses incurred by the renunciation of industry. The social need for mountains, shared by urban elites, and the economic and social distress of mountain areas, led people to believe that they could be reconciled. In fact, protecting nature implied a loss (of a territory to be exploited, with its forestry, hydraulic and mineralogical resources). Engaged, like all territories, and all the more so since the neoliberal turn of the 1970s, in a struggle for economic survival, the mountain valleys have at the same time had to accept the immobilization of part of their territory to compensate for the accelerated destruction of nature everywhere else. The compromise, posed in these terms, seems unrealistic.

The problem posed here is in fact inherent to societies that are based above all on the growing appropriation of natural resources, and thus feed on the degradation of ecosystems. The corrective measures introduced by nature conservation in France have occasionally saved spaces and species, as long as this did not fundamentally jeopardize the competitiveness of territories and the nation.

Today, nature protection still relies on tourism, although the tools have diversified considerably. The issue of the sector's carbon footprint is now doubling that of its impact on ecosystems (Ademe 2021). The mountains could, according to some, become a laboratory for ecological transition. The field of tourism contestation in the name of nature is expanding until now: domain extensions and artificial snow with rising global warming, airports, new roads, new resorts or resort extensions, contestations grow up as well as tourist economy. The main tourist projects are now challenged. Faced with this, experiments aimed at reconciling tourism with respect for the planet's limits are also multiplying: new positive-energy buildings, renovation of buildings, closure of roads or ski lifts, decarbonization of resorts, promotion of soft mobility, quotas for certain sites, carbon and ecological offsetting. Caught up in the same constraints of competitiveness, they could well only fuel a *greenwashing* that has become systemic.

References

ADEME (2021) Bilan des émissions de gaz à effet de serre du secteur du tourisme en France. ADEME, Paris

Anderson B (2016) Alpine agency: locals, mountaineers and tourism in the Eastern Alps, c. 1860–1914. Rural Hist 27:61–78. https://doi.org/10.1017/S0956793315000163

Basset K (2013) L'invention des parcs nationaux français entre modernisation et décolonisation (1850-1970). In: Mouhot J-F, Mathis C-F (eds) Une protection de l'environnement à la française? Champ Vallon, Seyssel, pp 170–181

Bergé G (1916) A propos des parcs nationaux. La Montagne 12:24–26

Besson L (1982) Rapport fait au nom de la commission d'enquête sur la situation de l'agriculture et de l'économie rurale dans les zones de montagne et défavorisées. Assemblée nationale, Paris

Blanc G et al (eds) (2022) Protéger et détruire. CNRS Editions, Paris

Bouchet JC (1990) Histoire de la chasse dans les Pyrénées françaises. Marrimpouey, Pau

Bouneau C (2008) Entre David et Goliath. La dynamique des réseaux régionaux. MSHA, Pessac

Briffaud, Serge, Emmanuelle Heaulmé, Véronique André-Lamat, Bernard Davasse, et Isabelle Sacareau. The Nature of Resources. Conflicts of Landscape in the Pyrenees During the Rise of Hydroelectric Power. In Renewable Energies and European Landscapes, 135–53. Dordrecht: Springer, 2016. https://doi.org/10.1007/978-94-017-9843-3_8

Butler R (1980) The concept of a tourist area cycle of evolution. Canadian Geogr 24:5–12. https://doi.org/10.1111/j.1541-0064.1980.tb00970.x

Cardot E (1909) Manuel de l'arbre. Touring Club de France, Paris

Charlier B (1999) La défense de l'environnement : entre espace et territoire: géographie des conflits environnementaux déclenchés en France depuis 1974. Thèse de géographie, Pau

Charvolin F (2012) L'affaire de la Vanoise et son analyste. Vingtième Siècle. Revue d'histoire 113:82–93

Childers M (2012) Colorado Powder Keg: ski resorts and the environmental movement. University Press of Kansas, Kansas City

Chimits P (1952) Inventaire piscicole des lacs pyrénéens français. Annales de la Fédération pyrénéenne d'économie montagnarde (AFPEM) 16:105–116

Chouard P (1936) Les réserves naturelles aux Pyrénées. Création de la réserve de Néouvielle. AFPEM 4:30–48

Cronon W (1996) The trouble with wilderness: or, getting back to the wrong nature. Environ Hist 1:7–28. https://doi.org/10.2307/3985059

DATAR (1974) La montagne. La Documentation française, Paris

DATAR (1978) Schéma d'orientation des Pyrénées. DATAR, Paris

de Clermont R (ed) (1926) Premier congrès international pour la protection de la nature. MNHN, Paris

de Franqueville H et al (2022) Lutter et gagner contre le tourisme. Silence! 514:12–14

de Gorsse P (1949) L'équipement hydro-électrique en face de la protection et du respect de l'esthétique. AFPEM 14:42–60

de Nussac L (ed) (1910) Congrès international pour la protection des paysages. SPPF, Paris

Debarbieux B (2001) Chamonix-Mont-Blanc (1860-2000). Édimontagne, Saint-Gervais

Debarbieux B et al (2010) Les faiseurs de montagne. Imaginaires politiques et territorialités (XVIIIe-XXIe siècle). CNRS, Paris

Denning A (2014) Skiing into modernity. University of California Press, Oakland

Deprest F (1997) Enquête sur le tourisme de masse. Belin, Paris

Etchelecou A (1981) Allo, la décentralisation, c'est quoi ? La Montagne et Alpinisme 128:346–349

Ferrand H (1907) La conservation des montagnes. Impr. Elie Rey et Cie, Grenoble

Fressoz JB et al (2020) Les révoltes du ciel. Seuil, Paris

Gaussen H (1939) Congrès de 1938 à Perpignan. AFPEM 7:295–318

Gigase M (2014) Le développement du rail et la construction du système touristique dans l'Arc lémanique (1852-1914). Thèse d'histoire, Université de Lausanne

Hagimont S (2018) Aménager et exploiter la montagne sportive hivernale. Entreprises et histoire 93:27–46. https://doi.org/10.3917/eh.093.0027
Hagimont S (2022) Pyrénées. Champ Vallon, Ceyzérieu
Hagimont S (2024) Décoloniser les montagnes? XX & XXI. Revue d'histoire (forthcoming work)
Heaulmé E (2014) Hydroélectricité et conflits paysagers dans la montagne pyrénéenne. Projets de paysage 10: [en ligne]. http://www.projetsdepaysage.fr/fr/hydroelectricite_et_conflits_paysagers_dans_la_montagne_pyreneenne_du_debut_du_xxe_siecle_a_la_creation_du_parc_national
Hoibian O (2000) Les alpinistes en France (1870-1950). L'Harmattan, Paris
Humair C et al (2018) Développement touristique et protection de l'environnement. In: Ambroise-Renssu A-C, Trespeuch-Berthelot A, Vrignon A (eds) Une histoire des conflits environnementaux. PULIM, Limoges, pp 91–109
Larrieu J (1944) L'équipement piscicole des Pyrénées. AFPEM 10:53–60
Le Bondidier L (1944) La protection des sites. AFPEM 10:61–147
Lenzen M et al (2018) The carbon footprint of global tourism. Nat Clim Change 8:522–528. https://doi.org/10.1038/s41558-018-0141-x
Martel EA (1913) La question des parcs nationaux en France. La Montagne 9:401–457
Mathis CF (2012) Mobiliser pour l'environnement en Europe et aux États-Unis. Vingtième Siècle. Revue d'histoire 113:15–27. https://doi.org/10.3917/vin.113.0015
Milian J (2004) Protection de la nature et développement territorial dans les Pyrénées. Thèse de géographie, Toulouse
Moranda S (2015) The emergence of an environmental history of tourism. J Tour Hist 7:268–289. https://doi.org/10.1080/1755182X.2015.1102975
Nash R (1982) Wilderness and the American mind. Yale University Press, Yale
Nifosi C (2021) Du marcheur au touriste : la mise en scène des Alpes dans la littérature du XIXe siècle. Revue italienne d'études françaises 11, Online. https://doi.org/10.4000/rief.8078
Piccioni L (2020) The Beloved Face of the Country. The White Horse Press, Winwick
Préau P (1964) Le parc national de la Vanoise. Revue de géographie alpine 52:393–436
Plas E (2020) Je n'accuse que l'homme. Romantisme 189:74–84
Puiseux P (1907) Une première victime : l'Eiger (3975 m.). La Montagne 3:537–552
Quin G (2023) Funiculaires, skilifts et téléphériques. Genèse et structure de l'essor d'un domaine skiable à St. Moritz (1928-1973). Traverse 2:64–78
Reclus E (1866) Du sentiment de la nature dans les sociétés modernes. Revue des Deux Mondes 62:352–381
Schrader F (1898) A quoi tient la beauté des montagnes ? Annuaire du CAF 25:555–577
Selmi A (2006) Le parc national de la Vanoise. Éd. de la MSH, Quae
Spont H (1914) Les Pyrénées. Perrin, Paris
SPPF (1909) La loi pour la protection des Sites et Monuments naturels. SPPF, Paris
Tizzoni E (2022) Tra Spiggia, Scoglio, Fiume e Collina. Unicopli, Milano
Vonnard P (2024) L'affirmation d'une posture conservationniste de la nature au sein de l'Union internationale des associations d'alpinisme (UIAA). In: Pouvoir et emprise du sport. Alphil, Lausanne, pp 145–155 (forthcoming work)
Urbain JD (2002) L'idiot du voyage. Payot, Paris
Young P (2009) A tasteful patrimony: landscape preservation and tourism in the 'sites and monuments' campaign, 1900-1935. French Hist Stud 32:447–477
Walton JK (2011) Seaside tourism in Europe: business, urban and comparative history. Bus Hist 53:900–916. https://doi.org/10.1080/00076791.2011.590936

Steve Hagimont is an Associate professor of Environmental History at the Institut d'études politiques de Toulouse (Occitanie, France). He work about the commodification of mountain environment through tourist activities and facilities since the nineteenth century. He published La Terre perdue. Une histoire de l'Occident et de la nature (18e-21e siècle), edited with Charles-François Mathis (Tallandier, 2025).

Chapter 3
Switzerland: A New Playground for Tourism in the Twentieth Century?

Laurent Tissot

Abstract Switzerland is a pioneer in the emergence of tourism in the nineteenth century, but its development over the following century is mixed. Forced to abandon certain strategies that made it successful due to changes in the economy (crises) and in the political situation (wars), faced with an increasingly competitive international market, it adopts new institutional, technical, and financial tools that gradually transform all aspects of the tourism sector. While the winter season is becoming predominant in the tourist calendar, more attention is also being paid to the cultural and historical diversity of the country. This has led to a change in the hotel stock, with new buildings attracting a socially and internationally diverse clientele. But more importantly, the intervention of the central government not only makes it possible to find ways of reducing the burden of debt, but also to solicit new financial resources to renovate infrastructures, many of which have become outdated.

Introduction

Making Switzerland a model for tourism development is certainly verifiable. This is clearly the case in the nineteenth century, when a number of elements combined to give this country a leading position in terms of accessibility to landscapes, means of transport and communication, hospitality infrastructure, governance, education and entertainment, not to mention the context of security and privacy associated with its peaceful and neutral attributes (Tissot 2004). Combining audacity and confidence, tradition and innovation, anticipation and imitation, Switzerland succeeds in winning over a clientele that is as financially well-off as it is economically loyal (Humair

L. Tissot (✉)
University of Neuchâtel, Neuenburg, Switzerland

Neuchâtel, Switzerland
e-mail: Laurent.Tissot@unine.ch

C. Larrinaga, D. Strangio (eds.), *Tourism Destinations and Policies in Europe During the 20th Century*, Contributions to Economics,
https://doi.org/10.1007/978-3-031-88447-4_3

et al. 2009). But is this exemplarity still relevant for the twentieth century, as many advertisements have claimed?

The question deserves to be raised. A glance at the evolution of the number of hotel beds and overnight stays is all it takes to realise the singularities of the country over the centuries (Graph 3.1). In complete contradiction to the second half of the nineteenth century, when the supply of beds follows a virtually linear curve and overnight stays more or less follow the same trajectory—marked upward trends are punctuated periodically by downward movements, illustrating the extreme sensitivity of the sector to the slightest economic swing—the twentieth century presents a striking contrast. Both bed supply and overnight stays are in a very complicated situation. Combined with the consequences of the First and Second World Wars and the crisis of the inter-war years, the depressing nature of these trends is evident well into the 1950s. Admissions are falling, as is the number of beds, indicating a serious depression. We are back to the figures of 1890–1900 (Humair 2011). While it is true that the first half of the twentieth century is extremely unfavourable for the tourism sector, the end of the Second World War marks the start of a period of prosperity that lasts almost 30 years. Referred to as the Trente Glorieuses, these years breathed new life into the industry and put Switzerland back on the global tourism map. Without describing them as calamitous, instability once again becomes the "norm" from the 1970s onwards. The sector's resilience during the fluctuating period that stretches to the end of the twentieth century is actually quite astonishing, given its particular characteristics (strong franc, globalisation, refusal to join the European Union, etc.). It cannot be dissociated from a capacity for adaptation, reinforced by changes in social and cultural behaviour, which give leisure activities, and tourism in particular, a growing importance in the scale of values.

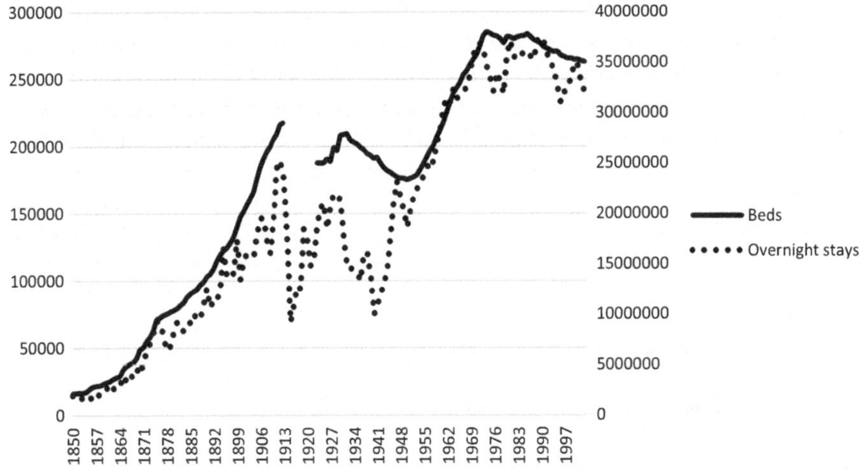

Graph 3.1 Trends in hotel supply (number of beds in thousands: left hand scale) and demand (overnight stays in millions: right hand scale). Source: Historical Statistics of Switzerland (HSSO)—Tourism: M.1–M.5

Beyond simply commenting on the statistics, we need to look more closely at the managerial and strategic implications of these figures for the Swiss tourism industry. Looking at Swiss tourism involves considering all the factors that explain its political and economic stature and, consequently, its influence on the recognition of the country's landscape and hospitality around the world. While the durability of a reputation is the challenge facing public authorities and developers, the resolution of these short-term disruptions is not uniformed. Calling on the State, taking better account of technological and cultural innovations, renewing political and economic conditions—the range of measures is very broad.

The Role of the State

Although Switzerland declared its neutrality, it was not immune from the consequences of the First World War for its economy and population. The impact on tourism is immediate. Directly affected by the measures taken in their countries of origin (closure of borders, mobilisation of soldiers, material restrictions, transport, and communication obstacles), the large number of visitors who were staying in Switzerland abandon their stay overnight to return home as quickly as possible. Hotels are helplessly faced with a real desertion. As a result, tourism service providers must contend with all kinds of obstacles: exchange rate fluctuations, customs and bureaucratic formalities, tax debts, transport fares, and so on (Tissot 2021).

One consolation comes from the war... itself. Although Switzerland's role is not limited to taking in the wounded and prisoners of all nationalities—above all French, Belgian, English and German—the hotels, boarding houses, and other buildings—barracks—provide a place of rest for some and consolation for others. As part of a range of initiatives that also include the Federal Post Office and the Federal railways, as well as the International Committee of the Red Cross (ICRC), the action of the central government is decisive (Cotter and Herrmann 2014). Its diplomatic and humanitarian actions don't only lead to concrete results in the admission of these victims, but it is also active in the requisitioning of reception buildings in collaboration with the Swiss Hoteliers' Association (Bondallaz 2021). The number of these guests is not enough to compensate for the losses caused by the conflict, but their welcome gives the Swiss hotel industry an image far removed from the one that clung to it, that of a destination for wealthy guests benefiting from the dividends of the Belle Epoque.

Uniting Despite Resistance

The weight of the Confederation increases from the end of the war (Narindal 2023). There are several reasons for this. Firstly, the global conflict leaves those involved in tourism in a state of shock, despite the spirit of solidarity that animates them as they welcome internees. From an economic point of view, there is only one adjective to describe the events: catastrophic. Marked by a strong liberal conviction in all the speeches and actions throughout the nineteenth century—political, financial, and economic—but sustained at the same time by continuous growth, the tourism sector saw no need for external intervention. Although tourism offices had been set up in a number of places—Zurich and Lausanne in 1885, Genève in 1889—demonstrating the desire of promoters, particularly hoteliers, to pool their forces for joint action, initiatives remained local and private (Tissot 2013). With the emergence of growing competition from neighbouring countries, as well as from other European and non-European countries, Switzerland finds itself less and less in a monopoly situation from the beginning of the twentieth century. This situation is reinforced during the inter-war period by growing protectionism and exacerbated nationalism. In Austria and France, there is a clear conviction that the forces of tourism should be united in a national body supported, more or less intensively, by the State.

Created in 1910, the Office national du tourisme (ONT) is the first step towards centralising national efforts to promote tourism in France. It is inspired directly by the Austrian model, where in July 1909 a "Section for the Movement of Foreigners" is set up within the Ministry of Public Works, with special responsibility for tourism issues. Even if the beginnings are difficult and do not diminish thereafter, the momentum is there (Larique 2007). The French case prompts, 1 year later, Alexandre Seiler, a Valais hotelier who runs several hotels and is also a member of the Swiss Parliament, to take action. His initiative leads to the creation in 1917 of the National Association for the Development of Tourism, which takes the name of the Swiss Central Office for Tourism in 1937 and becomes a public-law corporation domiciled in Zurich in 1940 (Amacher 2016). The organism is still very imperfect. But it marks the first step towards the institutionalisation of tourism and its recognition by the State as a decisive economic force for many regions, particularly in the mountains. Its primary aim is to promote Switzerland as a country for travel, holidays, and congresses. With this in mind, it attempts to bring together the interests and initiatives of all the tourism sectors in Switzerland. It's important to emphasise the word "attempt", as all the parties involved are putting their own interests before the defence of a national industry. The most immediate achievement is the opening of an office in Nice in 1923, to improve the association's presence abroad. The choice for being present there proves the Swiss Central Office for Tourism's aim of reaching an upper-class clientele. But no one asks whether tourism based on high-style, capital-intensive hotels and targeting a relatively socially restricted clientele is still relevant and appropriate for the times.

Helping Against All Odds

Another aspect of state intervention is linked to the deplorable situation of many hotels (Schneider 2022). Founded in 1921, the Société fiduciaire suisse pour l'hôtellerie (Swiss Trust Company for the Hotel Industry), which is revived, after a brief interruption, in 1932 under the name Société Suisse de Crédit Hôtelier (SSCH) has a dual objective: firstly, to stimulate the sector and limit the arrival of new competitors on the domestic market through protective measures (Narindal 2016) and, secondly, to reorganise hotel businesses that are in difficulty, but which meet all the conditions for viability (Schneider 2016). These measures are largely part of the vast cartelisation movement that the Swiss economy undergoes in the first half of the twentieth century (Cortat 2010). The main focus is on improving the financial situation, rationalising management, and advertising methods. In addition to internal methods (downsizing, cost-cutting, etc.), there are initiatives to improve professional training and knowledge of commercial accounting. The Federal Vocational Training Act of 1930, which comes into force in 1933, strengthens training in the hotel industry, which had seen the launch of the Ecole hôtelière de Lausanne in 1893 on the initiative of the Swiss Hoteliers' Association, and the Ecole hôtelière de Lucerne in 1909 under the supervision of Union Helvetia, the largest organisation representing employees in the hotel and catering industry.

The questioning of Keynesian theories during the second post-war period and the excitement generated by neo-liberal beliefs in the 1960s lead to a new interpretation of the socio-economic conditions under which prosperity should be envisaged (Narindal 2023). Globalisation as seen under the neo-liberal banner leaves little room for the State. Swiss tourism is no exception, in what can only be described as a tidal wave. In 1967, aid to the hotel industry—known under the German name of *Hotelhilfsaktion*—is abolished. Although the State had not said its last word, its influence is considerably reduced.

All these measures lead to a major strategic change. They raise awareness of the futility of a supply-side policy based on what had made Switzerland's tourism reputation in the nineteenth century. The construction of establishments far removed from the sumptuous standards of the Belle Epoque is combined with the arrival of less "prestigious" clients, particularly local ones. The proportion of foreign tourists falls sharply, illustrating the major changes in the consumption patterns of the Swiss population. With the return to normality in the 50s and the advent of the Trente Glorieuses, the attraction that Swiss tourism exerts on foreign customers once again becomes a fact (Graph 3.2). In other words, it is the domestic clientele that enables the sector to survive during the great moments of uncertainty of the wars and the inter-war period (Schneider 2022). Subsequently, foreign customers regain the momentum that ensure the revival of tourism, but on a different and broader basis from that of the Belle Epoque.

The Role of Transport

Transport is at the heart of tourism. It is the key element whenever a tourist activity involves travel (Tissot 2006). While Switzerland is able to rely, not without difficulty, on an efficient rail network with technical infrastructure and material support facilities closely associated with the strengthening of the sector, the creation of the

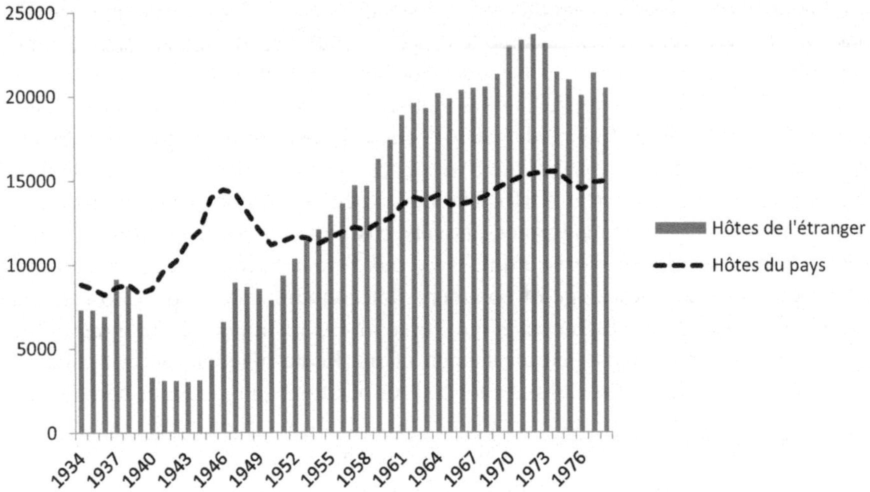

Graph 3.2 Hotels: overnight stays by domestic and foreign guests (in thousands). Source: Historical Statistics of Switzerland (HSSO): M.7b. Hotel Operations

mountain railways is certainly the trigger for Switzerland's prosperity as a tourist destination and its worldwide reputation.

Electrification of the Rail Network

In the difficult context created by the First World War and the years that followed, the railways don't remain passive. Still leading the way in transport before motorised vehicles competed head-on with them, but aware of the changes that were taking place, they were very active and initiated numerous measures.

While steam dominated the birth and consolidation of the railways in the nineteenth century, electrical technology is slowly making inroads into what is seen by many as the most appropriate solution for transporting passengers: no more inconveniences in the form of suffocation from smoke or dirt from soot residues. You can open the carriage window without fear and marvel at the scenery, soaking up the fresh mountain air. Travelling by electric train is clean, convenient, and invigorating. In this sense, it redefines the link between transport and the environment, giving it a whole new dimension for tourism. Although it requires colossal investment, electrification is an obvious choice and solves the nagging question of coal supplies, which was severely felt during the Great War (Humair and Chachereau 2024). The electrification of the Gotthard line in 1920 marks the real energy turning point. By 1936, over 70% of the Swiss network is electrified, compared with an average of 5% in other European countries. In 1960, the network is completely electrified. The consequences for tourism are just as decisive because they reinforce the idea that the conjunction of this activity with technical innovation underpins its attractiveness, but less so because, as we shall see below, another innovation, the motor vehicle, collides head-on with this electrical triumph.

An Attractive Supply Policy

Against this innovative backdrop, the railways, both public and private, take initiatives in advertising, fares, and the promotion of new offers. In 1922, sports and weekend tickets are introduced, which are transformed into Sunday tickets; the same year, special trains are introduced at reduced prices for company trips and school runs; in September 1933, travel weeks are launched, allowing people with an ordinary single ticket to benefit from a free return journey.

The most emblematic innovation in this respect is the launch in 1935 of the Red Arrows, the new lightweight electric railcars. They quickly become an icon. Their use is not only linked to their mobility, but they also have an immediate advertising function. Although they travel the length and breadth of the Swiss network, they carry with them what Switzerland wants to show off: modernity, cleanliness, speed, flexibility, comfort, accessibility—the praises keep piling up to describe the prowess of a machine that is seen by many as revolutionary. The interest they arise among the public is prompting the Federal railways to use them for other occasions that are becoming more and more important: in combination with the shipping companies and post buses, company trips, school runs, family or company excursions and organised tours are being offered. There are a number of different models, with improvements aimed primarily at making travel conditions more pleasant and increasing the number of places available. After all, the public uses this means of transport above all to enjoy, marvel and be entertained. The popularity of the Red Arrows continues to grow among the Swiss public, particularly children who, accompanied by their parents, give them considerable publicity. As future tourists, they provide strong support for the Federal railways at a time when competition from motorised vehicles is increasing.

This means that, by choice, the pricing policy is very advantageous, as the Federal Railways avoid making these trains luxury items reserved for an elite. Along with other measures, the Red Arrows contributes to the democratisation of travel in Switzerland, a process that benefits from social advances in terms of working hours, paid holidays, and access to leisure activities in several sectors of the economy: public administration, chemicals, metallurgy, watchmaking and banking.

The Triumph of the Automobile

Unlike the train, which is obliged to follow fixed trajectories through the territory and, unless new lines are built, which takes time, is limited in its horizons of exploration, the motor vehicle has a formidable advantage: it can go (almost) anywhere as long as the road is suitable and can suddenly take a side road to discover a new viewpoint. This flexibility is part of the individualisation of mobility, giving everyone the opportunity, real or pretended, to travel without a fixed timetable and as they please. The management of time and space is taking on a new dimension, summed up in a single word that justifies the use of motorised vehicles for tourism: freedom. Although up until the Second World War, freedom of movement remains limited for technical and social reasons, it explodes during the second half of the twentieth century.

It is not unreasonable to associate the period known as the "Trente Glorieuses" with a socio-technical revolution. What happens to mobility during this period remains of crucial importance for understanding the evolution of individual travel and its impact on both the cultural and natural environment. Even without a national manufacturer on its soil, Switzerland played a major role in the unbridled development of automobile transport. Following in the footsteps of other countries, it is making the most of the synergies that can be found between the automobile and tourism. The tourist argument is regularly put forward to describe the attractions of motorised access to the resorts. One of the main indicators of this gradual takeover of the car is the appearance in Switzerland of travel guides devoted entirely to its benefits.

André Beerli (1915–2004), a future professor of art history and architecture, wrote numerous articles on tourism for the Touring-Club de Suisse. In the midst of the war, he publishes a book entitled *La Suisse inconnue* (Unknown Switzerland), which sets out the 27 proposed itineraries that appear in the pre-war *Revue du Touring-Club de Suisse*. "Even if, [he writes,] draconian measures limit the use of petrol [...], the war must not prevent us from travelling and discovering the hidden treasures of our cantons". His vision of Switzerland as a tourist destination draws on the old clichés already widely used in the nineteenth century: the country's small size makes it easy to visit, the diversity of its cultures amplifies the desire to visit, "the tenacity of regional traditions" in no way excludes "a profound unity". He rejects the idea that Switzerland is inward-looking. On the contrary, "the variety of foreign influences superimposed on local particularities of style" is what gives it its originality and unity. He is aware that this unity is not easy to discern, but it can be seen in the political history of the country, in the long-term tendency for the regions between the Alps and the Jura to come together, and in the arts, in "a particular way of assimilating the waves of civilisation that have swept through our territory". This speech takes on a particular tone in the midst of a "spiritual defence" in which typically Swiss values are constantly being celebrated since the 30s, but Beerli is keen to set his speech in a European context, which is what makes it so original.

Other editions and publishers (notably the Michelin guide) will follow with the same emphasis on the benefits of the road in getting to know the hidden facets of Switzerland.

Second Homes Triumph

The car activates another alternative form of sedentary lifestyle, which can be found to a greater or lesser extent throughout the Alps: second homes in the form of chalets or flats. Second homes have a decisive impact on post-Second World War tourism. They are part of a transformation in Swiss tourism that has major consequences for land management, particularly in the Alps, and for the development of resorts. What has been called the "tourism transition" is based on a shift away from the traditional hotel business towards forms of accommodation combining stays of varying lengths in chalets and flats, whether owned or rented. For many resorts, this shift can be seen as a revolution in the way land is used, and in the activities of mountain populations.

Owned by local residents—some of whom already own hotels—or by the commune bourgeoise, these plots of land and the mayens that populate them, many of which are considered to be of no particular value, become a source of significant added value and, as new buildings are built, whet the appetite of other owners, as the coveted areas are limited only by altitude and access (Lorenzetti and Delmenico 2017). The lack of state intervention in land management and in regulating the land et property market is a key factor in the expansion of second homes. Awareness of the concept of a "development plan" emerges only slowly, first at municipal level and then at cantonal level, without any major restrictions. Faced with the rapid expansion of the phenomenon, the 1960s see the emergence of less timid federal regulations. Access to home ownership for non-Swiss residents, the promotion of territorial zoning and, until more recently, the imposition of a maximum threshold of 20% of these residences as a proportion of the total housing stock, all serve to highlight the attention paid to a problem that is considered to be very thorny. The patrimonial and emotional dimension felt by the world of property owners, especially indigenous ones, clashes head-on with the environmental and landscape dimension that is increasingly widespread in public opinion, and the conflict between private and public interests is exacerbated (Clivaz 2014).

The phenomenon of second homes is not confined to mountain areas and also affects certain lakeshores. However, one factor plays a decisive role in this sudden development of land that had previously been considered of little interest: the explosion of winter tourism, and particularly skiing, which is already perceptible during the inter-war years and which, from the 1950s onwards, exerts a real fascination on ever-wider sections of the population, both Swiss and foreign. As summer pastures are only used for a few months a year, the mountain pastures and their buildings are left unused in winter. With the popularity of winter sports, they have taken on a new appeal, with the former being annexed to these new areas of enjoyment and the latter being transformed into refreshment stands, mountain restaurants or converted chalets (Clivaz and Nahrath 2010).

The Role of Sports and Leisure

While the advent of sports represents a real revolution in the nineteenth century in educational, hygienic, military, ideological and social terms, their impact on tourism is central (*Entreprises et Histoire*, December 2018). Although not yet very visible during the summer season, it is mainly the emergence of winter sports that multiplies the effects. The result is a synergy that gives tourism an astonishing boost. This phenomenon is particularly precocious and vivid in Switzerland (Busset and Marcacci 2006). The question is not just how this merger comes about in terms of leisure activities, but also the strategic reasons why developers are opening resorts in winter and creating new infrastructures. That means that the issue cannot simply be reduced to demand versus supply.

Winter, the Other Summer

At the heart of the problem are the new relationships between the human body and the sun. The growing conviction that the sun is good for your health is tipping the balance in annual visits. Up to the end of the nineteenth century, many wealthy people take refuge in the mountains in the summer, or go there for holidays between June and September, to escape the heat. With the return of winter, they take shorter or longer stays by the sea, where the temperatures are milder and the climate more clement than in the mountains. At the heart of numerous debates and heated controversies, the beneficial effects of altitude on lung disease convince however many doctors as early as 1840. But it isn't until the 1880s that winter sojourns are considered as beneficial as those in Mediterranean climates (Reichler 2005). For some authors, this context explains the emergence of winter sports-related entertainment. Winter sports are first and foremost associated with health. The impetus comes from the sanatorium patients themselves, who, finding time long, indulge in them before they attract a more seasoned sporting clientele keen to detach themselves from any medical tone (Allen 2007).

For mountain tourism, which until then had been a summer activity, the huge challenge is to prove that the mountains can also be visited in winter for fun and leisure. The development of a winter season involves costly investment in infrastructure, particularly hotels, with the introduction of central heating, road clearing and the construction of facilities such as ice rinks, bobsleigh runs, sledging, skiing, and curling.

As the winter season develops, large-scale initiatives are being taken. The most notable of these comes from an English promoter, Henry Lunn. He sets up a full-fledged agency, the Public Schools Alpine Sports Club (PSASC), to organise organised trips to Swiss resorts. This agency is unique in that it admits only a very select clientele, chosen on the basis of their membership of the various institutions that cater for England's aristocratic, economic, political, medical, religious and administrative elite, most of whom are educated in the most renowned public schools. It takes up the social codes in force in these institutions and redeploys them into formulas combining elective sentiment and sporting conquest (Barton 2014).

From then on, Switzerland is the preferred playground. Lunn plans arrangements with hotels in numerous resorts where he does more than just book hotel rooms. It also organises bobsleigh, skiing, and ice hockey competitions. The arrival of Lunn's "tourists" gives the chosen locations the opportunity to develop their winter sports offer and build new establishments. The case study of Mürren is a good example (Feuz 2014). During the winter of 1912–1913, five of the resort's ten hotels are reserved exclusively for Lunn's clientele, a total of 400 guests. Lunn also invests personally in the hotel business. He buys the Hôtel des Alpes and extends it with a new building, the Palace, with a ballroom for 350 people. The hotel also has 10,000 m^2 of ice, as well as curling rinks and ice rinks. These achievements, reinforced by other initiatives in other places, particularly in the Lake Geneva region and the canton of Graubünden, make the Swiss Alps a major centre of development (Humair et al. 2009; Quin 2022).

They are illustrated in travel guides, which are quick to point out these new uses for winter. The famous Baedeker guide is one of the first to do so. It lists 34 resorts, including those in the Jura, that offer winter activity facilities. First and foremost is Saint-Moritz, "whose huge hotels are full all winter", and Davos "more tranquil, in an excellent location, which was once just a climate resort and now boasts sports centres" (Baedeker 1911: XXI).

Mass Leisure

As we have already mentioned, the advent of the "Trente Glorieuses" marks a turning point for tourism, with winter sports booming. The notion of mass consumption is not a misnomer when it comes to defining the real craze that characterised the 1980s. Skiing is the main vehicle for this trend, which continues to attract enthusiasts from Switzerland and elsewhere, whether on their own, with their families or as a group. There's nothing pretentious about describing the 1970s to the present day as the "heyday" of skiing. Every effort is made to multiply the number of resorts, extend the skiable area as far as possible by increasing the number of facilities, come up with new forms of skiing (snowboarding, freestyle, carving) that appeal to new generations tired of skiing like mum and dad, and update equipment (skis, clothing, boots, goggles, etc.) with the introduction of synthetic materials that make it much easier to use. By constantly reinventing itself, the industry benefits from a technology without which it would be neither feasible nor profitable. The mountains are measured only by their ability to provide ski lifts, which are in turn measured by their transport capacity (so many skiers per hour). Second homes are springing up all over the place, alongside hotels. It's filled with restaurants, bars, and cafés, and has to deal with the great après-ski hours, key moments of conviviality when alcohol, dancing, flirting, and other forms of fun lead to the creation of the 3 S (sun-snow-sex), parodies of a lifestyle that knows no limits (Quin et al. 2023).

With this in mind, skiing and all its associated activities are becoming formidable targets for investment from all over the world, seeking returns to match their ambitions at all costs. Its systemic aspect makes it a powerful element in the tourism value chain. The uncertainties associated with climate change (global warming, greenhouse effects, pollution, overexploitation) cast a shadow over the future of this activity (Tissot 2025).

The Role of Luxury and of Popular Tourism

The social aspect is associated with practices that are far from identical. Taking skiing as a case study, until the 50s it is mainly reserved for a privileged few in an increasingly complex and sometimes tragic world, but with the advent of the Trente Glorieuses, it becomes a mass sport. Alongside victories in competitions (Olympic Games, world championships), the nation and the general public begins to identify with the sport. Skiing is a way of showing that you are Swiss. But this phenomenon is also recognisable in the summer, when the joys of camping and discovering nature now dominate the free time of the majority of the population. This is not to say that, over the long term, Swiss tourism has indiscriminately brought together customers from different social backgrounds. We are dealing with social accumulations where new entrants do not question existing profiles. Distinction remains a key element in explaining the trends that are affecting tourism.

Jet Set and Peopolisation

Luxury summons specific attributes (both material and symbolic) in order to respond to the expectations and requirements of a wealthy clientele, the aristocracy, and the upper middle class. In that sense, luxury is not a superfluous value as it is experienced in other fields. It gives expression and meaning to a way of life, to behaviours which directly correspond to political, economic, cultural, and social authorities (Tissot 2018). St Moritz, Zermatt, Gstaad, Crans-Montana, Verbier, Davos, Villars-sur-Ollon, or Klosters are resorts where luxury is on display in all its splendour. This opulence is based on a number of criteria: the quality of sports and leisure facilities, the number of palaces and five-star hotels, the number of Michelin-starred restaurants and brand boutiques (clothing, watches, jewellery, cigars), the excellence of cultural events (festivals), the presence of luxury chalets and the ease of getting around. As a key element of resort strategy, the supply policy acts as a powerful magnet to attract a very wealthy clientele.

Finding the reasons for this also means looking at the demand, i.e. the celebrities who stay there, whether they come from showbiz, sport, politics, the media, the world of business and finance, the arts, the royal families, and so on. A resort's reputation is built on its ability to see these celebrities' parade through its streets or onto its ski slopes. Wrapped up in their coats and fur hats, they stroll nonchalantly with their families or couples before slipping on the latest boots and donning the latest ski outfits. This "peopolisation" goes back a long way, and bears witness to the rise of skiing as a social marker. Originally, only the very wealthy classes could afford winter holidays, but the resorts were already making the point. It was not uncommon to publish a list of foreigners staying in the resorts. Showing who you were hosting was also proof of visibility and notoriety.

In search of places where they can stay in complete safety, they make the condition, however, that this publicity must be accompanied by respect for their privacy. The photographers and other journalists sent by the celebrity magazines are never far away, but never too close. If treating yourself to such a luxury shows that you belong to a select community, being seen in such a resort shows everyone else that you are different from them. Showing off without being disturbed is not trivial, but the act is not without risk: by trying too hard to show off, you lose your sense of status, and by living reclusively in your hotel suite or chalet, you distance yourself from the media spotlight. This elite adopts common codes and likes to socialise. They adhere to a form of excellence where money is used to make all demands and solve all problems (Quin et al. 2023).

The Impact of Social Tourism

We cannot be content with this one-sided view of things. The concept of social tourism, which emerges in England at the end of the nineteenth century and is popularised between the wars, really comes into its own in the second half of the twentieth century. The initial aim is to preserve or restore the working capacity of those affected by the infernal pace of factory work, by giving them adequate free time. Added to this is the compensation for the sacrifices made during the war and the improvement in living standards thanks to increased productivity. By regenerating bodies, social tourism also gives the people who embody them the opportunity to enjoy unique experiences in a different way, even for a limited time. Social tourism therefore activates a series of mechanisms designed to guarantee widespread access to leisure activities. There are many measures aimed at widening the circle of beneficiaries. It is only their scope that is being discussed (Schumacher 2002).

From this perspective, the railways play a decisive role, particularly the Federal railways in accordance with its status as a state-owned company. Social objectives are nevertheless coupled with commercial considerations. The forms taken by social rail tourism are diverse, with journeys promoting excursions with different outward and return journeys rubbing shoulders with direct, fast journeys between home and holiday destination. But in all cases, the collective dimension predominates to the detriment of individual travel. The case of the Red Arrows, analysed above, is also part of this social craze for tourism in Switzerland. It is a perfect illustration of the link between technical change and social change.

The fact remains that, willy-nilly, initiatives have sprung up that enable the railways to drive leisure traffic. It's worth mentioning the players who are working to promote this social extension of tourism, and who are using the railways, among other means, to achieve their aims. There are around ten of them: the "Friends of Nature", the Swiss Railway Workers' Holiday Home Cooperative, the Industry, Construction and Services Union, the Federation of Wood and Building Workers, the holiday homes of the Swiss Union of Consumer Cooperatives, the Swiss Union of Trade Unions' Holiday Foundation, the Christian Social Holiday Home Cooperative, the Swiss Association of Family Hostels, holiday flats and the Association of Swiss Youth Hostels. Some of these associations were already active at the turn of the nineteenth and twentieth centuries, others at the end of the Second World War, but they were all committed to social tourism. Added to these are the initiatives taken by Hotelplan, the Swiss Travel Fund and the Popularis Tours travel agency set up after the war. A real backbone is being put in place, including trade unions, philanthropic and religious organisations, and private companies.

The transition is easy from this point of view, except that social pressures are still growing. A few factors give an idea of the rise in living standards and its repercussions on the possibilities of participating in what is becoming a normality.

There is a downside to this enthusiasm: inflation upsets the wonderful plans for achievement. However, much it may have been desired, the opening up of leisure activities has come up against this major obstacle. By pressure, therefore, we also mean the pressure that forced the railway companies to tackle the sharp deterioration in their financial situation at the end of the war. The situation is the same, if not worse, in private companies. The public authorities find themselves caught between the social hammer and the financial anvil: responding to the legitimate demands of the working classes and satisfying the business community, which is increasingly concerned about the profitability of public services. In other words, every new service is accompanied by measures to increase fares, in a mutually reinforcing effect.

The Role of Coaches and Camping

Coaches and, to a lesser extent, boats are essential complements to the rail network, branching out where trains are unable to go. In both cases, collective travel remains predominant, and it is understandable that their role should not be overlooked, particularly in the affirmation of social tourism. In other words, what happens within the rail companies has a direct impact on road traffic and, to a lesser extent, lake traffic. Despite the car, coach travel is literally exploding. Not only tourists, of course, but also schoolchildren and commuters.

While it is true that the economic crisis of the 1930s keeps demand for coaches at constant levels, the Trente Glorieuses see it increase considerably, which also leads to an increase in supply. Vehicles operating under the supervision of the PTT provide services required by law. But private companies can also be concessionaires for lines that must provide a certain number of services to the local population (transport of letters, parcels, etc.) as well as offering other services. Tourism soon becomes a highly lucrative business. New private companies enter this field, either by initially operating postal lines or transporting goods, then diversifying into tourist excursions, and expanding their range. For many of these companies, the creation of a travel agency ensures a lasting presence in tourism. What is new, however, is that less affluent sections of the population have access to leisure travel in the context of social tourism. Shooting clubs, singing clubs, youth clubs, brass bands and sports teams from town and country are all taking advantage of the services on offer. They fill the coaches and travel along the roads of Switzerland and beyond for 1 or 2 days or more.

Often labelled as cultural tourists from the affluent classes, choosing well-located and well-equipped hotels, motorists were not the only ones to take to the road. That's what makes the post-war years so special. Driving is certainly a means to an end, but it also has a specific purpose: to find a destination where they can relax and enjoy the sun and snow. Tourism doesn't necessarily mean an accumulation of visits and sights. Immersion in nature, enjoyment of the landscape, freedom of behaviour and movement—camping lends itself to every kind of fantasy and imagination. Let's beware of limiting camping to an alternative sedentary lifestyle. It is a term that covers a wide range of living arrangements and habitats. Moving from one pitch to another, many motorhome and caravan enthusiasts criss-cross the countryside and are not afraid to add up the kilometres to see something new. For those who prefer a fixed pitch, tents, and caravans sit alongside chalets, mobile homes, and cabins. Camping is also associated with different means of locomotion: walking, horse riding, train, bicycle, motorbike.... But it is true that the car gives it an undeniable boost. Leaving the city to take up spaces free of all constraints is a way of understanding and defending them (Tissot 2023).

Conclusion

For a long time, the Belle Epoque is like a ridge that the tourism industry tries desperately to reclaim, and which, despite all its efforts, becomes more distant the closer you think you are approaching it. Once the First World War breaks out, certainties and uncertainties continue to exist side by side. It is in the middle of this turbulent backdrop that we must try to understand the reasons why Switzerland's tourism sector finds the resources it needs, first to survive and then to revive. Accumulating and sometimes even contradicting or excluding each other, different strategies are recognisable, drawing on different sources. It is probably fair to say that throughout the twentieth century, tourism in Switzerland undergoes profound changes in terms of its governance, its practices, and its customer base, even if there are perceptible continuities, supported by the presence of the mountains remaining an intangible point.

While state intervention comes as no surprise, as it can be found elsewhere and in other Swiss economic sectors, the intensity of the measures is noteworthy. Tourism is following in the footsteps of other sectors for which the State is no longer an enemy to be kept as far away from as possible, but a welcome, albeit temporary, aid in these troubled times. State intervention is accompanied by a strengthening of the links between tourism players, leading to the creation of a cartel in which the very notion of laissez-faire/laissez-aller is no more than a pipe dream.

The survival of tourism in Switzerland is also the prerogative of those involved in transport. While the effects are clearly visible in an advantageous pricing policy, the Swiss Federal Railways are conquering a new market thanks to technical innovations in the form of the Red Arrows, light electric railcars that are rapidly winning over the Swiss public. No doubt that, in the long term, the motorised vehicle will be the most important vector. As much an object of independence as of individualisation, the car has shattered all our points of reference. In the space of just a few years, as in many countries around the world, the car determines new ways of life and opens the door to new experiences. The case study of winter sports and skiing is sufficient to demonstrate the strength of this mode of transport, which brings thousands of skiers and snowboarders to the slopes. All the mountain resorts are involved, giving free rein to the devouring ambitions of property developers who know how to meet the expectations of customers looking for second homes.

The concept of luxury, which is based on a number of different aspects, largely determines the trajectory of Swiss tourism. While it is the foundation of its development in the second half of the nineteenth century, it continues to dominate the twentieth century, and even more strongly. Political, fiscal, economic, ideological, and symbolic aspects all combine to explain Switzerland's appeal. This is not to say that less "prestigious" profiles are not taken into account. Even if the notion of social tourism is perhaps more restrictive than it is in other countries, it does define the tourism trajectories that have welcomed Swiss people—families, workers, employees—in search of moments of conviviality and happiness in the Alps.

References

Allen EJB (2007) The culture and sport of skiing: from antiquity to World War II. University of Massachusetts Press, Amherst

Amacher A (2016) The beginnings of the Federal Tourism Policy 1917-1939. An institutional history of Switzerland's national tourist office, the Schweizerische Verkehrszentrale (SVZ), University of Neuchâtel, unpublished doctoral thesis

Baedeker K (1911) La Suisse et les parties limitrophes de la Savoie et de l'Italie. Manuel du voyageur, 27e ed. Baedeker, Leipzig

Barton S (2014) Healthy living in the Alps. The origins of winter tourism in Switzerland, 1860-1914. Manchester University Press, Manchester

Bondallaz P (2021) «Inter Arma Helvetia». L'action humanitaire suisse pendant la Grande Guerre. Alphil, Neuchâtel

Busset T, Marcacci M (eds) (2006) Pour une histoire des sports d'hiver. CIES, Neuchâtel

Clivaz C, Nahrath S (2010) Le retour de la question foncière dans l'aménagement des stations touristiques alpines en Suisse. J Alpine Res. Revue de géographie alpine. En ligne, 98-2 | 2010, mis en ligne le 14 septembre 2010. http://journals.openedition.org/rga/1220; https://doi.org/10.4000/rga.1220, consulté le 26.12.2023

Clivaz C (2014) Acceptation de l'initiative sur les résidences secondaires. J Alpine Res. Revue de géographie alpine. En ligne, Hors-Série | 2013, mis en ligne le 08 avril 2014. http://journals.openedition.org/rga/1866, consulté 26.12.2023.

Cortat A (2010) Contribution à une histoire des cartels en Suisse. Alphil, Neuchâtel

Cotter C, Herrmann I (2014) Quand secourir sert à se protéger. La Suisse et les œuvres humanitaires. In: Rossefeld R, Buomberger T, Kury P (eds) 14/18. La Suisse et la Grande Guerre. Hier und Jetzt, Baden, pp 241–265

Entreprises et Histoire (2018) Sports et tourisme. Editions ESKA, Paris, no 93, December

Feuz P (ed) (2014) Kronleuchter vor der Jungfrau. Mürren. Eine Tourismusgeschichte. Hier und Jetzt, Baden

Humair C et al (2009) Système touristique et culture technique dans l'arc lémanique. Analyse d'une success story et de ses effets sur l'économie régionale (1852-1914). Alphil, Neuchâtel, pp 19–50

Humair C (2011) Introduction. In: Humair C, Tissot L (eds) Le tourisme suisse et son rayonnement international, « Switzerland, the Playground of the World ». Antipodes, Lausanne, pp 9–54

Humair C Chachereau N (2024) L'énergie en Suisse. De 1800 à nos jours. Savoir Suisse, Lausanne

Larique B (2007) Les débuts et déboires de l'organisation officielle du tourisme en France : l'expérience malheureuse de l'Office National du Tourisme (1910-1935). Entreprises et histoire 47:73–92

Lorenzetti L, Delmenico D (2017) La transition touristique d'une "station-village". Multipositionnalité et gestion foncière à Champéry (Valais), 1870-1970. J Alpine Res. Revue de géographie alpine 105(4). https://doi.org/10.4000/rga.3643

Narindal M (2016) Limiter la concurrence pour mieux surmonter la crise : la régulation de l'hôtellerie suisse (1915-1954). In: Andrieux JY, Harismendy P (eds) Pension complète ! Tourisme et hôtellerie, XVIIIe XXe siècle. Presses universitaires de Rennes, Rennes, pp 145–154

Narindal M (2023) State intervention in the Swiss hospitality industry: from the end of Laissez-Faire to the beginnings of neoliberalism (1915–1967). In: Larrinaga C, Strangio D (eds) The development of the hotel and tourism industry in the twentieth century comparative perspectives from Western Europe, 1900–1970. Palgrave/Macmillan, London, pp 33–55

Quin G (2022) The hotelier, the politician and the skier. On the founding moment of alpine skiing in St. Moritz. Sport in History: 213–234.

Quin G, Tissot L, Leresche JP (eds) (2023) Le ski en Suisse. Une histoire. Château&Attinger, Orbe/Colombier

Reichler C (2005) Le bon air des Alpes. Institut de géographie alpine, Grenoble

Schneider G (2016) Configurations et reconfigurations sociales du modèle hôtelier suisse (1914-1953). In: Andrieux JY, Harismendy P (eds) Pension complète ! Tourisme et hôtellerie, XVIIIe XXe siècle. Presses universitaires de Rennes, Rennes, pp 135–144

Schneider G (2022) Comment renouveler l'hôtellerie au sortir de la guerre ? Une enquête de la Société suisse de crédit hôtelier (1943-1952), Mondes du Tourisme [En ligne], 22 | 2022, mis en ligne le 15 décembre 2022, consulté le 19 décembre 2023. http://journals.openedition.org/tourisme/5538; https://doi.org/10.4000/tourisme.5538

Schumacher B (2002) Ferien: Interpretationen und Popularisierung eines Bedürfnisses: Schweiz 1890-1950. Böhlau, Wien

Tissot L (2004) Le tourisme en Suisse ou l'avènement d'un modèle d'excellence (19ème – 20ème siècle). Le Globe 144:103–121

Tissot L (2006) Développement des transports et tourisme : quelles relations ? Revue suisse d'histoire 56:33–39

Tissot L (2013) Dictionnaire historique de la Suisse (DHS), version du 28.03.2013. Offices du tourisme. https://hls-dhs-dss.ch/fr/articles/016456/2013-03-28/, consulté le 16.12.2023

Tissot L (2018) Exclusively for the happy few. Luxury hotels and globalisation: the emergence of a new sector (1980-2010). In: Donzé P-Y, Fujioka R (eds) Global luxury: organizational change and emerging markets since the 1970s. Palgrave Macmillan, London, pp 239–256

Tissot L (2021) La Suisse en tant que destination touristique. In: Halbeisen P, Müller M, Veyrassat B (eds) Histoire économique de la Suisse au XXe siècle. Alphil, Neuchâtel, pp 585–599

Tissot L (2023) La Suisse se découvre. Trois siècles de tourisme en question (1730 à nos jours). Alphil, Neuchâtel

Tissot L (2025) "Towards a New Type of Tourism? From Conventional Tourism to Ecotourism in the Alps" in Teresa da Silva Lopes, Robert Fredona, and Paul Duguid (dir.), Climate Change and Business: Historical Perspectives. London, Routledge, 199–217

Laurent Tissot is Emeritus professor of contemporary history at the University of Neuchâtel since 2018. Studied at universities in Lausanne, London and Paris. Adjunct professor at the University of Lausanne (1987) and the University of Geneva (1997–1999). Lecturer at the University of Fribourg (1994–2005). Professor at the Doctoral School of Social Sciences in Bucharest (2002–2003). Visiting professor at the University of Ottawa (2016). Treasurer of the International Committee for Historical Sciences (2008–2018). Member of the Executive Board of the International Committee for Philosophy and Human Sciences (2013–2020).

Chapter 4
Public Policies and Tourism Development in Spain in the First Third of the Twentieth Century

Carlos Larrinaga

Abstract In the configuration of the tourist systems, the Administration constitutes an agent of special importance, together with the private actors themselves. For this reason, this chapter intends to analyse which were the official national agencies of Spanish tourism, studying the tourism policies they carried out, as well as the degree of satisfaction that these policies generated in the aforementioned private actors. To do this, we start from the hypothesis that these policies were not really satisfactory and that, at the time when Spain was incorporated into the birth of modern tourism, with the birth of the first Spanish tourism system, these private actors saw their expectations lowered regarding of state action.

Introduction

In the configuration of tourist systems, the Administration constitutes a particularly important agent, together with the different private actors. For this reason, this chapter seeks to analyse the official national agencies of Spanish tourism, studying the tourism policies they carried out, as well as the degree of satisfaction that these policies generated among the aforementioned private actors. To do this, we start from the hypothesis that these policies were not wholly satisfactory and that, at the time when Spain was incorporated into the birth of modern tourism, with the emergence of the first Spanish tourism system, these private actors saw their expectations lowered regarding state action.

PID2021-122476NB-I00 research project, financed by MCIN/AEI /10.13039/501100011033/ and the FEDER/ERDF Una manera de hacer Europa / A way of making Europe.

C. Larrinaga (✉)
Department of Economic Theory and Economic History, University of Granada, Granada, Spain

C. Larrinaga, D. Strangio (eds.), *Tourism Destinations and Policies in Europe During the 20th Century*, Contributions to Economics,
https://doi.org/10.1007/978-3-031-88447-4_4

The Spanish Tourism System and the First Official Tourism Body

During the first third of the twentieth century, a first tourism system began to take shape in Spain, based on the agents, destinations and tourism products that had emerged mostly in the last quarter of the nineteenth century. At this time, in the same way as in other European countries, the foundations were laid of what has become known as modern tourism, a term that we will explore later on. In the first decades of this century, Spain could not be considered as a tourism country as such, that is, one that receives foreign tourists and has a tourism balance surplus. This is because national tourism was much more important than inbound tourism, which was still scarce, although it gradually began to gain weight. According to the data available for 1931—1934, it represented between 10% and 17% of total tourism (Vallejo et al. 2016: 150). Unfortunately there are no estimates for the whole of the first third of the twentieth century. All in all, during these years, Spain could be classified more as an outbound tourism country as its nationals predominantly travelled abroad and it had a tourism balance deficit. However, this does not mean that Spain did not have an inbound tourism industry.

In fact, the tourism sector grew slightly until the outbreak of the Civil War in July 1936. Therefore, in the first third of the twentieth century, as previously mentioned, modern tourism began to develop, characterised by the desire to travel for pleasure, the increase in the number of tourists and the development of an entire industry at their service (accommodation, transport, travel agencies, all kinds of entertainment, etc.) (Vallejo 2018: 68; Vallejo and Larrinaga 2018). In this respect, Spain was not unaffected by the tourist flows of these years and the cycles described for other countries of the European continent could also be observed in Spain (Ogilvie 1933; Vallejo et al. 2016: 143). Therefore, tourism as a social practice and as an industry was present in Spain before 1936 in the same way as in other nearby countries, such as France and Italy, although with a lower intensity. This practice gained economic importance and social diffusion and modern tourism gave rise to the emergence of a tourism industry or an industrial organisation of tourism (Norval 1936). As indicated by this author in his classic study, modern tourism was conceived as an industry and had to be promoted due to its economic implications. Therefore, we would be referring to tourism conceived as a business. Focusing on the Spanish case, the emergence of modern tourism brought about the birth of a Spanish tourism system with different regional developments (Vallejo and Larrinaga 2018; Vallejo 2018, 2019). However, it was heavily affected by the outbreak of the Civil War, which plunged it into a severe crisis. Nevertheless, it did not completely disappear, and at the end of the war the Spanish tourism system was reorganised (Larrinaga 2020) (Table 4.1).

In accordance with the objective of this chapter, here we will focus on the Administration. In other words, on its evolution, actions and interaction with private agents. First, however, it is worth mentioning how, from the beginning of the twentieth century, some leading voices noted the relevance that tourism should have for

Table 4.1 The components of the tourism system in the first third of the twentieth century

Tourism system	Destinations and products	
	Market (informal, formal)	
	Agents	Tourists (consumers)
		Active tourism associations
		Inbound tourism associations
		Administration
		Companies (suppliers)
	Tourism organisation	

Source: Vallejo (2018: 85)

the Spanish economy. A prominent defender of this conception of modern tourism as an industry was Bartolomé Amengual. He was the secretary of the Chamber of Commerce and Navigation of Barcelona and had close connections with the economic life of this city and of his native island, Mallorca. Already in 1903, Amengual insisted on the need to organise an inbound tourism industry (Amengual 1903). In his opinion, this industry would not only be beneficial for the hoteliers but also for all of the citizens and different administrations. The foreign tourism industry had to be seen as another sector of economic activity and, therefore, it had to be promoted so as to attract the highest number of tourists possible in order to reactivate the hotel business and also retail, industry or agriculture, as the visitors consumed all types of goods and services. This vision that Amengual had of tourism at the beginning of the twentieth century fully coincided with the definition of modern tourism and was perfectly matched with the path that tourism had begun to take in certain European countries such as Switzerland, France or Italy, for example. A few years later in 1909, Carlos Arcos published a study analysing the economic advantages that tourism should bring to Spain, studying the fundamental causes of its scarce development and the need to promote it and improve the hotel supply of the country, which was vilified by foreign visitors (Arcos 1909).

These studies reveal that, at least in the private economic sphere, the debate on the need to promote tourism in Spain existed. In light of the economic impact that this activity represented for a country such as Italy, for example (Incerpi 2019: 289), the different private Spanish agents, mostly connected to the hotel industry, saw an opportunity in tourism to relaunch their businesses and reactivate the national economy after the strong decline caused by the loss of the last colonies in 1898. Therefore, in parallel with the work of Amengual, it should be noted that the first interest in tourism among the political classes was also generated early on. Between 1903 and 1904, Pablo de Alzola published a report titled "El saneamiento de la moneda (Informe de la Liga de Productores Vizcaína ante la Comisión Parlamentaria)" (*Nuestro Tiempo,* 1903–1904, issues 35: 26 and 37). Pablo de Alzola was a civil engineer and had close connections with the industrial sector in particular and with the economy in general. Born in San Sebastián, the tourism capital of Spain, he had a perfect knowledge of the tourism boom experienced by this town during the last third of the nineteenth century and early years of the twentieth century. In fact, prior to this report, he had published an article titled "La industria del turismo" (*El Pueblo Vasco*, 13 August 1903: 1), in which he advocated the promotion of this sector, not only in the provincial capital of Guipuzcoa, but also in the Basque Country in general (and, by extension, in the rest of Spain), indicating the need for Spanish tourists to spend their summer holidays in Spain and not abroad, due to the losses that this meant for the Spanish economy. According to Alzola, by promoting tourism, Spain could achieve a good financial situation similar to that of Switzerland, France and Italy.

As part of the debate in the Courts on monetary stability, Alzola, the ex-Director General of Public Works, defended the incorporation of the peseta into the gold standard and the need to reinforce it at a time when it had depreciated and to re-establish the balance of payments for which the currencies obtained through foreign inbound tourism could play an important role. The tenets of this engineer were immediately taken up by the Minister of Finance José Echegaray, who established a direct relationship between tourism, external balance and appreciation of the peseta. Immediately after this a commission was created to promote tourism as the first public body. Specifically, the national commission responsible for promoting, using all means available to it, artistic and recreational excursions for foreigners, was created through the Royal Decree of 6 October 1905 (*Gaceta de Madrid*, 7 October 1905: 79). It was the first intervention of the State in the tourism sector and, seemingly at a relatively early date. In fact, the decree specified the tasks and who would form part of this commission, but it ended up being a fiasco as the commission never actually met (Cal 1997: 126–127; González Morales 2003: 61–64; Moreno 2018: 319–320).

Amegual, Alzola, and Echegaray were regenerationists who introduced tourism into the national debate, although the action of the national commission was minimum and several years went by until a new initiative of this type was implemented. However, this was not an obstacle for the emergence of the first sectoral legislation. In 1906, a Royal Order was enacted to create special commissions in every municipality to propagate and promote tourism. A good example of this was the Comisión de Atracción de Forasteros y Turistas de Barcelona (Palou 2023). In 1909, the Circular Royal Order was passed to protect the traveller against fraud, both in places of accommodation and by those transporting their luggage. And, in 1910, the member of parliament Francisco Prieto Mera presented a law proposal for promoting tourism, which did not prosper (Moreno 2018: 320–321). Ultimately, the ideal context was being generated so that an official tourism body could be finally created in Spain, although this did not happen until 1911.

The Comisaría Regia del Turismo

On 19 June 1911, the then president of the council of ministers, José Canalejas, proposed the creation through Royal Decree of the Comisaría Regia del Turismo y Cultura Artística Popular, which existed until 1928 (*Gaceta de Madrid*, 20 June

1911: 805). After the failed attempt of 1905, Spain finally had an administrative body dedicated to tourism at a moment when the tourism activity was gaining relevance not only in the political debate, as previously mentioned, but also in the private initiative, with an increasingly significant increase in the number of hotel establishments, for example (Vallejo et al. 2016: 156–157; Larrinaga 2021: 45–52). Therefore, this initiative seemed to respond to a growing demand by professionals in the sector who increasingly saw the need for the involvement of the government in the industry (Moreno 2007: 74). Everything seems to indicate that the context was favourable for the creation of an organisation of these characteristics, although its origin is not so clear. For authors such as Rosa Cal (1997: 131) and Luis Fernández Fuster (1991: 214), the Comisaría Regia was created during the 4th International Tourism Congress held in Lisbon between 12 and 19 May 1911. During the debate in one of the sessions of the congress, the appropriateness of creating tourism bodies in countries participating in this congress was discussed. The Sociedad de Atracción de Forasteros de Barcelona proposed the creation of an organisation in Spain that would be responsible for the development of tourism. However, for González Morales, after conducting a detailed analysis of the minutes of this congress, this was not so clear. Although it is true that, at the end of this publication, there is a paragraph written after the congress indicating the implementation of the Comisaría Regia del Turismo (González Morales 2003: 79).

Irrespective of the origin of this body, during the whole of its existence it was closely connected to the Marquis of Vega-Inclán. Benigno de la Vega-Inclán was a retired military man and was close to the courtier circle of King Alfonso XIII. He was passionate about archaeology and fine arts. Not only was he a politician and militant in the Partido Liberal, but he also became one of the principal merchants of his time, being named royal commissioner, and, therefore, responsible for official tourism in Spain in 1911 (Menéndez Robles 2006). His enormous interest in art meant that he had many contacts among artists, dealers and collectors, to the point where his interest in El Greco led him to buy a house in ruins and an estate in the Jewish quarter of Toledo in 1905 with the intention of refurbishing them as a house-museum of the Cretan painter. When the Greco House-Museum opened in 1907, Vega-Inclán had become a cultural entrepreneur. The Baedeker Guide (1908: 147) refers to it as a commemorative museum of the painter, indicating that Doménikos Theotokópoulos had lived there. However, in a letter sent to the congress in the same year, he expressed his intention to donate the building to the State. Therefore, by Royal Order of 27 April 1910, the government accepted this donation and created the El Greco Museum, which opened on 12 June 1910 (Moreno 2022: 152–153). A few days later he was named as Royal Commissioner.

The Comisaría Regia (Royal Delegate) was formed to generate wealth through the activity of tourism, which had to bring in new revenue to the country. The objective was to attract the largest possible number of tourists to a country which, due to its tradition, history and monuments, was worth visiting. In this respect, tourism was basically being developed around culture, responding to the personal interests in this field of the Royal Commissioner, who fully became identified with the official body which was directed in a highly personalist way. Vega-Inclán directed the

Comisaría as he saw fit and did so without payment. However, a higher board had to be constituted to assist the Royal Commissioner, whose members were named by the Presidency of the Council of Ministers. Furthermore, it would have eight civil servants, two for each of the ministries involved (State, Governance, Development, and Instruction). That said, as these civil servants provided their services without leaving their positions and responsibilities in their respective ministries, Vega-Inclán undertook the management of the Spanish tourism industry alone (Moreno 2005: 32). In addition, the economic issue was always a problem, as the Comisaría Regia did not have an office and was not assigned a budget between June 1911 and January 1913. From that moment, it was assigned a very low budget for carrying out its mandated tasks. In some cases, Vega-Inclán even paid for the actions of the Comisaría from his own pocket (Moreno 2005: 39; 2018: 322). Even so, after 1914, the amount assigned was reduced to 75,000 pesetas, due to the special circumstances being experienced by Spain in those years: continuous changes of government, the Moroccan war, the increase in social conflict and specific ministerial decisions, such as the investment of large amounts in hydraulic works. All of these factors meant that the Comisaría Regia had very scarce resources at its disposal (González Morales 2003: 83). In addition, the failure of the tourism exhibition of London in 1914 must have also influenced this budgetary cut, as the Marquis was accused of wasting an excellent opportunity to promote Spanish tourism (Villaverde 2018: 157–158).

The tasks or responsibilities of the Comisaría Regia were the following: the dissemination of a basic knowledge of art and the enhancement of collective artistic culture; the proper preservation and exhibition of artistic, monumental and picturesque Spain; the promotion and maintenance of international relations required at the time in the artistic field; facilitating knowledge and studies on Spain, ensuring comfortable accommodation, safety and fast communications and access to the natural and artistic splendours of the country; and the development of spiritual, social and economic relations between Spain and America (*Gaceta de Madrid*, 20 June 1911: 805). It seems that tourism was understood as an artistic and cultural element and there was a somewhat reductionist view of the activity and, it was still far from being considered as a major national business (Moreno 2005: 32). Again, the personal interests and concerns of Vega-Inclán were predominant.

In this respect, it is worth mentioning that the principal specialisation of the Comisaría Regia was, as previously mentioned, cultural tourism, although we should not forget that, between 1911 and 1928, the foundations of what would later be known as natural or ecological tourism were laid, with the declaration of the national parks (1918), the natural sites and monuments of national interest (1922) or the construction of paths, shelters or mountain infrastructures in the 1920s (Moreno 2007: 35; 2022: 157–160; Sánchez Picón and Gómez García 2018). With respect to cultural tourism, the most fertile stage of its activity took place between 1911 and 1920, after which and until 1928, when it disappeared, its activity was languid and almost non-existent. Undoubtedly, one of the most noteworthy actions of the Comisaría was that related to heritage. After the success of the El Greco house-museum and the Tránsito Synagogue also in Toledo, the house of Cervantes in

Valladolid was bought and refurbished coinciding with the third centenary anniversary of the death of this distinguished writer in 1916. Miguel de Cervantes had lived in the house between 1604 and 1606 and it was restored and staged according to the criteria used for the El Greco house in Toledo. Vega-Inclán bought it on behalf of and with the funds of Alfonso XIII in 1912, also acquiring another two adjacent houses on behalf of the well-known New York hispanophile Archer Huntington and a fourth house for himself. The House of Cervantes was opened in this complex, closely connected to the strong national discourse of the day (Moreno 2007: 77; 2022: 156–157).

Apart from a few disperse actions in Granada or the opening of the Romantic Museum in Madrid in 1924, for example, between 1912 and 1920, the Comisaría Regia was focused on the renovation of the Santa Cruz neighbourhood in Seville, the first of the Spanish medieval historical quarters to be reformed for tourism purposes. This neighbourhood, which had been the former Jewish quarter of the city, was extended to incorporate land from the Alcázar gardens. Furthermore, its streets were embellished, cobbled, and cleaned, the street names were replaced and the façades were whitewashed. Gardens and small Andalusian-style squares were also created. Street lighting with gas streetlamps was even installed. In short, it was the first experience of this kind in Spain and also served to save a neighbourhood which, almost certainly, would have disappeared (Moreno 2007: 77–78).

Another of the fields of activity of the Comisaría Regia was the promotion of Spanish tourism abroad. The strategy was not so much based on the publication of leaflets and posters, but, most of all, on personal trips (of particular note was the trip lasting several months that Vega-Inclán made in 1912 to the United States in order to strengthen ties with the Hispanic community and use tourism as an instrument of cultural diplomacy) or the participation in international events, such as the tourism exhibitions of the day (the unsuccessful one of London in 1914, New York in 1922–1923 and Philadelphia in 1926). Furthermore, the tourism propaganda carried out by the Comisaría should also be mentioned, which was based on promoting the national delights to attract foreign tourists. In this section, particularly noteworthy was the publishing activity carried out by the institution, with works such as the collection of booklets *El Arte en España*: 36 titles with brief texts in three language written by specialists and accompanied by many postcards. This action contributed to enhancing Spain's monumental heritage and constituted a commendable informative effort. The other two tourist series published by the Comisaría Regia were *Propaganda de viajes por España* (which featured popular itineraries and excursions) and *Sección de montaña* (with informative leaflets about different mountain ranges of the country). It also published, although possibly of less interest for the tourism activity, literary works, texts on social issues, museum catalogues, and official publications (Moreno 2007: 78–79).

Finally, one of the most significant legacies of the Comisaría's activities was the creation of the Parador network, that is, a network of public hotel establishments. These hotels were intended to satisfy the needs of the growing motorist tourism and to cover the accommodation needs in remote places and in those of interest to tourists where the private supply was insufficient. They provided tourist accommodation to middle-class tourists who demanded a high level of quality. The first parador was opened in 1928 in the Sierra de Gredos, close to Madrid, in a mountain location, ideal for mountaineering, hiking, and hunting. This establishment was the only one that opened during the life of the Comisaría Regia, but it laid the foundations of a network which, over time, was reinforced and still exists today (Moreno and Pellejero 2015).

Although some of the aforementioned actions were important, in general, the efforts of Vega-Inclán did not meet the needs of modern tourism. In fact, the Marquis was a man with a mindset closer to the nineteenth century than the twentieth century. He did not understand what the tourism industry was starting to require in those years: accommodation, infrastructures and propaganda. Therefore, the fact that he had been the leader of the official body responsible for tourism for such a long time caused a delay in Spain's tourism industry. Vega-Inclán did not comprehend that tourism in the twentieth century was related to the development of infrastructures, the promotion of the car as a middle-class vehicle and the promotion of the private activity based on associationism and international contacts. In short, he was unaware of the demands of the professionals in the sector, who, except in a few cases (related to the art world), hardly saw their needs satisfied. Modern tourism, conceived as an industry posed new challenges that Vega-Inclán did not acknowledge. As a result, the number of foreign tourists did not increase as had been initially expected. Moreover, his own very personalist way of managing the Comisaría Regia, without accepting the help of anyone and guided by secrecy and a lack of clarity, did not help the development of Spanish tourism in those years and he was reproached by his adversaries who did not share the way he directed the organisation (Moreno 2005: 34–35). Many of the private agents who formed part of this first Spanish tourism system that was taking shape in those years saw the Comisaría Regio more as an obstacle than a valid instrument to place Spain at the forefront of modern tourism in Europe (Villaverde 2018). From this point of view, it could be said that it was mainly the private agents who really promoted the tourism activity in Spain in this period, thanks to their investments, their initiatives, and their publications and propaganda, etc.

The Patronato Nacional del Turismo

After the First World War, the tourism policy of many of the European governments was characterised by an increase in state intervention in the sector. Before the conflict, many of these countries had created public bodies for managing tourism, but in the inter-war year, their function became fully defined and they all benefited from an increase in their budgets (González Morales 2003: 94; Paloscia 2004: 41). In this respect, Spain was an exception, because, as previously mentioned, due largely to the failure of the tourism exhibition of London, the Comisaría Regia's budget was cut. Vega-Inclán became increasingly isolated and in the second half of the 1920s, this official organisation had lost all of its effectiveness. With two major events on the horizon, namely the Ibero-American Exhibition of Seville and the International Exhibition of Barcelona, the time had come to remove the Marquis and the Comisaría Regia and create a new body, the Patronato Nacional del Turismo, that would boost the sector and measure up to the task.

By way of the Royal Decree of 25 April 1928, the new official Spanish tourism organisation was formed, dependent on the presidency of the council of ministers at the height of the dictatorship of Primo de Rivera. Its spirit was very different to that of the Comisaría Regia, as the Patronato represented a professional model of understanding tourism management in which all the dimensions of the sector were given the same consideration. While the Comisaría Regia had been fundamentally identified with elite tourism and the personalism of Vega-Inclán, in the 1920s a democratisation process of tourism began, in which increasingly wider layers of society began to enjoy this activity. As tourism began to be conceived as a broad and diverse activity, with many agents and industries involved, the Patronato Nacional de Turismo adopted a complex structure with regional delegations. Between 1928 and 1931, that is, the years of the monarchy of Alfonso XIII, this structure was remodelled twice, which reveals the organisational problems that this body experienced (Fernández Fúster 1991: 284–288; Moreno 2007: 43).

The creation of the Consejo General del Turismo (General Tourism Council), which had an advisory role, was highly interesting for the tourism sector in general. It brought together not only the representatives of general directorates of the National State Administration, but also of certain private entities and sectors with an interest in tourism (González Morales 2003: 100–101). In this way, the foundations were laid of a true tourism organisation in Spain, in which a formalised collaboration prevailed between civil society and the government (Vallejo 2018: 87). Before this, the private agents had complained of the low level of involvement of the government in tourism matters, so the Consejo General del Turismo opened the doors to a collaboration between the public and private sectors to better shape the tourism policies. Representatives of the railway and shipping companies, banking or the hotel industry, for example, came together in this advisory body, which provided them with an opportunity to influence the decisions of the Patronato.

The principal functions of the Patronato were the following: to disseminate knowledge about Spain, promoting publications; to support initiatives aimed at improving tourism; to stimulate the development of the hotel industry; to study the possibility of creating tourism schools; to establish tourism centres and agencies in places where there were none in Spain; and to contribute to promoting the prestige of Spain among the visitors (PNT 1930: 193). However, in order to carry out all of these functions, the Patronato had problems with finance, as had also been the case with the Comisaría Regia. As it did not have a budget assigned to it by the State, it was forced to recur to self-funding. Specifically, from 1 November 1928, its principal source of finance were the resources obtained from the imposition of the mandatory insurance of travellers transported by the railways and shipping companies and the insurance of live cattle transported by rail (Moreno 2005: 43).

Unlike the Comisaría Regia, which, as mentioned, was basically focused on cultural tourism, the Patronato expanded its lines of action slightly, in line with a booming tourism and because of the time factor due to the two international exhibitions that were to be held in Seville and Barcelona (Fernández Fúster 1991: 296–298; González Morales 2003: 106–116; Moreno 2007: 122–125). First, the Patronato urgently addressed the accommodation issue, which was an aspect of particular concern to the tourism authorities on the eve of the aforementioned exhibitions. In fact, accommodation had constituted one of the principal obstacles to Spanish tourism development, evident in the travel guides of the beginning of the twentieth century. Therefore, the Patronato drew up a series of tourism action plans and projects addressing this issue. More specifically, the State became directly involved in the construction of hotels, continuing with the line of action begun by the Comisaría Regia, increasing the number of establishments of the public accommodation network. Furthermore, the Patronato initiated a hotel control policy. To do this, in implemented the complaints book and legislated on hotel process and the creation of plates for establishments recommended by the Patronato. Moreover, it created the hotel loan concept whereby low-interest loans were granted to companies or individuals who wished to open a hotel. The objective was to improve the country's hotel infrastructure, providing investment incentives to accommodation entrepreneurs.

The publication and propaganda service was also fundamental. Thanks to the Patronato, the first state tourism promotional campaign was designed, with the edition of different series of publications. These were complemented with exhibitions, press advertisements, official invitations to foreign journalists to Spain and the making of films. However, undoubtedly, one of the most striking contributions was propaganda through posters. At that time, the Spanish tourism poster was enjoying is golden age. Twenty-five large-scale motifs were designed with a highly generic slogan "Visit Spain" in four languages.

Also noteworthy, on the other hand, was the novelty and relevance of the information service, particularly with respect to two aspects. On the one hand, the regulation of the Servicio de Guías, Intérpretes, y Correos (Tourism Guides, Interpreters, and Postal Service), which, for the first time in Spain, offered professionals with these characteristics. The Patronato now defined their activities and fees, distinguishing between three categories: interpreters (who could carry out their profession across the whole country), guides and interpreter-guides (who could be local, regional or national, depending on the demarcation of their action) and the postal service (engaged in courier tasks). Candidates for these positions had to pass an exam and then had to be clearly uniformed and identified with a badge. The second aspect was the creation of the tourist information offices. In the Comisaría Regia, there had been a predominance of personal contacts and trips made by Vega-Inclán broad. Now, the Patronato opted to open offices in Spain and abroad. The objective of the latter was the promotion of Spain, with offices opened in Paris, London, Rome, Munich, Gibraltar, New York, and Buenos Aires. By February 1929, 18 offices had been opened across Spain. Their mission was to provide information to the visitors, distribute propaganda and present monthly statistics for the Patronato. This last point is particularly interesting, as one of the principal novelties of the Patronato was the implementation of a Statistics Service and the first official statistics of foreign visitors to Spain were published in 1929. These statistics only referred to foreign tourists, not national visitors within their own country.

In general terms, the actions of the Patronato can be considered as being fairly effective. The principal objective of the government was, through tourism, to contribute to the economic expansion of the country. The military regime used the promotion of the hotel industry as a propaganda instrument for its political actions, but with the creation of an organisation so as to put an end to the improvisation in tourism management and improve procedures in order to increase the number of international tourists. It also sought to promote national tourism, in order to counteract the trips that Spaniards were making abroad. There was a desire for Spanish tourists to practice tourism in Spain. In this respect, the creation of the Patronato Nacional del Turismo implied the participation of professionals in the task of promoting tourism, with a predominance of the aristocratic and financial elite who were responsible for designing tourism policy, removing the specialists, the critics of the reign, associations, middle classes and trade unions from the decision-making. The Patronato was even accused of diverting economic resources to finance the campaign of the monarchic parties in the municipal elections of April 1931, which gave rise to the proclamation of the Second Republic. Although there is no concrete evidence, the details that we have available seem to point in this direction (González Morales 2003: 117–118).

In fact, the economic crisis in which the Patronato Nacional del Turismo was immersed, together with the accusations of cronyism and nepotism, led the new republican authorities to dissolve it, creating in its place the Dirección General de Turismo, responsible for investigating the body and its managers, while the new government made a decision. The revenue derived from the mandatory insurance of travellers had diminished due to the railway crisis. However, the expenditure of the Patronato had not reduced, so it was literally bankrupt. The new Dirección General de Turismo harshly criticised the Patronato, cut its spending drastically and reduced its workforce. However, the life of this Dirección General de Turismo was short, due to the whims of the policy changes in the government. On 4 December 1931, it was removed and the Patronato Nacional del Turismo was reinstated (*Gaceta de Madrid*, 5 December 1931: 1445–1446). A new phase began which left behind the provisional stage that had begun in April. The immediate effect was the restructuring of the organisational chart of the Patronato with respect to the dictatorship period. However, there were very little substantial changes in the objectives of the organisation with respect to the previous period, so its lines of action were practically the same until the outbreak of the Civil War in 1936. The principal transformation in the actions of the new Patronato was based on a greater state control in terms of its budget and administration. The Patronato depended on the presidency of the Council of Ministers and was financed by the general budgets of the State. Therefore, once again it did not have is own budget (Moreno 2005: 48–49).

With the re-establishment of the Patronato, a biennium began that was characterised by the economic austerity policy of the government and it was subject to the general administrative law and a reduction in its workforce, in its local and international presence and in its budget. The most relevant effect on its infrastructure was the closure of the information offices in London, Rome, Munich, New York and Buenos Aires. At a time when Italy, Germany, the Soviet Union, or the United States, for example, were becoming more committed to the industry of pleasure trips, particularly national tourism, the Spanish government, and certain parliamentarians considered that the tourism budget should be cut. In fact, they also believed that those offices in Spain that had no funding from the local institutions should be closed. In the case of Catalonia, after the passing of the Statute of Autonomy of 1932, the Patronato conferred is representation to the Catalan executive for the organisation and development of tourism in that region, granting it the usufruct of its offices on Catalan soil (Pellejero 2018: 355–356 and 362; 2021). Therefore, in the years of the Republic, tourism policy in Spain was decentralised for the first time (Palou 2018). Despite the austerity measures that had been imposed, the Patronato continued to publish tourist leaflets and, although the advertising in the Spanish press was reduced, and even suspended in 1935, it maintained a presence abroad. Furthermore, the network of public accommodation establishments also continued to grow and the principal commitment of that period was made to the roadside inns. Between 1932 and 1935, eight establishments of this kind were opened, at a time when automobile tourism was gaining prominence (Pellejero 2018: 367–368 and 371).

Similarly to the proceedings in 1928, the provisional regulations of 12 January 1932 of the new Patronato Nacional del Turismo also contemplated a strictly advisory body, the Consejo General de Turismo. This council included representatives of the government and also those of the different sectors involved in the tourism activity in Spain (*Gaceta de Madrid*, 14 January 1932). In the same way as before, the Consejo constituted a good opportunity to influence the decisions of the Patronato, although it was too broad and, unsurprisingly, not very operative (Pellejero 2018: 354). In fact, among the modifications introduced in the regulations of 31 January 1934, (*Gaceta de Madrid*, 1 February 1934), the Consejo General de Turismo was abolished. On the contrary, the Board of the Patronato, which was also an advisory body, was renewed and extended and the representatives of some private agents directly interested in tourism participated in it, namely: railway companies, shipping companies, the Federation of Travel Agencies of Spain, the hotel association, and the Automobile Club of Spain. Apart from the operability of the board, which was dragged down by the economic difficulties and by the many changes that were taking place within the Patronato, Spain's tourism muscle in the 1930s, on an organisational level, actually took a considerable leap forward (Vallejo 2018: 88).

The Decree of 31 January 1934 referred to the beginning of a third phase, after the years of the dictatorship and the early years of the Second Republic, during which the promotion of tourism was characterised by greater efficiency, less bureaucracy and the backing of initiatives. The modification of the regulations of the Patronato sought to adapt this organisation to this new reality and to make the norms more flexible. Undoubtedly, the intentions were good, but the context did not favour them. In fact, the entire tourism policy of the years of the Second Republic was marked by the effects of the Great Depression and by the strong political instability of the period. As a result, tourism was not really a priority in Spain during those years. Despite the restoration of the Patronato Nacional del Turismo as an official tourism body in Spain, it is true that nor the left-wing or right-wing forces reinforced it, but rather converted it into a service of the Presidency of the Council of Ministers. Furthermore, the Patronato had an increasingly smaller budget at its disposal to carry out its functions. The republican governments did not see the potential of the incipient tourism industry in Spain and did not promote it adequately (Pellejero 2018: 373–374). In short, the tourism policy was basically oriented towards foreign tourism and was highly centralised, poorly funded and highly politicised (Vallejo 2022: 276–279).

These limitations in the tourism policy clashed with the aspirations of the private agents, who, from the beginning of the twentieth century, had been working in favour of developing tourism in Spain and attracting the largest number of tourists possible. Therefore, the Spanish Federation of Tourism Initiative Trade Unions, which had been constituted in 1932 to group these inbound tourism associations together, soon expressed its unease with respect to the closure of the Patronato offices. The Federation, without a doubt, represented the opinion of a large part of the private initiative related to tourism. Moreover, the increasing state intervention in certain matters, such as accommodation, was also a cause for concern. Specifically, the expansion of the network of public establishments, which was criticised, for example, by the Association of Innkeepers and Similar of Madrid in 1935, which requested that these establishments were not located in areas where they would compete with the private initiative, limiting their positioning to places where the accommodation entrepreneurs did not have a presence (Pellejero 2018: 372). All in all, and despite the difficulties, the different agents of the Spanish tourism system were able to advance considerably in terms of its development and its organisation, only truncated by the outbreak of the Civil War.

Conclusions

From the end of the nineteenth century and beginning of the twentieth century, what has become to be known as modern tourism emerged in a good part of Europe. Spain was no exception, although its development was somewhat delayed with respect to the pioneer countries, such as Italy, Switzerland, or France. However, from 1900, the first tourism system began to take shape, in which, as could be expected, the State was called to play an important role. At the beginning of the century, certain intellectuals connected to the economic life of the country began to write about the importance of promoting tourism in Spain. It seems that these reflections did not fall on deaf ears and in 1905 the first official tourism body was constituted, a national commission created for its promotion. This Commission never actually met and therefore did not fulfil the needs of a sector that was gradually showing signs of a greater dynamism (establishment of the first travel agencies, hotel development, etc.). In this way, with a private sector that was becoming increasingly involved in the tourism activity, the creation of the Comisaría Regia del Turismo, contrary to what the private agents had hoped for, was not able to establish a tourism policy that truly satisfied the interests of the private companies. With a clear personalist approach, the Comisaría Regio focused its activity on safeguarding the cultural heritage and, to a lesser extent, the promotion of nature tourism. Only with the creation of the Patronato Nacional del Turismo in 1928 did Spain, for the first time in its history, have an official body characterised by a responsible and professional management. This could be considered as real tourism administration. Now, all dimensions of tourism were given the same level of importance. With the creation of the Consejo General de Turismo at its heart as an advisory body, at last a real tourism organisation was formed providing the different public and private agents related to tourism with the appropriate channels. However, in reality, the actions with respect to tourism policy were less bold and effective than what the private agents would have liked, even taking into account the achievements in terms of promotion, the training of professionals in the sector, publications or the promotion of tourist accommodation. All in all, the budget cuts, the constant political to-ing and fro-ing, and the implications of the shift from an elite tourism to mass tourism were reflected in the limitations of the actions of the Patronato Nacional del Turismo.

References

Amengual B (1903) La industria de los forasteros. Amengual y Montaner, Palma de Mallorca

Arcos C (1909) De las grandes ventajas económicas que produciría el desarrollo del turismo en España. Imp., Lib. y Enc. de Nemesio Aramburu, Pamplona

Baedeker K (1908) Espagne et Portugal. Manuel de voyageur. Karl Baedeker Publisher, Leipzig

Cal R (1997) La propaganda del turismo en España. Primeras organizaciones. Historia y Comunicación Social 2:125–134

Fernández Fúster L (1991) Historia general del turismo de masas. Alianza, Madrid

González Morales JC (2003) Turismo en España 1905-1931. Universidad Carlos III de Madrid, unpublished doctoral thesis

Incerpi A (2019) Balancing the current account: remittances and tourism in Italy, 1861-1914. Rivista di Storia Economica, XXXV 3:269–294

Larrinaga C (2020) El turismo en España entre 1939 y 1953. La reorganización del sistema turístico antes del turismo de masas. In: Barrientos A, Parradas E, Martínez JA (eds) Investigaciones actuales en Ciencias Sociales y en Turismo. Valencia, Tirant lo Blanch, pp 217–229

Larrinaga C (2021) De la fonda al hotel. Turismo y hotelería privada en España entre 1900 y 1959. Granada, Comares

Menéndez Robles ML (2006) El marqués de la Vega Inclán y los orígenes del turismo en España. Ministerio de Industria, Turismo y Comercio, Madrid

Moreno A (2005) Turismo de élite y administración turística de la época (1911-1936). Estudios Turísticos 163–164:31–53

Moreno A (2007) Historia del turismo en España en el siglo XX. Síntesis, Madrid

Moreno A (2018) La política turística, 1905-1931. In: Vallejo R, Larrinaga C (eds) Los orígenes del turismo moderno en España. El nacimiento de un país turístico, 1900-1939. Sílex, Madrid, pp 315–344

Moreno A (2022) De forasteros y turistas. Una historia del turismo en España (1880-1936). Marcial Pons, Madrid

Moreno A, Pellejero C (2015) La red de establecimientos turísticos del Estado (1928-1977), ¿necesidad hotelera o política turística? Revista de Historia Industrial 59:147–178

Norval AJ (1936) The tourist industry. Sir Isacc Pitman, London

Ogilvie FW (1933) The tourist movement. An economic study. P.S. King, London

Paloscia F (2004) Il turismo nell'economia italiana. AGRA, Roma

Palou S (2018) La primera experiencia de política turística autonómica en Cataluña. In: Vallejo R, Larrinaga C (eds) Los orígenes del turismo moderno en España. El nacimiento de un país turístico, 1900-1939. Sílex, Madrid, pp 421–446

Palou S (2023) Los inicios del fomento turístico institucional en Barcelona: Agentes, actuaciones, narrativas e imágenes en la obra de la Comisión de Atracción de Forasteros y Turistas (1906-1909). Investigaciones Históricas 43:699–726

Patronato Nacional de Turismo (1930) Memoria de los trabajos realizados por el Patronato Nacional del Turismo desde julio de 1928 a 31 de diciembre de 1929. Talleres Voluntad, Madrid

Pellejero C (2018) La política turística durante la República, 1931-1936. In: Vallejo R, Larrinaga C (eds) Los orígenes del turismo moderno en España. El nacimiento de un país turístico, 1900-1939. Sílex, Madrid, pp 345–380

Pellejero C (2021) El Patronato Nacional de Turismo republicano: caos organizativo y austeridad presupuestaria. Ayer 123:233–258

Sánchez Picón A, Gómez García JJ (2018) Los espacios naturales: los primeros pasos de un nuevo producto turístico durante el primer tercio del siglo XX. In: Vallejo R, Larrinaga C (eds) Los orígenes del turismo moderno en España. El nacimiento de un país turístico, 1900-1939. Sílex, Madrid, pp 841–864

Vallejo R (2018) La formación de un sistema turístico nacional con diferentes desarrollos regionales entre 1900 y 1939. In: Vallejo R, Larrinaga C (eds) Los orígenes del turismo moderno en España. El nacimiento de un país turístico, 1900-1939. Sílex, Madrid, pp 67–170

Vallejo R (2019) Turismo en España durante el primer tercio del siglo XX: la conformación de un sistema turístico. Ayer 114:175–211

Vallejo R (2022) Historia del turismo en España, 1928-1962. Sílex, Madrid

Vallejo R, Larrinaga C (eds) (2018) Los orígenes del turismo moderno en España. Sílex, Madrid

Vallejo R, Lindoso E, Vilar M (2016) Los antecedentes del turismo de masas en España, 1900-1936. Revista de la Historia de la Economía y de la Empresa 10:137–188

Villaverde J (2018) La Comisaría Regia de Turismo (1911-1928). ¿Ejemplo de España oficial? In: Yun Casalilla B, Luengo J (eds) Pensar el poder: "Liber amicorum" de Pedro Carasa. PUV, Valencia, pp 149–170

Carlos Larrinaga is Full Professor of Economic History at the University of Granada (Andalusia, Spain). He is the Main Researcher of the project "Tourism in Spain in the first third of the twentieth century. Characteristics and evolution of an economic activity and a social practice in comparative perspective", funded by the Government of Spain and ERDF.

Chapter 5
Tourism Policies in Post-WWII Yugoslavia

Tomi Brezovec and Aleksandra Brezovec

Abstract The central planning of economic activity was characteristic of the socialist states that emerged in Eastern Europe after the Second World War. The nationalization of enterprises and state ownership of the means of industrial production and agriculture were accompanied by a series of 5-year plans with which the socialist governments in Eastern Europe directed the economic development of their countries. Yugoslavia, which is neither a free market economy nor a member of the Soviet-controlled Eastern bloc, has developed its own economic model. Although the state followed the socialist model of nationalization of industry and central planning, the Yugoslav economic system was less rigid than in other Eastern European countries. Although the country maintained economic relations with the countries of the Eastern Bloc, the Yugoslav economy was heavily dependent on Western markets.

In the 5-year plans introduced in 1947, tourism was always addressed in some way. However, the importance given to tourism has changed over time. In the first 5-year plan, tourism was viewed primarily from the perspective of the Yugoslav working class—as a tool for the regeneration and recreation of workers, who were considered the cornerstone of society. This view changed when tourism was recognized as a potential foreign exchange earner. In the 1960s and early 1970s, 5-year plans allocated large funds for investment in new tourism infrastructure, mainly built on the Adriatic coast. These investments were targeting the growing tourist demand from Western European markets. Within a few years, the share of foreign visitors in the Yugoslavian tourism market doubled. Tourism soon became a key contributor to country's balance of payments. In the 1980s, the consolidation of the country's stagnating economy required large sums of foreign currency. This put pressure on tourism, which continued to rely on mass tourism without making new investments or maintaining the existing infrastructure. With the emergence of new competition on the global tourism markets (e.g. Southeast Asia and southern

T. Brezovec (✉) · A. Brezovec
Faculty of Tourism Studies, University of Primorska, Koper, Slovenia
e-mail: tomi.brezovec@upr.si; aleksandra.brezovec@upr.si

C. Larrinaga, D. Strangio (eds.), *Tourism Destinations and Policies in Europe During the 20th Century*, Contributions to Economics,
https://doi.org/10.1007/978-3-031-88447-4_5

Mediterranean countries), Yugoslavia's tourism offer began to lose its attractiveness. In the last years of the decade, tourism demand began to decline and collapsed completely in 1991 with the break-up of Yugoslavia.

Introduction

Yugoslavia played an important role in the post-WWII development of tourism in Europe. A country that had been severely devastated during the war, whose railroad and road networks were in ruins and with no significant industrial background, developed into one of the most important European tourist destinations of the second half of the twentieth century. The country's reconstruction process was based on government policies summarized in a series of 5-year plans, which were crucial documents of the country's central planning system. The new Yugoslav socialist system was designed similarly to the system applied in the Soviet Union and other Eastern European countries, where the Communist Party controlled all aspects of society. In Yugoslavia, however, a modified version was introduced in which the people (society) were declared the owners of the country under the leadership of the Communist Party. In this scenario, the working class had the decision-making power and the government was supposed to run the country in a way that maximized the benefits for all citizens. Based on these declaratory principles, the government began to coordinate the process of reconstruction and adopted administrative approach to the development of Yugoslav society. In this process, the government wanted to create a solid economic basis for the further development of society by nationalizing the means of production. The first nationalization process (1946) concerned all large private industrial plants and mines. Smaller companies were nationalized in 1948 as part of the second nationalization cycle. Due to the socialist demand to raise the standard of living and culture of the people, medical facilities, hospitals, sanatoriums, hotels, spas, health resorts, print shops and cinemas were also nationalized in the course of the second nationalization. By 1950, the socialist economic sector united 93% of all economic enterprises, which employed 99.3% of all workers. Only small craft businesses and workshops remained in private ownership.

The companies and organizations had to follow the government's decisions and pursue the goals set by the government in a 5-year development plan. Central planning was considered by the government to be the best method for coordinating and optimizing the use of available resources. Drawing up a central plan for all activities for the next 5 years became one of the government's most important tasks. However, due to the large number of entities involved in this process and the not always clear communication between them, this proved to be a difficult task. The government's views and expectations set out in the 5-year plans were not always fully met and the targets often proved to be too optimistic or even unrealistic. Nevertheless, the 5-year plans and the policies, measures and targets they contained were the starting point for today's political and economic reality. They also reflect the changes that have occurred over time, whether caused by external or internal factors. The development of tourism in Yugoslavia was also guided by 5-year plans. They set priorities for development, material and financial goals to be achieved and allocated funds for investment in tourism. Less tourism-specific goals and policies such as the introduction of self-management of companies by employees or the process of integrating companies into larger entities also had an impact on tourism. The analysis of these plans therefore provides an insight into the government's attitude towards tourism and its development.

Yugoslav tourism has been studied by domestic and foreign scholars both during its development (e.g. Allcock 1986; Kobašić 1987; Pirjevec 1988; Radišić 1981; Stanković 1990) and after the dissolution of Yugoslavia (e.g. Duda 2010, 2016; Sitar 2020; Yeomans 2010). The authors often describe the development of Yugoslav tourism in stages. Although they do not always agree on the duration or the beginning of a particular period (Tchukarine 2010), they usually divide it into 4–5 phases. These phases fit perfectly into Butler's Tourism Area Life Cycle (TALC) model (Butler 1980). The model explains the development of a tourism area through six stages—involvement, exploration, development, consolidation, stagnation, and decline/rejuvenation. Yugoslav tourism has evolved through all of these stages but with different dynamics and duration of each stage. Five-year plans played an important role in determining the dynamics and course of tourism development. They reflect the government's expectations of tourism and present government's response to changes in the political and economic factors affecting tourism. Analysing the tourism-related content of the 5-year plans can reveal the transition between the different stages of tourism development.

1947–1951: Administrative Management of the Economy

The war led to a complete cessation of tourist activities on Yugoslav territory, and most of the infrastructure was destroyed or abandoned. The reconstruction of tourism after the war had to start from scratch (Alfier and Domanik 1955). The reconstruction of tourism began with the adoption of the first 5-year plan (1947–1951). In the immediate post-war years, the government's main objective was to rebuild the country's infrastructure, which had been destroyed during the war. The reconstruction of industrial facilities and the railroad and road network did not include the reconstruction of tourist facilities, even though most of the pre-war tourism infrastructure had been destroyed and could no longer fulfil its purpose. In 1946, the available hotel capacity was estimated at only around 16,000 beds (Radišić 1981). At this period, tourism was considered as part of the health and recreation agenda and not as a commercial activity. The recreation of the working class and the strengthening of national unity and fraternity of the Yugoslav people were considered as the main task of tourism (Allcock 1986; Yeomans 2010). For this reason, the government's efforts in tourism were focused almost exclusively on the domestic market.

The demand for foreign tourism was almost non-existent. In 1947, there were only 62,000 foreign visitors, which corresponded to 4.7% of total arrivals. These were mainly visitors from other Eastern European socialist countries, especially Czechoslovakia and Hungary, who visited Yugoslavia as part of the holiday exchange programme between the countries' trade unions. For visitors from Western European countries, Yugoslavia was not attractive due to the lack of suitable accommodation, the poor transport network and the rationalization of food.

After the break with the Soviet Union in 1948, Yugoslavia was excluded from the Cominform (a coordinating body of Marxist-Leninist communist parties in Europe during the Cold War). As a result, citizens from Eastern European countries were banned from travelling to Yugoslavia. The number of foreign tourists decreased significantly, and in 1949 only 32,000 foreign visitors were counted in Yugoslavia (share of 1.6%). The political situation in post-war Europe was also not exactly stimulating for foreign visitors to Yugoslavia. The unresolved border issue with Italy and Austria, the drought, and the shortage of goods did not stimulate foreign visitors to visit Yugoslavia (Tchoukarine 2010).

In contrast to the low foreign arrivals, the demand for domestic tourism grew rapidly and 2.3 million arrivals were registered in 1950, up from 1.2 million in 1947. Domestic tourists were mainly members of the working class who spent their vacations in facilities run by the trade unions. Under the premise that tourism should primarily benefit the working class, the government introduced a paid holiday scheme as early as 1946, as well as a voucher system to encourage workers to travel and take vacations. Train, bus and boat fares were reduced from 50% to 75% for domestic vacationers. Airline tickets were also subsidized by up to 50%. The subsidies were financed from the federal budget (for rail travel) and from the budgets of the individual republics (for bus fares). In this first planning period, most of the investments in tourism also went into the development of holiday facilities for workers, a "socialist type of tourist accommodation" (Kavrečič and Šuligoj 2021:155) and the construction of youth holiday centres.

In 1949, the Federal Committee for Tourism and Hospitality, founded in 1948, attempted to draw up a general plan and regulate workers' vacations (Kobašič 1987). The plan stipulated that about 90% of the available tourist accommodation facilities should be available for workers' vacations, and only the remaining part should be made available on a commercial basis for other domestic and foreign vacationers. However, due to non-existent or poorly coordinated plans for holiday activities in various enterprises and organizations, some unfavourable weather conditions and overly optimistic plans for the use of holiday facilities during the summer months, the objectives of the plan were not achieved. Such general planning of holiday activities for employees was soon abandoned.

1952–1965: Growing Importance of Tourism

After the period of administrative management of the economy (including tourism), Yugoslavia entered a period of economic reforms (1952, 1956, 1961 and 1965) aimed at improving overall productivity and introducing entrepreneurial principles in the economy (Radišić 1981: 77). After the 1952 reform, companies had to adopt a more market-oriented business approach. The pricing policy for goods and services, which had previously been set by the government, was now the responsibility of individual companies. This led to a general increase in the prices of goods and services. The tourism and hospitality sector, including holiday facilities for workers and holiday homes for young people, was no exception. The introduction of market-driven prices led to a decline in demand for domestic tourism. In 1952, there were 1.3 million fewer overnight stays by domestic tourists than in the previous year, a decline of 16%. The government attempted to mitigate the negative effects of higher prices by introducing subsidies for domestic tourists. Prices for listed accommodation were reduced by 40% in the high season and by 60% in the low season (Pirjevec 1988; Stanković 1990). The tourism and hotel companies then received a refund from the federal budget. These measures helped to maintain the growth of domestic tourism and enabled tourism and hotel companies to raise funds for the necessary renovation and/or expansion of their facilities. In 1953, domestic demand increased by 22% to around 8.5 million overnight stays.

The devaluation of the Yugoslav dinar in 1952 from 50 to 300 dinars to USD1 made Yugoslavia very affordable for foreign tourists. The number of their arrivals and overnight stays increased immediately by around 80% (Tchoukarine 2010). In 1954, there were about 320 thousand foreign tourists (compared to 130,000 in 1952) who spent more than 1 million nights (compared to 460 thousand in 1952). Their share of total arrivals rose to 10% (compared to 4.9% in 1952), and the increase in their market share continued in the following years.

In 1953, Yugoslavia established its national tourism office—the Tourist Association of Yugoslavia—with the task of promoting Yugoslavia as a tourism destination. Soon after, representative offices were opened in the most important European cities (Čulić 1965). The Tourist Association of Yugoslavia promoted the beauty of the country as well as the new political system and the successes of post-war reconstruction (Yeomans 2010).

In the second half of the 1950s, the government's general attitude towards tourism changed. Tourism was recognized as an important foreign exchange earner and contributed to the country's gross domestic product. These changes are documented in the second 5-year plan for social development, which was not adopted until 1957 (Društveni… 1957). Due to the political situation in 1948 and the break with the Eastern European bloc led by the Soviet Union, the validity of the plan was extended from 1947 to 1951 until 1952. Finally, it remained in force until 1956 (Pirjevec 1988). With the second plan, the government recognized the need to rebuild and modernize the tourism infrastructure and provided funds for the necessary investments. The funds were allocated to established tourism resorts as well as to other towns and industrial centres throughout the country.

In addition to investment in tourism infrastructure, the plan also recognized the need for a qualified workforce to meet the growing demand for tourism. In the early post-war period, tourism and hospitality workers acquired the necessary skills in intensive courses organized in the main tourism destinations to ensure at least some qualifications for the workforce employed during the tourism season. As tourism demand developed, it became clear that a more systematic approach was needed to provide a sufficiently skilled workforce for the hospitality and tourism industry. Vocational schools soon became part of the country's education system. These were schools with 2- to 3-year training programmes in the catering, hotel and tourism office sectors. Hotel management schools and some university-level courses were designed to provide higher-level knowledge to middle and upper-level managers in hospitality and tourism companies. The system was well designed and provided a qualified workforce until the end of Yugoslavia.

The initiatives introduced with the second 5-year plan were further developed with the third plan from 1961 (Društveni… 1961). The plan aimed to increase tourism capacities and strengthen the competitiveness of Yugoslav tourism companies on the tourism market. The plan supported the development of new tourism destinations and campsites. The funds allocated for direct investment in hospitality and tourism amounted to 90 billion dinars, or about 2% of total investment. The policy also stimulated private initiative in tourism, which led to an immediate increase in the supply of accommodation for tourists. In 1965, there were a total of about 450,000 beds available, of which one third (150,000 beds) were in private accommodation. The second largest segment were capacity in holiday centres for workers and/or young people with 100,000 beds available (24%), followed by capacity in campsites (70,000 or 16%) and hotels with 66,000 beds (14%).

Another goal of the 1961–1965 plan was to increase the competitiveness of Yugoslav tourism enterprises. To achieve this goal, the government encouraged the establishment of large companies and pushed for the integration of small tourism companies into larger groups, as well as cooperation between tourism companies to create holistic tourism products. The main reason for this policy was the need to strengthen the position of Yugoslav tourism companies in the competitive European market.

The further devaluation of the Yugoslav dinar in 1961 (from 300 to 600 dinars for USD1) and 1962 (to 750 dinars for USD1) led to a further slump in tourism demand. In the first half of the 1960s, the number of overnight stays abroad rose with an average annual increase of 25% from 4.5 million (1961) to 11.2 million (1965), with overnight stays abroad accounting for a third of the total number of overnight stays. Domestic tourism recorded more moderate growth, and in the same period the number of domestic overnight stays rose from 19.5 million (1961) to 21.5 million (1965). The dynamics of domestic and foreign tourism demand (nights spent) is shown in (Fig. 5.1).

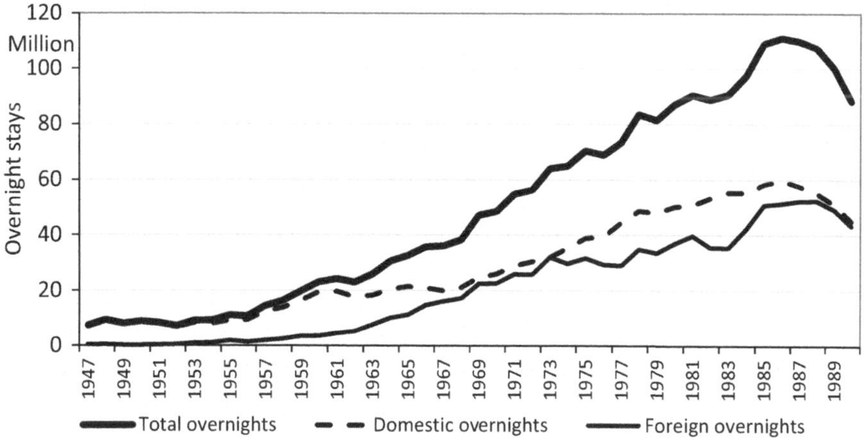

Fig. 5.1 Number of domestic and foreign overnight stays in Yugoslavia 1947–1990. Source: Statistical Yearbook of Yugoslavia (1954–1990)

1966–1975: Tourism Recognized as Main Foreign Currency Earner

In the mid-1960s, the government changed its paradigm of seeing domestic tourism as a social category and began to view it as an economic category determined by purchasing power and the level of personal consumption (Kobašić 1987: 14). In the Five-Year Plan 1966–1970 (Društveni… 1966), tourism was not only officially recognized as a viable economic activity, but was also declared one of the most important sectors of the Yugoslav economy. The plan envisaged an increase in accommodation capacity by around 300,000 beds by 1970 and an increase in tourism demand to 30 million overnight stays by domestic tourists and 32 million overnight stays by foreign visitors. It was also expected that tourism would contribute 75% to covering the country's trade deficit (Repe 2018).

To achieve these goals, the planned funds for investment in tourism were almost three times higher than in the previous 5-year plan. Between 3% and 5% of total annual investment in Yugoslavia were allocated to tourism. The funds were primarily used for the development of new accommodation facilities. This trend continued in the following 5-year period (1971–1975), but with a slowdown in investment from a share of 5.4% of total investment in 1971 to 2.2% in 1975 (Društveni… 1972). As a result of increased investment in tourism infrastructure, available tourism capacity grew from around 450,000 in 1966 to 700,000 in 1970 and more than doubled to almost 1 million by 1975. About one-third of the new capacity was accounted for by hotels and similar facilities, the rest by new additional capacity, mainly in private accommodation and new campsites. Most of the investment was concentrated on the Adriatic coast, which has become a major destination for both domestic and foreign tourists. In 1975, the coastal region accounted for 62.4% of all available capacity in hotels and similar establishments and 80% of the capacity of campsites and private accommodation.

Following the new paradigm, the government abandoned the system of subsidies for accommodation and travel of domestic tourists, which had been introduced in the past to stimulate domestic tourism demand. As a result, the volume of domestic tourism decreased by around 10% in the next 2 years. To maintain the growth momentum of domestic tourism, tourism companies, which set their prices based on seasonal demand and the quality of services offered, introduced "dual pricing" for domestic and foreign tourists. The companies introduced discounts on the stated prices that only applied to domestic guests. Depending on the pricing policy of the individual companies, the discounts could range from 10% in the high season for accommodation in a five-star hotel to 60% in the low season in a three-star hotel. After 1967, domestic demand picked up again, with an average annual growth rate of 9% until 1975, when about 10 million domestic tourists spent almost 39 million nights in all available types of accommodation (See also Fig. 5.1).

The strong inflow of foreign currency has led to measures being taken to further increase the demand for foreign tourism. Border crossings have become much easier due to less stringent controls and the liberalization of entry visa procedures. Tourist visas were lifted for citizens from 43 countries in Europe and other continents, making Yugoslavia's borders the most open in the world. In addition, in 1967, the year proclaimed as the International Tourist Year, Yugoslavia temporarily lifted the visa requirement for citizens from all countries of the world (Radišić 1981). A further devaluation of the Yugoslav dinar in 1965 (to 900 dinars for USD1) gave an additional boost to demand for foreign tourism by making vacations in Yugoslavia even more affordable. The demand for foreign tourism grew rapidly and by 1975 its market share almost equaled the demand on the domestic market.

In the second half of the 1960s, the government introduced a number of specific economic measures to encourage investment in tourism and targeting foreign tourism markets (Zečević 1973). One of the most important measures was interest payments from the federal budget to individual companies for investments in tourism facilities. If investments increased foreign demand for tourism, the interest rate was higher. With such measures, the government tried to facilitate the growth of foreign tourism demand and thus the inflow of foreign currency. Another measure was retention quotas. In contrast to other export companies, which were allowed to keep 7% of their revenues earned in Western markets in foreign currency (the rest had to be converted into dinars), tourism companies could keep 60% of these revenues. These funds could then be used to repay loans for investments in tourism. Inflation and the devaluation of the Yugoslav dinar meant that companies benefited from the exchange rate difference when the loan repayment was due. The tax breaks were also used to stimulate tourism. Taxable income earned on foreign markets was reduced by 10%, allowing companies to operate with a higher net profit. Commercial banks were also allowed to receive loans from foreign banks if they invested in tourism. The required deposit for bank loans for investments in tourism were only 1% of the invested funds, while a 10% deposit was required for loans for other investments. These measures were decided for the duration of the 5-year plan. After 1970, the federal government transferred part of the responsibility for stimulating the tourism industry to the level of the republics (Stanković 1990).

1976–1990: Tourism for Masses and Changing Role of the Government

In the second half of the 1970s, tourism continued to enjoy a privileged status among the economic sectors. Its ability to generate foreign exchange was considered crucial for the further economic development of the country (Kobašić 1987). Like the previous plan, the Five-Year Plan 1976–1980 also supported further growth of accommodation facilities (Društveni... 1976). The overall tourism demand was optimistically expected to grow by 7% per year, while foreign tourism revenues were expected to reach an average annual growth of 15%. It was also expected that by 1980 Yugoslavia would have a total of 1.15 million accommodation capacities, 98 million overnight stays, 44 million of which would be by foreign visitors, and an income from international tourism of about USD1.6 billion (Kobašić 1987; Radišić 1981). The plan was overly optimistic, and since the federal government introduced the decentralization of federal investment funds in the early 1970s and lost its direct authority to intervene, the plan was actually a sum of targets set and agreed upon by the governments of the individual republics. The federal government had no funds for investment and was limited to using stimulating measures such as tax breaks, minimizing import duties, co-financing tourism promotion and maintaining Yugoslav tourism offices abroad, and reducing gas prices for foreign tourists.

The republics that were now responsible for investing in tourism had their own agenda, and the measures adopted could vary depending on the importance of tourism to their economies. Croatia was by far the most important of the republics. With its long Adriatic coast, it attracted about 45% of all tourist arrivals and had a share of about 60% of total overnight stays in Yugoslavia. Croatia's position was even stronger when foreign tourism demand was taken into account. About 65% of foreigners visiting Yugoslavia ended up in Croatia, where they spent about 80% of all overnight stays by foreign visitors. In contrast, the Republic of Bosnia and Herzegovina accounted for around 5% of total arrivals and less than 1.5% of total overnight stays by foreigners in Yugoslavia. Due to these differences in the importance of tourism, it was difficult to reach agreement at the federal level on investments and other measures in tourism.

The 1976–1980 plan did not bring the desired results. In 1980, the total number of overnight stays reached only 88 million, about 10 million below the planned figure. Overnight stays abroad amounted to 37 million, 16% below the planned figure. The additional overnight stays amounted to 171,000, of which only 43,000 were in hotels and similar establishments. The remainder was accounted for by increases in available private accommodation and new campsites. Income from international tourism also fell short of the target figures. Instead of the expected USD1.6 billion, international tourism only brought in USD1.2 billion.

The 1980s began with major political and economic changes in Yugoslav society. The death of President Tito, who had been a leading political figure since the Second World War, in May 1980 marked the beginning of an open political confrontation between the governments of the individual republics, which led to political instability. This were compounded by economic problems—stagnation in the country's economic development, inflation and shortages of consumer and industrial goods. In addition, there were high energy prices due to the international oil crisis triggered by the Iranian revolution (1978–1979) and the Iran-Iraq war (1980–1988). This situation put pressure on tourism to export as many services as possible. In Yugoslavia's development plan for the period 1981–1985, further growth in tourism was expected (Društveni… 1981). For 1985, 64 million overnight stays by foreign tourists were forecast, a very optimistic goal considering that the figure in 1980 was only 37 million. The plan was fulfilled to about 80%, although the number of foreign overnight stays was 14 million less than planned (Kobašić 1987) (see also Fig. 5.1).

The government maintained some of the economic measures to stimulate foreign tourism, such as retention quotas and tax breaks. It also continued to stimulate investment in the expansion of accommodation facilities, which grew by a further 195,000 beds to 1.26 million beds in 1985, of which 380,000 were private rooms and 350,000 were campsite capacity. The introduction of fuel vouchers ensured the availability of gasoline for tourists during the oil shortage. A further devaluation of the dinar in 1981 and the abandonment of the fixed exchange rate increased the purchasing power of the foreign currency and also made the dinar less attractive for the citizens of Yugoslavia.

At the beginning of the 1980s, Yugoslavia promoted its tourism through Tourism Association of Yugoslavia. This was not a commercial promotion, but rather a series of image campaigns that promoted some of the country's most important regions as a destination for an affordable holiday in a beautiful natural and cultural environment. The government's policy of encouraging the concentration of companies in order to build robust organizations led to the development of large travel agencies and tour operators that dominated the market. Six leading Yugoslav travel agencies—Atlas, Centroturist, Generalturist, Kompas, Kvarner-Express and Putnik—had over 230 offices in all major tourist centres in Yugoslavia (Rešetar 1981). Some of these companies also operated as tour operators with representative offices abroad. The largest Yugoslav tour operator operating in foreign markets was Yugotours, with agencies in 11 countries. At the beginning of the 1980s, Yugotours was the fourth largest tour operator on the British market.

In the mid-1980s, the Yugoslav tourism sector was at its historic peak. Demand for domestic and foreign tourism, which was concentrated in two summer months, reached record levels in 1986 and 1988 respectively. In the remaining years until the end of the decade, tourism demand began to decline rapidly. The constant pressure to obtain foreign currency in ever-increasing quantities led the tourism sector to focus on increasing the number of incoming tourists, disregarding the need to develop tourism products. The formula of the sunny Adriatic and low prices, which was successful in the past, has lost its attractiveness. Consumers have become more demanding, competition in the tourism market has intensified and visitors were not willing to pay higher prices for only basic services. The price-benefit advantage of Yugoslav tourism was lost. In addition to the loss of competition on the global tourism market, tourism companies also had to contend with the difficult economic situation in the country. Yugoslavia struggled with high inflation and the dinar lost its value. The shortage of raw materials for industrial production and the shortage of some consumer goods also had a negative impact on tourism. The federal government, which was supposed to take care of these problems, lost its political power against the governments of the republics. The political situation in the country finally led to the dissolution of Yugoslavia in 1991.

Discussion on the Post-World War Two Tourism Policies in Yugoslavia

The reconstruction of the country required a lot of financial and material resources, which were scarce. In the distribution of available funds, priority was given to the reconstruction of the country's industrial base as well as the railroad and road networks. Tourism was not considered a priority unless it was for the regeneration and recreation of the local working class, which was considered the cornerstone of society.

During the World War Two, Yugoslavia lost most of its pre-war tourism infrastructure. The first stage of tourism development (1946–1951) can be seen as the period of renovation of the damaged tourism infrastructure and the construction of holiday facilities for the working class. It could also be described as the rejuvenation of pre-war tourism or the initial phase of a new tourism life cycle as suggested by Butler's TALC model (1980).

The main priority was the development of domestic tourism demand. Workers benefited from government measures to stimulate domestic tourism and holidaying of the socialist workers. Discounts on travel prices, paid vacations, free or cheap holiday accommodation and meals were introduced to enable domestic tourists to travel and turn them into tourists. Pre-war Yugoslavia was predominantly agricultural, and workers and farmers were not used to holidaying.

The second stage (1952–1965) would fit into the exploration phase of Butler's model. This period shows an early orientation towards foreign markets. The strict entry policy was abandoned and the number of foreign visitors began to grow. As the existing tourism infrastructure was insufficient and did not meet international standards, the federal government began to invest in accommodation facilities to meet this demand. On the other hand, the government abandoned its direct involvement in stimulating domestic tourism demand. Domestic tourism, which used to be a social category that ensured workers' recreation, has slowly become an economic category, similar to foreign tourism. Hospitality and tourism companies that were previously run by the government can now operate on commercial principles. The government continued to promote domestic tourism, but with more indirect measures such as funding discounts on tourism services for domestic tourists from the federal budget.

The third stage (1966–1975) can be described as the development phase in Butler's model. It was a period of intensive investment in tourism infrastructure. The government recognized the economic benefits of international tourism and began to invest in the development of accommodation facilities built primarily for foreign tourists. Since the construction of hotels and similar facilities required large amounts of funds and the construction process took a long time, the government found the solution for a rapid increase in available capacity in investing in the development of campsites along the Adriatic coast and in stimulating the development of private accommodation facilities. The decentralization of the federal investment budget to the republican level was another step towards reducing the direct involvement of the federal government in tourism. However, the federal government introduced economic measures to encourage investment that would have a positive impact on the inflow of foreign tourists, such as tax breaks, subsidized interest rates on loans, and foreign currency retention quotas. The development of new infrastructure was always given priority over the modernization and renovation of existing facilities.

The period from 1976 to the dissolution of Yugoslavia in 1991 is a period of consolidation and stagnation in tourism development, which ended with a decline in tourism (see Butler 1980). Some of the measures taken by the Yugoslav government in the previous period to stimulate the inflow of foreign tourists were continued during this period. With the process of political decentralization, the development of tourism became the responsibility of the individual republics, which pursued their own development agendas. The government withdrew from planning investments in tourism and focused on coordinating the activities of the republics to create a common agenda for tourism development. It financed tourism promotion and representative offices for tourism abroad. The deterioration of the economic and political situation in the country, which began after the death of President Tito in 1980, made it difficult, if not impossible, to develop a coherent tourism policy. The lack of coordinated tourism development and the lack of investment made the Yugoslav tourism product less attractive and led to a decline in tourism demand in the last years of the 1980s.

The development process of Yugoslav tourism clearly shows the changes in the government's attitude towards tourism. The initial focus on ensuring the qualitative regeneration of the Yugoslav working class had almost neglected foreign tourism. Visitors from abroad were not prohibited from coming to the country for holiday, but no effort was made to stimulate these activities. Travel for pleasure was a symbol of the old, capitalist system and was not compatible with the new socialist ideology, in which workers were seen as the most important part of society. It was therefore the government's responsibility to provide everything necessary for their recreation and regeneration. After the break with the Soviet Union in 1948, Yugoslavia began to seek the support of Western European countries and the United

States, but retained its socialist system. Although tourists from Western Europe began to visit Yugoslavia, the government still focused mainly on promoting domestic tourism in the 1950s. Organized vacations to places where workers could meet people from other parts of Yugoslavia also served the government's political agenda of strengthening national pride and building a new socialist society in Yugoslavia.

Competition on the world market was a challenge for the developing Yugoslav industry, and exporting products to Western European markets was no easy task. The foreign currency required for the further development of the economy and the import of goods was not easy to obtain. At the end of the 1950s, the government recognized the foreign exchange-generating power of tourism. Investments in tourism infrastructure soon proved profitable and by the mid-1960s tourism was recognized as one of the country's most important economic sectors. This led to even greater sums being invested in tourism infrastructure, particularly in accommodation facilities. A decade of intensive development left a considerable burden on the national budget and made Yugoslavia even more dependent on foreign income from tourism. The government delegated the responsibility for tourism development and its financing to the lower levels (republics and municipalities). Its main activities now focused on promoting investments in tourism that would lead to an increase in foreign visitor numbers. It introduced some tax measures and adopted some banking regulations to make investment in tourism an attractive alternative. On the international market, the federal government maintained a network of tourism offices and invested considerable sums in tourism promotion.

From the outset, investment in tourism infrastructure was almost exclusively focused on accommodation facilities. Although this has led to an increase in available bed capacity, it has not contributed to the development of various tourism products. Investment in facilities for sport and recreation, entertainment and other tourist attractions (amusement parks, museums and galleries, etc.) was much lower or nonexistent. As a result, the Yugoslav tourism product conveyed only natural beauty, which was not enough to attract a large number of visitors. Therefore, the government pursued a low-price approach to make vacationing in Yugoslavia attractive and fill a large number of accommodations. Instead of investing in other infrastructures for which no funds were available, the government pursued a policy of price attractiveness. The frequent devaluation of the fixed exchange rate in earlier periods and the premature devaluation of the dinar in the 1980s made Yugoslavia a destination for cheap holidays and tourists from Western European countries came in millions. Yugoslavia openly promoted cheap holidays on the Adriatic coast (Brezovec and Brezovec 2021) and developed a network of travel agencies and tour operators that attracted foreign tourists in masses.

Eventually, the development of competition in the global tourism market and Yugoslavia's already outdated tourism product led to a rapid decline in tourism demand after the peak years in 1986 with over 111 million overnight stays, of which 51 million (46%) were accounted for by foreign visitors. By 1990, i.e. in just 4 years, the number of overnight stays had fallen to 88 million (43 million of which were from abroad, 49%). The political events of the early 1990s and the disintegration of Yugoslavia put an end to Yugoslav tourism.

References

Allcock JB (1986) Yugoslavia's tourist trade. Pot of gold or pig in a poke? Ann Tour Res 13:565–588
Alfier D, Domanik R (1955) Osnovne postavke o ekonomici i unapređenju našeg turizma. In: Zbornik rasprava o problemima turističke privrede. Društvo ekonomista, Zagreb
Brezovec T, Brezovec A (2021) Yugoslavia awaits you: Post-WW2 tourism promotion of the Yugoslav coast. In: Batillani P, Larrinaga C (eds) Coastal tourism in Southern Europe in the XXth century. Peter Lang, Berlin, pp 171–186
Butler RW (1980) The concept of a tourist area cycle of evolution: implications for management of resources. Canadian Geogr, XXIV 1:5–12
Čulić DJ (1965) Turistička propaganda. Panorama, Zagreb
Društveni plan privrednog razvoja Jugoslavije od 1957. do 1961. godine. (1957) Službeni list
Društveni plan privrednog razvoja Jugoslavije od 1961. do 1965 godine. (1961) Službeni list
Društveni plan Jugoslavije za razdoblje od 1971. do 1975. godine. (1972) Službeni list, 35/1972
Društveni plan Jugoslavije za razdoblje od 1976. do 1980. godine. (1976) Službeni list, 33/1976
Društveni plan Jugoslavije za razdoblje od 1981. do 1985. godine. (1981) Službeni list, 17/1981
Društveni plan razvoja Jugoslavije od 1966. do 1970. godine. (1966) Službeni list, 28/1966
Duda I (2010) Workers into tourists. Entitlements, desires, and the realities of social tourism under Yugoslav socialism. In: Grandits H, Taylor K (eds) Yugoslavia's sunny side. A history of tourism in socialism (1950s–1980s). Central European University Press, Budapest, pp 33–68
Duda I (2016) When capitalism and socialism get along best: tourism, consumer culture and the idea of progress in Malo misto. In: Taylor K, Duda I, Stubbs P (eds) Social inequalities and discontent in Yugoslav socialism. Routledge, London, pp 173–192
Kavrečič P, Šuligoj M (2021) Socialist style tourist accommodation. In: Batillani P, Larrinaga C (eds) Coastal tourism in Southern Europe in the XXth Century. Peter Lang, Berlin, pp 155–170
Kobašić A (1987) Turizam u Jugoslaviji. Informator, Zagreb
Pirjevec B (1988) Ekonomski aspekti jugoslavenskog turizma. Školska knjiga, Zagreb
Radišić F (1981) Turizam i turistička politika. Istarska naklada, Pula
Repe B (2018) "We Cannot be Satisfied with the Development of Tourism in Slovenia so Far": Impact of tourism legislation, regulations and other texts on the development of Slovene Tourism in contemporary history. Retrospektive 1(1):57–95
Rešetar M (1981) Turističke agencije. Informator, Zagreb
Sitar P (2020) Workers becoming tourists and consumers: social history of tourism in socialist Slovenia and Yugoslavia. J Tour Hist 12(3):254–274
Stanković SM (1990) Turizam u Jugoslaviji. Beograd, Turistička štampa
Statistical Yearbook of Yugoslavia (1954–1990) various years. Beograd, Statistical Office
Tchoukarine I (2010) The Yugoslav road to international tourism. Opening, decentralization, and propaganda in the early 1950s. In: Grandits H, Taylor K (eds) Yugoslavia's sunny side. A history of tourism in socialism (1950s-1980s). Central European University Press, Budapest, pp 107–138
Yeomans R (2010) From comrades to consumers. Holiday, leisure time, and ideology in communist Yugoslavia. In: Grandits H, Taylor K (eds) Yugoslavia's sunny side. A history of tourism in socialism (1950s-1980s). Central European University Press, Budapest, pp 69–106
Zečević M (1973) Investicije i razvoj turizma u Jugoslaviji. Institut za spoljnu trgovina, Beograd

Tomi Brezovec is Senior Lecture University of Primorska, Koper, Slovenia · Faculty of Tourism Studies—TURISTICA, Portoroz.

Aleksandra Brezovec is an Associate Professor of Communication Studies and Marketing Communications in Tourism at the University of Primorska, Faculty of Tourism Studies—TURISTICA (Slovenia, EU). Her research field connects tourism, communication studies and marketing. Aleksandra has worked on several international research projects in the field of tourism. She was a dean of the faculty (2008–2012), and in 2014, she was a visiting scholar at San Diego State University (USA). She is a member of UNWTO Panel of Tourism Experts, a member of European Communication Research and Education Association, and a member of Chair of Cultural Tourism within UNESCO-UNITWIN Chair of Culture, Tourism, Development (Paris Sorbonne).

Chapter 6
The First World War and the Crisis of International Investment in Tourism in Italy

Annunziata Berrino

Abstract In the history of tourism in Italy, the First World War represented a moment of profound transformations in the structure of investments in tourist services and in accommodation. After the national unification and the proclamation of the Kingdom of Italy (1861), the Italian peninsula, already very attractive for European and American tourism, had also become more accessible and interesting for foreign investors, who actively participated in the expansive and liberal phase of the early twentieth century. The outbreak of the First World War interrupted many economic circuits and cultural and professional relationships. This chapter seeks to analyse two important phenomena. The first is the interruption of the flow of foreign capital—Swiss, French, and Belgian—invested in the grand hotels of the cities of art and spa towns in Italy. The second is the interruption of economic relations in the tourist services of Bolzano and Trento, when these two provinces, following the treaties of Paris, passed from the Austro-Hungarian Empire to the Kingdom of Italy.

Introduction

In Europe, already in the early decades of nineteenth-century, travel and sojourn practices had suffered the adverse effects of revolutions and the Napoleonic wars (Towner 1985; Large 2015). However, the ban on travel and the long period of conflict and consequent economic and political changes had generated the modern figures of the *traveller* and *tourist* and the whole range of facilities to meet their needs, giving an enormous boost to the maturation of tourism (Berrino 2019). From the

PID2021-122476NB-I00 research project, financed by MCIN/AEI/10.13039/501100011033/ and the FEDER/ERDF Una manera de hacer Europa/A way of making Europe.

A. Berrino (✉)
University of Naples Federico II, Naples, Italy
e-mail: annunziata.berrino@unina.it

C. Larrinaga, D. Strangio (eds.), *Tourism Destinations and Policies in Europe During the 20th Century*, Contributions to Economics,
https://doi.org/10.1007/978-3-031-88447-4_6

middle of the century, European tourism, which was already in place as a system, showed its rapid capacity to adapt to changing geopolitical contexts such as, for example, those generated by the Crimean war from 1853 to 1856, the wars of the Risorgimento in Italy between 1848 and 1866 and the violent Franco-Prussian conflict of 1870 (Large 2015). But the First World War and the Russian Revolution, which left deep scars on the society and economy of the countries involved, had devastating effects despite the fact that tourism was firmly established, having reached extraordinary levels of development in the Euro-Mediterranean region.

The intense rivalry between the powers at war, the unexpected closure of the frontiers of the former Tsarist Empire and the aggressiveness of the defence lines that ran through the heart of Europe paused or slowed down general travelling, which had been accelerating up to that point thanks to technological advances during the second industrial revolution and the new perspectives of expansion that opened up with the first globalization.

The Italian tourism property suffered material damage in relatively limited areas, the eastern Alps and Pre-Alps, but the violence and worldwide dimension of the conflict interrupted the economic, cultural and professional circuits that had fostered the expansion of international tourism into which Italy had become integrated.

Italy—already very attractive from the point of view of European and American tourism—after national unification and the proclamation of the Kingdom of Italy in 1861, had become more accessible and interesting not just for travellers and sojourners, but also for foreign operators and investors.

In 1996 Richard Bosworth, pointing out the lack of studies reconstructing the history of tourism in Italy and offering an initial brief interpretation of it, highlighted the importance of the later years of the First World War, when the liberal state became aware of the economic weight of tourism and, launching a policy of intervention, underlined the importance of public intervention also in the hotel sector.

Studies and research in this last decade have enriched our knowledge of the hotel world (Tissot 2007; James et al. 2017; James 2018; Larrinaga 2018a, b, 2021) and enabled us to advance more detailed interpretations of the effects that the First World War had on the world of high-level *hôtellerie* in the Italian context as well as others (Leonardi 2014).

There have been some important reflections on the effects of the First World War on tourism, in the short and medium term and in particular on the assets of hospitality sector (Walton 2013; Zuelow 2016; Large 2015; James 2018). The most recent one from Carlos Larrinaga, dedicated to the birth and consolidation of the hotel supply in San Sebastián from the second half of the nineteenth century to the First World War, offers an accurate and up-to-date historiographic overview (Larrinaga 2023: 3–4).

We also have studies analysing the impact of the Great War on tourism in Italy (Bosworth 1996; Capuzzo 2020; Pasini 2021) and reconstructing the debate that opened up in country, leading to the first public interventions in the sector (Treves 1989; Bosworth 1996; Teodori 2007; Cavalcanti 2004, 2022). There are also many works devoted to the provinces of Trento and Bolzano, which passed from the Austro-Hungarian Empire to Italy in 1919 with the treaty of Saint-Germain and which were already acknowledged as being of great value for tourism (Rohrer 2003; Leonardi 2007, 2010, 2014; Gasser et al. 2014; Gasser 2016; Capuzzo 2019), as well as works dealing with subsidiary hospitality infrastructures present in the regions affected by acts of war (Strangio 2014; Dal Negro 2016).

This study refers to these analyses and interpretations and, after a brief sketch of the panorama of the growing presence of foreign professionalisms and capital in tourism services in Italy from the mid-nineteenth century onwards, it analyses how the outbreak of the war interrupted those transnational networks that had supported the development of tourism during the first globalization years. Starting from these premises, this work attempts to identify what medium-term effects the First World War had on the Italian tourism system, besides those of a political nature, and it tries to determine how the hospitality sector, weakened by the removal of overseas capital and the departure of foreign professionalisms, was placed in the context of disorder and economic crisis of the dramatic post-war period.

Italy and the Transnational Tourism Networks of the First Globalization

On the eve of the First World War, tourism in Italy comprised an important economic sector: by the end of the nineteenth century, tourist revenues, along with remittances from emigrants, had successfully covered the entire balance of payments deficit (Cavalcanti 2022: 29). The attraction of Italy was undisputed and had its roots in the centuries of the modern age. Between 1860 and 1861 the old States into which Italy was divided had been unified in the Kingdom of Italy, and national unity had further facilitated the development of tourism, which had been slowed down up to that point by the diversity of administrative institutions and systems. Tourist facilities grew from the 1870s onwards, converging and becoming part of the increasingly close-knit transnational networks. Italy had already gained experience in the founding stage of mid-century tourism and was therefore also able to participate actively in the subsequent phase of expansion, generated by the second industrial revolution; it assimilated the development of services and the widespread use of technological innovation, participated in the integration of markets and the acceleration of consumption, while still being rather slow in the active tourism practice.

Its central geographical position on the Mediterranean Sea was strategic in broadening and reinforcing links between Europe and the continents of Africa and Asia, which started with cutting of the Suez isthmus in 1869. And Italy was even more favoured by the creation of easier crossings through the Alps, which had started back in the early nineteenth century, but reached levels of functionality from mid-century onwards; the Frejus railway line of 1871 and the Saint Gotthard, completed in 1882, are cases in point, followed by the Simplon tunnel, completed in 1905.

The development of railway lines and navigation routes enhanced the resorts with intermodal functions, such as the large port cities like Naples and Genoa, or the lakeside and valley resorts of the Pre-Alps, which, although smaller in size, were in a strategic geographical position, being located between different provinces and countries. These resorts were able to set up specific services, also of a high standard, to welcome travellers and tourists moving within the regions or on intercontinental routes.

Italy therefore moved from a geography of tourism that had been established in the late eighteenth and early nineteenth centuries, when the search for different landscapes, climates and antiquities had led to the success of certain resorts, to a richer geography, outlined by the reinforcement of communications between Europe, the Mediterranean, and other centres involved in the modernization process, above all North America (Bosworth 1996).

The methods and intensity with which Italian tourism participated in transnational networks of professionalisms and services from the last quarter of the nineteenth century onwards is a subject of extreme interest and in the present study it forms the necessary premise in order to understand the impact and the effects that the First World War had on this trading system.

We can identify at least three transnational networks that directly involved tourism in the 1870s until the outbreak of the war: the first one mobilized the use of professionalisms, technological innovation, and capital in the hospitality sector; the other two linked the professionalisms and capital bound up in the railways and in navigation to those deployed in the hotel business.

We start from a rapid overview of the professional and financial networks in the hospitality sector. The hotel business in Italy, traditionally characterized by a marked economic individualism (Carera 2002a: 10), had been reinforced through the efforts of local operators, who in many cases had had forms of backing from foreign subjects; times and methods had been specified on a case-by-case basis, but the synergic action between local businesses and external forces is an undisputed fact (Leonardi 2016: 12; Cavalcanti 2022: 176). The subject has not yet received a systematic airing, and it is undoubtedly difficult to estimate the financial and cultural contribution given by these presences; however, research focusing closely on the history of high-end hotels in Italy, in respect of both the history of the business (Carera 2004a, b; Zanini 2014, 2016, 2020, 2022; Gerbardo 2015) and that of territorial development, (Selvafolta 2016) or the circulation of culture (Naccarato 2002), very frequently documents foreign shareholdings. It should be added that recent research confirms the entrepreneurial presence and professional contribution of Italians in other countries which are slower to participate in the tourism system, such as Spain, for instance (Larrinaga 2023).

In Italy the first areas to be involved and integrated in the professional and financial transnational networks were those of the pre-alpine lakes and the northern Tyrrhenian coastal areas, where communications between regions, which had always been facilitated by lake and maritime navigation, was soon favoured by steam technology applied to transport, bringing them even closer to the great north European centres. In addition, these coasts also had an obvious value in their landscapes and climate, which had been rediscovered in the Romantic period. Historiography identifies some of the major trading routes which facilitated tourist development processes: the first crossed the Alps and was aimed at the North-west, towards Switzerland; the second again crossed the Alps and, looking to the North-east, was connected to the lands of Austria and Germany; the third involved the northern Mediterranean coasts, exploiting the acceleration of trade links by land and sea between the Ligurian and French coasts.

The financial and professional wealth of neighbouring Switzerland found its way into the tourist enhancement of Lake Maggiore, whose shores already received investments by the aristocracy and then from the Piedmontese and Lombard middle classes (Cirio 2016). Foreign presence in these regions is documented in the history of the impressive *Grand Hôtel et des Iles Borromées* in Stresa, starting from its first relaunch in 1863 initiated by Italian and German entrepreneurs (Leonardi 2016: 12; Cirio 2016: 177).

Lake Como, too, called upon international presences and resources: along its shores, during the nineteenth century, European *high life* acquired historic sites and villas established by Lombard aristocracy, and many of these were thus included in tourist circuits (Carera 2002b). At the end of the century this was added to by capital from the city of Milan, with its industrial development well under way (Mosca 2002; Prosperi 2002): in many cases the management of the hotel facilities was given to Swiss professionals (Kawamura 2004: 33). Large hospitality facilities were built at Bellagio, such as the *Grand Hôtel Bellagio*, and then the *Grand Hôtel Villa Serbelloni* and the *Hôtel Grande Bretagne*, or the *Grand Hôtel Victoria*, opened in Menaggio in 1885; or the *Grand Hôtel Tremezzo*, which opened in 1910 in Tremezzo. In 1873 a company comprising members from the institutional, financial and entrepreneurial world of Milan transformed a sixteenth-century property on the lake shores of Cernobbio, another destination already identified by the culture of Romanticism, into the luxury *Grand Hôtel Villa d'Este* (Leonardi 2016: 13; Zanini 2016; Selvafolta 2016: 106).

Further east, Lake Garda had always acted as a line of communication between the Germanic world and the Italian peninsula and the Mediterranean. It attracted different visitors and economic interests; the mild climate on its shores drew the Hapsburg nobility to it, closely followed by the Austrian and German business community. Arco, Riva, and Torbole were the resorts that were soon thriving (Gregorini 2011: 64; Leonardi 2016; Pasini 2021).

On the northern Tyrrhenian coast of the Mediterranean, Swiss, and French professional experiences combined with the intuition and commitment of local figures were the driving force behind the success of tourism on the western Ligurian Riviera. This area has been the subject of detailed studies by the economic historian Andrea Zanini, who has documented the presence of French and Swiss capital and professional skills that, in synergy with local ones, enabled numerous coastal resorts and many entrepreneurs to achieve international success in tourism. This is the case of the extraordinary rise of the Piedmontese Lorenzo Bertolini (1832–1905) who, on emigrating to Switzerland while still young, entered the tourism scene starting as a hotel servant, and then ended up by managing, purchasing and creating, with the support of his Swiss wife Julie, luxury hotels in Courmayeur, Sanremo, Aosta, Milan, Florence, Rome and Naples. In the early years of the twentieth century Lorenzo Bertolini and his sons had seven prestigious luxury hotels, totalling 1100 beds (Zanini 2020). Major amounts of foreign capital also arrived on the Ligurian Riviera, such as at Ospedaletti, a fishing village that received investment in the 1880s from the French Société Foncière Lyonnaise which, along with the local Société Française Ligurienne, transformed the little resort into an international tourist destination (Zanini 2022: 48–49). And it was Swiss businessman Adolf Angst (1845–1928) who, in 1887 in Bordighera, opened the monumental *Hotel Angst*, one of the most prestigious hotels on the Ligurian Riviera, and then in 1890 we find Swiss and German professionals alongside Italians in the *Grand Hôtel Bellevue* in Sanremo (Zanini 2022: 53).

In those same years, Italian cities such as Rome, Florence, and Venice, whose tourist attraction was historically never in doubt, were integrated in the transnational networks that supported tourism, attracting foreign operators who were able to bring skills and financial resources. Facilities for high-level *hôtellerie* were also built in these resorts. In the capital, Rome, the Swiss presence was probably the most important. Of the many hotels there we would mention the *Hôtel Quirinal* of Bucher & Durrer, which later passed to Heinrich Wirth & Bucher. Friends and associates Franz-Josef Bucher (1834–1906) and Josef Durrer (1841–1919) started from the trade and processing of wood and became involved in furniture production and the construction and management of hotels, finally venturing into the world of transport and building tram, cable car and chairlift networks. We also recall the *Hôtel Hassler* belonging to the Hassler family, who originated in the Grisons canton, and the *Hôtel Eden* belonging to Nistelweck & Wirth—the former, a German, had married Berta of the Swiss Hassler family of hoteliers. In 1894 the already legendary César Ritz (1850–1918), well-known as the owner of the *Hôtel Savoy* in London, invested his capital in the *Grand Hôtel de Rome*, with 300 bedrooms and open all year round; from its inauguration, this presented itself as a model of absolute luxury for other Italian hotels. Between 1903 and 1906, still in Rome, the Swiss baron Alphons von Pfyffer (1863–1920) built the *Hôtel Excelsior* in Via Veneto to a design by Swiss architects (Girelli Bocci 2006). From the mid-nineteenth century until the war, the names of the hotels, the families and the companies involved in hospitality created an extraordinary, variegated pattern, because in many cases they were interlinked, mixing individual biographies of men and women with the histories of the families and the businesses. The pioneers were almost all born in the 1830s.

The expansion of railway networks and consequent urban modernization produced a ripple effect of enhancing local transport systems. From the 1870s onwards, major foreign entrepreneurs and investors, some originating from Belgium, were also involved in these sectors that were so strategic for tourism. In Naples, there were Oscar de Mesnil de Volkrange (1836–1897), a diplomat, patron of the arts, as well as administrator of the thermal spa town of Spa, and his brother Herman Charles (1837–1918); the de Mesnils invested in tram networks and lift systems in Naples, where they accomplished an impressive redevelopment of the shoreline, creating areas for construction of residential buildings and for hotels on the model of the activities carried out in Paris by the Pereire brothers, Jacob Emile (1800–1875) and Isaac Rodrigue (1806–1880) (Tessier 2012: 23). At the end of the 1870s in Naples, Oscar de Mesnil invested in the luxury thermal establishment of *Bagni del Chiatamone*, later transformed into a hotel, and in the *Hôtel du Vésuve*, both on the sea-front, stating publicly that they intended to compete with the Swiss supply, offering excellent service at reasonable prices. De Mesnil built the *Vésuve* in partnership with another Belgian, Théophile Finet (1837–1910), an engineer who was active in constructing special structures necessary for railway construction in the regions of southern Italy and in various other Mediterranean countries, including Algeria and Egypt. Finet had founded the Régie Générale des Chemins de Fer et des Travaux Publics in 1870, together with one of his brothers-in law Philippe Vitali (1830–1909), also an engineer and builder of railways, among other things, in Sicily and Calabria. For professional reasons and because of his business commitments, Finet, also a senator of the Belgian liberal party, travelled extensively and stayed at the grand hotels in European cities and Mediterranean ports. In Rome, he used to stay at the *Grand Hôtel*, which he admired and which in his opinion was "Un des plus perfect hôtel de l'Europe". In the management of their hotel, the Belgians in Naples followed a model that was also common in other parts of Italy: ownership of the building, either newly created or the result of radical restructuring, remained the property of foreign investors, who received a secure income from it, while the management was given to Italians. This was also the case on the Ligurian Riviera (Zanini 2016: 39, 2022: 36).

Other Belgian entrepreneurs operated around Palermo, where an Italo-Belgian company designed a luxury bathing establishment at Mondello, which was partly built. Naples and Palermo were seaports of interest, because, like Genoa, they were reinforcing their function as intermodal centres for trade between railways and navigation.

The economic ferment pervading Italy when it was at its industrial take-off stage, began to mobilize big national capital to get involved in tourism. Like the foreign investors, it was seeking opportunities for investment in resorts located at convenient distances with respect to the transport available, so as not to risk connections being broken (Carera 2002a: 10).

The injection of Swiss capital and professionalisms in the hotel sector was undoubtedly the most evident and probably the most profitable. We owe the only systematic analysis of the Swiss presence in Italian *hôtellerie* and in some tourism services to the art and architecture historian Ewa Kawamura. Based on a large volume of data, Kawamura has conducted a census of the Swiss presence in the various professional roles and in the different Italian resorts and has compiled a chart of them. Her analyses show that the Swiss were present not just in Italian businesses located in the adjacent Italian lake regions, but over the whole of Italy (Kawamura 2004: 31–36). Gérard Kraft (1858–1943), the son of a Bern hotelier, emerged as a one of the many Swiss hoteliers in Florence. In 1883, Kraft purchased two Florentine hotels on the Lungarno, the *Hôtel d'Italie* and the *Hôtel Royal de la Paix* which he renamed the *Grand Hôtel* (Kawamura 2004: 21). In the early years of the twentieth century Kraft made other acquisitions in Florence and opened hotels in Turin, Nice and Bern, confirming the transnational nature of his businesses.

The major Swiss operators were also awake to the potential of Italian spa resources. In 1901 César Ritz and the baron Alphons von Pfyffer, who were already active in Rome, collaborated at Salsomaggiore in the management of the *Grand Hôtel des Thermes*, the investment of Giuseppe Magnaghi (1850–1895), a Milanese entrepreneur who died prematurely; the two French professionals who had worked alongside Magnaghi in designing the building, equipped with 300 rooms and state-of-the art facilities, took over the property in 1910.

On the eve of the outbreak of the war, incidences of foreign investment offered significant examples for Italian capitalism: as already mentioned, when reinforced by industrial development in the early part of the twentieth century, Italian capital also began to invest in tourism, following the experiences of France and Switzerland, although it obviously happened later.

The indisputable inventiveness that the Italians had expressed in the development of tourism was then accompanied by an initial financial participation. In 1908 a review of the banks and active capital in Italy recorded 27 companies whose purpose was the construction and management of hotels, all established in the early years of the century (Branzoli-Zappi and Mazza 1908). However, the review recorded that only very few family-sized hotel businesses had managed to evolve into companies, such as, for example, the Lorenzo Bertolini hotel company, with just over one million in capital, which owned the *Bertolini's Hôtels*. Several other companies were present in spa resorts, and had a long management history, such as at San Pellegrino and at Montecatini, where the Swiss company Spatz-Suardi controlled major sites for the town's expansion. The company with the largest amounts of capital was Ciga, the Compagnia Italiana Grandi Alberghi, founded in 1906 by the diplomat and banker Alberto Treves (1855–1921) with four-and-a-half million of initial capital; it was significant that Ciga originated in the world of Italian finance, through the Banca Commerciale Italiana, and in the national electricity industry with was growing strongly. With this power behind it, Ciga took over the famous *Hôtel des Bains* on the Venice Lido and the properties of the London company Venice Hotel Limited, acquiring the already legendary Venetian hotels, the *Danieli* and the *Grand Hôtel*, thus creating the first high-end *hôtellerie* chain that was entirely under Italian control (Gerbardo 2015: XIII). Reflecting the intensity of trade, company-owned hotels were concentrated especially in the northern cities, mainly in Milan; added to these were those in small regions with high value in landscape, climate, and culture, namely the Ligurian Riviera, the Pre-alpine lakes and the spa resorts, even if the latter had not achieved an international reputation.

This process made the Italian hospitality scene even more complex. The various business histories and the panorama of companies that emerged in the early twentieth century confirm how on the eve of the First World War the geography of Italy was composed of the tourist region concentrated in the North, the cities of art, a significant enclave in the gulf of Naples (Kawamura 2017; Giannico 2007) and a few destinations in Sicily (Bosworth 1996, 159).

It was an important system that, according to an efficient summary produced by Marco Avancini for the Italian government in 1925, had brought over 590 thousand foreigners to Italy back in 1910. In 1923, the first year of official data collection, arrivals had gone up to 700 thousand, or 14 million presences, because it was considered that every tourist would stay on average 20 nights and would generally make three stops. An average expenditure of 175 lire per day, or 2.5 billion lire a year, was estimated; this contributed positively to Italy's trade balance (Avancini 1925). Nevertheless, tourism had never been held in much esteem among the Italian political élite, who instead put their faith more in industrial development.

Therefore, the outbreak of the war devastated a sector that had grown considerably (Cavalcanti 2022: 180), but that was in a delicate phase of transformation, because it was absorbing the entry of Italian capitalism and facing other, equally important changes in context.

The Italian government had very little understanding of the system. Hospitality businesses had always had to dialogue with local administrations in order to establish roots in their areas, but until that moment they had never needed to foster relations with central government, focusing as they did on innovation and control of the competition.

The Material Damage of War

In May 1915 Italy also entered the war and, siding with the Triple Entente, had the Austro-Hungarian and German Empires as its prime enemy countries; visitors to Italy traditionally came from these countries, so their absence was felt starting in Venice, where 80% of personnel employed in hotels and boarding houses were already out of work in the second half of 1914. The Associazione italiana albergatori then tried to sensitize the government to obtain extraordinary measures, such as, for example, a suspension of tax on incomes for hotel companies and above all favourable credit terms, but these requests were ineffective. Only from the middle of 1915 did hoteliers, after a long period of exerting pressure, obtain from the government permission to postpone payment of rents on buildings and payment of mortgage interests. However, their needs were clear: those who had suffered material damage must be supported by accelerating payments of damages and support must be given to those who had difficulty in accessing credit because, having been part of the expansion phase in the early twentieth century and maybe planned innovations and investments, now found themselves burdened by instalments of rents and mortgages.

Very slowly, and after seemingly endless resistance, the Italian government began to consider the needs of tourism.

In 1917 the Italian government decided to include tourism in the subjects for study of the post-war Commission, considering that a policy of intervention was now necessary. However, Italian tourism was not represented by the hospitality business, but by active tourism associations, meaning the Touring Club Italiano and the Movimento dei Forestieri, which had already represented the government on international occasions in the years before the war. These representatives were also divided and had conflicting opinions concerning their view of tourism. Luigi Vittorio Bertarelli, director of the Touring Club Italiano prevailed, expressing scepticism regarding public intervention in tourism and instead proposing his complex, holistic view of the phenomenon. Thanks to his approach, Bertarelli was able to understand and condemn the fact that hospitality businesses in Italy were not associated and did not act as one single group, as happened, for example, in Switzerland, and that this situation was a serious critical issue. Unsurprisingly, no proposal was offered by the entire private sector in the post-war Commission; on the other hand, the Associazione italiana albergatori, founded in 1899, did not represent all the category and presented itself rather as a narrow club of a few big hoteliers; there had been 144 at its foundation and they were largely from the Lombardy region and in particular the area of Lake Como, one of the most advanced from a tourism point of view.

Anyway, conflicts, disputes and misunderstandings pushed the government to set up a commission in 1919 with the aim of studying the actions needed to support the recovery of the sector. So Enit, Ente nazionale per l'incremento delle industrie turistiche, the Italian national tourist board, was set up to boost the tourist industries. It was substantially inspired by the liberal vision of Luigi Vittorio Bertarelli, who firmly believed in tourism as a process to foster civil growth and an opportunity for economic growth. And thus began public state intervention in tourism.

Italy's tourist system in the meantime was experiencing deep uncertainty caused by the dramatic and structural changes resulting from the war.

In the areas involved in the fighting there was also material damage and rebuilding was necessary: in Trentino region alone, around 130 of the best hotels were unusable (Cavalcanti 2022: 184). The war had generated distrust not only of tourists, but also of the professionals and workers who came from German-speaking countries, and who were generically defined as "Germans"; the Swiss were also included with these (Raspadori 2014: 111). Thus, while the war had imposed more and more severe restrictions on the movement of people, propaganda and national solidarity assumed more and more heated tones: in many cases foreigners were discriminated against and removed from hospitality premises.

The interruption in transnational circuits inevitably also brought about a change in ownership structures. Ewa Kawamura, processing the data published by the Touring Club Italiano, records that in 1919 in Liguria on the western Riviera, one of the areas where Swiss operators were most active, 18 hotels with around 1630 beds were closed, and she reports that the hope for an immediate recovery in the post-war period very soon vanished: in 1922 six hotels out of ten closed the financial year in debt (Kawamura 2004: 29).

Big foreign capital then withdrew its commitments: in Rome, ownership of the *Grand Hôtel Excelsior* and that of the *Grand Hôtel* was transferred to the Sindacato Italiano Sviluppo Alberghi; serious problems were experienced by high-end operators, such as, for example, the Hasslers, in businesses located in several Italian cities; in 1917 at Salsomaggiore, the Italian government, following the recent regulations relating to the exploitation of underground resources, revoked the mining concession to the Magnaghi company and the site passed out of Swiss hands and into state ownership.

Many Belgian investors, too, gave up their shareholdings in Italy, because communications and financial transfers were interrupted for a long time due to the German occupation. In 1922 the proprietors of the *Grand Hôtel du Vésuve* in Naples decided to sell the ownership of the building, which was purchased, with a great deal of effort, by the Neapolitan hotels company, appropriately set up by the Fiorentino family, who already managed the hotel and owned the fixtures and fittings (Berrino 2022).

Transfers of properties in the provinces of Bolzano and Trento were also painful: following the treaties of Paris, they passed from the Austro-Hungarian Empire to the Kingdom of Italy.

The war had also overthrown the old organization of the labour market, which had long nourished some precise expectations, such as the achievement of the eight-hour shift, the abolition of tips, and the introduction of fixed salaries for waiters and porters, as well as the establishment of employment exchanges and compulsory accident insurance; moreover, it was a world that was already exhausted by calls to arms and the ban on travel. Between 1919 and 1920 the hotel personnel sector took part in the wave of strikes that swept over the country, standing alongside workers in the fields of transport, industry and agriculture (Bosworth 1996).

The economic crisis generated by the conflict continued to weaken the Italian hospitality system, which struggled in the midst of the difficulties of devastation, the decline in flows of tourists, the discontinuation of international investments and unrest among the workforces.

It must be said that the effects of the war were uneven in various areas comprising the Italian hospitality system. First of all the dynamics of the conflict put foreign interests in a weak position, as they were more difficult to protect and inevitably left the field free for national interests: in Alto Adige and in many other resorts in the tourist regions of the North, national operators had the chance to take over the ownership and management of top-class hotels from Austrian entrepreneurs and, "according to contemporary testimonies, the majority of hotels managed by Germans or Swiss-Germans were repurchased" (Cavalcanti 2022: 186).

In addition, although the government had imposed a ceiling price on rooms in 1918, and the hoteliers had grossly increased this to combat inflation, this provision did not in reality affect luxury hotels. Also, the closure of many hotels that were unable to hold on allowed those remaining active to operate almost under monopoly conditions; in fact, internationally favoured resorts welcomed those Italians who had been used to frequent the élite resorts abroad. And in some cases, the requisitioning of prestigious hotels located far from the combat zones acted as a kind of support for businesses. The *Grand Hôtel Vittoria* in Sorrento was requisitioned from November 1917 until February 1918: during the three-year period 1915–1917 it had lost two-thirds of its traditionally international attendances, which had fallen from 13 thousand in 1914 to around 5 thousand a year. In Rome, two floors of the *Hôtel Excelsior* were used by the Red Cross as a hospital for officers; in Bordighera the *Hotel Angst* was converted into a military hospital (Zanini 2014: 318–319). Even the *Grand Hôtel Miramare et de la Ville* in Genoa belonging to the Swiss company Italienisch-Scweizerische Hotelgesellschaft accepted the proposal of the Italian military authorities to lease the building and designate it as a hospital.

Following these many changes, most of the Italian hotel sector came out of the war with a profoundly altered profile, but one that was above all even less cohesive. However, while fascism rose to power, Enit continued to carry out its activities which, according to its charter, were spread over a broad range of areas: all those that concerned tourism, from roads to railways and from education to advertising, but one of its primary and greatest tasks was to supply a knowledge of the national hotel system. This involved collecting and publishing data, facilities, and prices of hotels in Italy, not only for statistic reasons, but above all to offer guarantees of clear prices, especially to foreign markets. Hoteliers put up enormous resistance, to the extent that Enit, without beating about the bush, expressed on several occasions the difficulty in intervening in the sector. This led to the start of a new course for Italian tourism.

Between the two world wars, Italy quickly recovered the numbers for international tourism by means of new promotional strategies, but the continuous structural innovation required by tourism particularly in the hotel sector became slow and laborious. The numbers immediately appeared positive, because foreign tourists' expenditure in Italy trebled between 1919 and 1926 (Cavalcanti 2022), but one detail seems significant and that is the expenditure of American tourists, considered as the most generous revenue streams between the two wars: more than three quarters of the dollars brought into Europe by American tourists between 1927 and 1937 was distributed among just five countries: excluding Switzerland and Germany which received around 5% of American dollars, France collected more than all the others, with over 60%; Great Britain between 13% and 20% and Italy only came third with percentages estimated at between 5% and 15% (10.5% in 1927; 13% in 1929; 5.7% in 1933; 15% in 1937) (Le tourisme international en Europe 1950).

Conclusion

History produced a tourism system combining interests, investments, and skills that, as an expression of modernity, was also able to adapt to the speed of transformations in what was known as the "long century", but the First World War represented a break which the weakest profiles, the most intrepid companies and the most determined survivors could not handle. However, there was no natural selection, because Italy at thc time of the outbreak of the war had a structural critical issue because, unlike France and Switzerland, it had never worked out a policy for tourism. From the early eighteenth century onwards, many businesses had certainly been reinforced and made autonomous with foreign backing, but they had focused above all on growing and controlling the competition, without realizing the need to keep an eye on the politics.

The war, on the other hand, dictated the urgency to protect their own interests, although it was not easy to act in the light of a common view that considered tourism, and first and foremost hotels, as useful for the balance of payments and taxation. In any case that contrast between entrepreneurs and government during the war years, more than contributing to putting down a basis for an Italian tourism policy (Zanini 2014: 314), steered the most exposed tourism operators towards a greater commitment to political relations.

The long twenty-year period of fascism started in 1922; the dictatorship, convinced of the effectiveness of tourism as a space for advertising and propaganda, decisively pursued a promotional activity abroad. On the other hand, interventions in the hotel sector were incoherent, being aimed especially at fact-finding and statistical surveys and at fiscal measures, but anyway with a view of tourism that was more and more dominated by the urgency to bring a monetary contribution to the trade balance, by political control and the search for consensus, rather than by organic, social, economic, and cultural growth.

In any case there was no lack of support for national businesses of particular prestige, so that luxury hospitality in the common imagination started to be associated with Ciga (Kawamura 2019); its hotel network in Italy had replaced the many businesses with foreign shareholdings, representing many liberal and really international spaces that were no longer coherent with the aims of the regime. The real inability to intervene to support mid-range hospitality and the absence of a view of the country's development, except in specific areas of interest to the regime, widened the differences in quality levels, in categories and areas; they were historical differences, already evident since the time of national unification and exacerbated by the impetuous growth that occurred in the liberal age.

It is not surprising that in 1947, after the fall of the fascist dictatorship and the Second World War, the world of Italian tourism reiterated the terms of the debate that had taken place following the First War, coalescing again around that ideal holistic view of tourism that had been proposed by Vittorio Bertarelli's Touring Club Italiano.

Meanwhile, however, the hospitality sector had changed greatly and, although interest groups remained within it that had grown up in the shadow of the regime, it was now quite clear that in order to operate in the new free and democratic context, newly opened to an international dimension, it was necessary to have a constant dialogue with the government, and this is what happened, because when, in 1947, after a long debate, the government of Alcide De Gasperi established the Commissariato del turismo, the strongest pressures came from all hotel businesses—not only luxury one—which proposed themselves as representatives of the entire world of Italian tourism and the main actors and interlocutors with the post-World War II government (Berrino 2020).

References

Avancini M (1925) Entità e svolgimento del traffico turistico in Italia: dati e congetture. Tipografia del Senato, Roma

Berrino A (2019) Dalle pratiche di viaggio e di soggiorno al turismo: categorie interpretative. In: Bohmel Fichera U, Giovannini E (eds) Spazi, orizzonti e confini. Nuove prospettive del viaggio in Italia (1750-1850). Istituto italiano di studi germanici, Roma, pp 13–21

Berrino A (2020) L'istituzione dell'Alto commissariato per il turismo nell'Italia del secondo dopoguerra. In: Berrino A, Larrinaga C (eds) Italia e Spagna nel turismo del secondo dopoguerra. Società, politiche, istituzioni ed economia. Franco Angeli, Milano, pp 19–36

Berrino A (2022) Grand Hotel Vesuvio. Napoli, 1882–2022. Guida editori, Napoli

Bosworth R (1996) Italy and the wider world: 1860–1960. Taylor & Francis Group, London

Branzoli-Zappi E, Mazza L (eds) (1908) Manuale bancario. Annuario generale delle banche e del capitale. Stab. Tip. G. Scotti e C, Roma

Capuzzo E (2019) Italiani. Visitate l'Italia. Politiche e dinamiche turistiche in Italia tra le due guerre mondiali. Luni editrice, Milano

Capuzzo E (2020) War tourism in Italy (1919-1939). In: Pellejero C, Luque M (eds) Inter and post-war tourism in Western Europe 1916–1960. Palgrave Macmillan, Cham, pp 35–65

Carera A (2002a) Premessa. In: Carera A (ed) Temi di storia economica del turismo lombardo (XIX-XX secolo). Vita e Pensiero, Milano, pp 7–18

Carera A (2002b) Linee di evoluzione economica del movimento turistico lombardo tra XIX e XX secolo. In: Carera A (ed) Temi di storia economica del turismo lombardo (XIX-XX secolo). Vita e Pensiero, Milano, pp 21–64

Carera A (ed) (2004a) L'alta hotellerie nell'Italia di inizio Novecento. Organizzazione e gestione manageriale in uno studio di Willy Dombré (1922). Pubblicazioni dell'I.S.U. Università Cattolica, Milano

Carera A (2004b) Manager e management alberghiero di inizio Novecento. In: Carera A (ed) L'alta hotellerie nell'Italia di inizio Novecento. Organizzazione e gestione manageriale in uno studio di Willy Dombré (1922). Pubblicazioni dell'I.S.U. Università Cattolica, Milano, pp 13–42

Cavalcanti ML (2004) Riflessioni sulle vacanze degli italiani nella belle époque. Storia del turismo Annale 4:55–70

Cavalcanti ML (2022) Il turismo d'élite in Italia. Dall'età liberale al regime fascista. Storia, economia, istituzioni, Bologna, Il Mulino

Cirio V (2016) Una rassegna dei Grand Hotel del lago Maggiore (1870-1930). In: Aresi M (ed) I Grand Hotel come generatori di cambiamento tra il 1870 e 1930. Indagini nei contesti alpini e subalpini tra laghi e monti. MAG Museo Alto Garda, Rovereto, pp 175–191

Dal Negro F (2016) Alberghi alpini ed infrastrutture. Rapporti reciproci. In: Aresi M (ed) I Grand Hotel come generatori di cambiamento tra il 1870 e 1930. Indagini nei contesti alpini e subalpini tra laghi e monti. MAG Museo Alto Garda, Rovereto, pp 123–134

Gasser P (2016) Da borgo rurale a "località di cura di fama mondiale": Merano e i suoi Grand Hotel tra 1870 e 1925. In: Aresi M (ed) I Grand Hotel come generatori di cambiamento tra il 1870 e 1930. Indagini nei contesti alpini e subalpini tra laghi e monti. MAG Museo Alto Garda, Rovereto, pp 51–65

Gasser P, Leonardi A, Barth-Scalmani G (eds) (2014) Krieg und Tourismus im Spannungsfeld des Ersten Weltkrieges / Guerra e turismo nell'area di tensione della Prima Guerra Mondiale. Studien Verlag, Innsbruck-Wien-Bozen

Gerbardo P (2015) Compagnia italiana dei grandi alberghi. Un sogno italiano dalla Belle époque al miracolo economico (CIGA, 1906-1979). G. Giappichelli editore, Torino

Giannico G (2007) Investimenti nella ricettività alberghiera nel sud Italia: dai primi albergatori di Capri all'arrivo dei "milanesi. Storia del turismo Annale 6:35–51

Girelli Bocci AM (2006) Roma: hotel e sistema ricettivo in età liberale. In: Girelli Bocci AM (ed) L'industria dell'ospitalità a Roma. Secoli XIX-XX, Padova, CEDAM, 21–212

Gregorini G (2011) Tra Ottocento e Novecento. In: Taccolini M (ed) Il turismo bresciano tra passato e futuro. Vita e Pensiero, Milano, pp 61–75

James KJ, Sandoval-Strausz AK, Maudlin D, Peleggi M, Humair C, Berger MW (2017) The hotel in history: evolving perspectives. J Tour Hist 9(1):92–111

James K (2018) Histories, meanings and representations of the modern hotel. Channel View Publications, Bristol

Kawamura E (2004) Alberghi e albergatori svizzeri in Italia tra Ottocento e Novecento. Storia del turismo Annale 4:11–42

Kawamura E (2017) Storia degli alberghi napoletani. Dal Grand Tour alla Belle époque nell'ospitalità della Napoli "gentile". Napoli, Clean edizioni

Kawamura E (2019) Strategia artistica nelle stampe pubblicitarie degli alberghi della Compagnia Italia dei Grandi Alberghi (CIGA) negli anni 1906-1938. In: Gemma Belli AC (ed) Le città e il turismo. Hotel tra Ottocento e Novecento. Arte'm, Napoli, pp 75–85

Large DC (2015) The Grand Spas of Central Europe. A history of intrigue, politics, art, and healing. Lanham, Rowman & Litterfield

Larrinaga C (2018a) La hotelería de lujo en Madrid, 1892-1914. Pasado Abierto, 8, julio-diciembre, 8–26

Larrinaga C (2018b) La hotelería turística y las primeras cadenas hoteleras en la España del primer tercio del siglo XX. In: Vallejo R, Larrinaga C (eds) Los orígenes del turismo moderno en España. El nacimiento de un país turístico 1900–1939. Sílex, Madrid, pp 679–722

Larrinaga C (2021) De la fonda al hotel. Turismo y hotelería privada en España entre 1900 y 1959, Comares, Granada

Larrinaga C (2023) Origin and consolidation of the hotel sector in the capital of Spanish tourism: San Sebastián between 1868 and 1914. Manage Org Hist 18(2–3):223–243. https://doi.org/10.1080/17449359.2023.2259885

Leonardi A (2007) Turismo e sviluppo in area alpina. Una lettura socioeconomica delle trasformazioni intervenute tra Ottocento e Novecento. Storia del turismo, Annale 6:53–83

Leonardi A (2010) Entrepreneurial mobility in the development of the Austrian Kurorte in the nineteenth century. J Tour Hist 2(2):99–116

Leonardi A (2014) La Prima guerra mondiale e la vulnerabilità del fenomeno turistico. In: Gasser P, Leonardi A, Barth-Scalmani G (eds) Krieg und Tourismus im Spannungsfeld des Ersten Weltkrieges / Guerra e turismo nell'area di tensione della Prima Guerra Mondiale. Studien Verlag, Innsbruck-Wien-Bozen, pp 57–98

Leonardi A (2016) I grand hotel come motore dello sviluppo turistico in area alpina. In: Aresi M (ed) I Grand Hotel come generatori di cambiamento tra il 1870 e 1930. Indagini nei contesti alpini e subalpini tra laghi e monti. MAG Museo Alto Garda, Rovereto, pp 9–36

Le Tourisme international en Europe (1950) Etudes et conjoncture - Economie mondiale 4:21–58

Mosca M (2002) Il turismo degli affari a Milano negli anni della prima industrializzazione (1871-1914). In: Carera A (ed) Temi di storia economica del turismo lombardo (XIX-XX secolo). Vita e Pensiero, Milano, pp 109–136

Naccarato C (2002) Il turismo d'élite sul lago di Como: il Grand Hotel Villa d'Este (1873-1963). In: Carera A (ed) Temi di storia economica del turismo lombardo (XIX-XX secolo). Vita e Pensiero, Milano, pp 165–198

Pasini MP (2021) Turismo e Grande Guerra tra rivendicazioni patriottiche e nuove istanze di modernizzazione. L'impegno del Touring Club Italiano. In: Gregorini G, Semeraro R (eds) Turismo 4.0. Storia, digitalizzazione, territorio. Vita e Pensiero, Milano, pp 95–108

Prosperi L (2002) L'offerta turistica a Milano fra la Prima e la Seconda guerra mondiale (1918-1938). In: Carera A (ed) Temi di storia economica del turismo lombardo (XIX-XX secolo). Vita e Pensiero, Milano, pp 137–164

Raspadori P (2014) Ospitare servire ristorare. Storia dei lavoratori di alberghi e ristoranti in Italia dalla fine dell'Ottocento alla metà del Novecento, Rubbettino, Soveria Mannelli

Rohrer J (2003) Camere libere. Il libro del Touriseum, Merano, Museo del turismo Touriseum

Selvafolta O (2016) I Grand Hotel e la tradizione dell'accoglienza sul lago di Como tra Otto e Novecento. In: Aresi M (ed) I Grand Hotel come generatori di cambiamento tra 1870 e 1930. Indagini nei contesti alpini e subalpini tra laghi e monti, Rovereto, MAG Museo Alto Garda, 99–121

Strangio D (2014) Turismo e infrastrutture. In: Gasser P, Leonardi A, Barth-Scalmani G (eds) Krieg und Tourismus im Spannungsfeld des Ersten Weltkrieges / Guerra e turismo nell'area di tensione della Prima Guerra Mondiale. Studien Verlag, Innsbruck-Wien-Bozen, pp 209–228

Teodori M (2007) La politica economica dell'accoglienza. La legislazione turistico-alberghiera in Italia tra le due guerre. In: Lopane I, Ritrovato E (eds) Tra vecchi e nuovi equilibri: domanda e offerta di servizi in Italia in età moderna e contemporanea. Atti del quinto Convegno Nazionale Torino 12–13 novembre 2004, Bari, Cacucci editore, 551–566

Tessier A (2012) Le Grand Hôtel. L'invention du luxe hôtelier (1862–1972), Rennes-Tours, Presses universitaires François-Rabelais de Tours and Presses universitaires de Rennes

Tissot L (2007) L'hôtellerie de luxe à Genève (1830-2000). De ses espaces à ses usages. Entreprises et histoire 46:17–34

Towner J (1985) The grand tour: a key phase in the history of tourismo. Ann Tour Res 12(3):297–333

Treves A (1989) Anni di guerra, anni di svolta. Il turismo italiano durante la Prima guerra mondiale. In: Botta G (ed) *Studi geografici sul paesaggio*. Cisalpino, Milano, pp 249–299

Walton KJ (2013) War and tourism: the nineteenth and twentieth centuries. In: Butler R, Suntikul W (eds) Tourism and war. Routledge, London, pp 64–74

Zanini A (2014) Verso una politica turistica nazionale. Gli albergatori italiani di fronte alla Prima guerra mondiale. In: Gasser P, Leonardi A, Barth-Scalmani G (eds) Krieg und Tourismus im Spannungsfeld des Ersten Weltkrieges / Guerra e turismo nell'area di tensione della Prima Guerra Mondiale. Studien Verlag, Innsbruck-Wien-Bozen, pp 313–331

Zanini A (2016) Grandi alberghi e organizzazione turistica in Italia tra Otto e Novecento. Il ruolo pionieristico dell'esperienza lariana. In: Aresi M (ed) I Grand Hotel come generatori di cambiamento tra il 1870 e 1930. Indagini nei contesti alpini e subalpini tra laghi e monti. MAG Museo Alto Garda, Rovereto, pp 37–50

Zanini A (2020) Un pioniere dell'alta hôtellerie: Lorenzo Bertolini (1832-1905). Atti dell'Accademia ligure di scienze e lettere 2(serie VII):253–272

Zanini A (2022) L'alta hôtellerie nella Riviera di Ponente durante la Belle Époque: capitali e imprenditori. In: Bagnoli L, Carassale A (eds) Riviera italiana e francese: similitudini e differenze. Una storia comparativa delle riviere francese e italiana / Riviera fraçaise et italienne: similitudes et differences. Une histoire comparative des rivieras italienne et francaise, Bordighera, Istituto Internazionale di studi liguri, pp 43–60

Zuelow E (2016) A history of modern tourism. Palgrave Macmillan, London

Annunziata Berrino is Professor of Contemporary History at the University of Naples Federico II, Italy. Her main research topic is the history of tourism in the Euro-Mediterranean area, to which she has dedicated books, essays, and scholarly articles.

Chapter 7
French Perspectives of the Genesis of a New International Tourism in the Interwar Period

Johan Vincent and Yves-Marie Evanno

Abstract The First World War shattered European national public finances. Even before the end of the conflict, the belligerent states realize that tourism is one of the few economic activities capable of quickly repatriating the gold spent for almost 5 years. In France, to attract international tourists, the government thus decides to promote memorial tourism of the Great War while continuing to promote the picturesque sites which had forged its fame in the past. But the success of such an enterprise was impossible without a favourable context. Tourism, which had benefited from nationalist perspectives to organize itself during the nineteenth century (see articles by Adrian Franklin), became a national economic actor. In the 1920s, the country took advantage of the weakness of the franc against other foreign currencies (in particular the pound sterling and the US dollar) to attract foreign customers. While continuing to develop its national clientele (with the progressive diffusion of paid vacation), France is becoming tourist. If the economic crisis of 1929 suddenly changed the outlook by favouring a nationalist withdrawal, including in the field of tourism, as the League of Nations regrets in a 1934 report, the development of international tourism did not stop entirely. In fact, it is encouraged by international structures. The conditions are now ripe for the emergence of a new international tourism (this time perceived as a transnational exchange and not between foreign destinations) which will not materialize, as Olivier Dehoorne specifies, after the Second World War.

J. Vincent (✉)
ESTHUA, University of Angers, Angers, France
e-mail: johan.vincent@univ-angers.fr

Y.-M. Evanno
Catholic University of the Western, South Brittany, UCO-BS, Arradon, France
e-mail: yevanno@uco.fr

C. Larrinaga, D. Strangio (eds.), *Tourism Destinations and Policies in Europe During the 20th Century*, Contributions to Economics,
https://doi.org/10.1007/978-3-031-88447-4_7

Introduction

The word "tourism" did not become part of the French vocabulary until the nineteenth century, almost two hundred years after the emergence of modern tourism practices in Europe (Boyer 2000: 9). At that time, its definition was limited to its international dimension. In 1873, in his *Dictionnaire de la langue française*, Émile Littré accurately reflected the thinking of the time when he reduced tourists to travellers who "wander through foreign countries […] out of curiosity and idleness" (Gay and Decroly 2018: 102). It was not until the turn of the twentieth century that domestic tourism, performed internally by national residents, gained recognition from tourism professionals who understood the economic potential of such demand. It was with this in mind that the Touring Clubs were created in the 1890s in Europe (in France in 1890, in Italy in 1894, in Belgium in 1895, in Luxembourg (Jeck 2008), etc.), as well as other specific associations (such as the Alpine Clubs) and local associations (tourist offices). This greater awareness of tourism coincided with the growth of the sport.

A few decades later, tourism was firmly established in the Western world. Yet the 1920s and 1930s seemed like a paradox between elitist permanence and growing popularity of this activity. John Walton, in *Tourism and Crisis in Europe, XIX-XXI centuries* (Dritsas 2014), using examples from the coasts of Europe and South America, even analyses the Inter-War Depression as a revelation for tourism. He highlights the widespread success of coastal destinations in extending their markets, both domestic and international, in some cases by tapping into working-class demand flows, while adapting their health and recreation provision, and their repertoire of attractions, to changing technologies, tastes and preferences. Resort publicity, transport improvements and the innovatory provision of entertainment and amenities were in evidence throughout the inter-war years but can be seen to have accelerated during the 1930s, after a brief hiatus at the beginning of the Great Depression. For the French anthropologist Saskia Cousin (2008), these two decades are a pivotal period for international tourism. At this time, tourism was seen as a political and financial issue, this until the end of the 1960s. In the 1970s, economic and cultural values collided. However, she does not dwell on the beginnings of this phase 1920s–1960s.

The French archives show that governments were very active in the tourism sector, particularly in its international dimension. For example, the Diplomatic Archives centre in La Courneuve has a special file on tourism during the inter-war period. It is also the case at the departmental archive centres, which keep bundles (in series M or T) where the word "tourism" appears in the inventories, generally to bring together documents from the 1930s (in connection with the law on paid holidays of June 1936). Although these files are not very thick, they are evidence of the State's growing awareness of the importance of tourism. Historians have long neglected tourism, as they were more focused on the private sector. Until the end of the nineteenth century, this activity was mainly driven by private interests (the Consiglio d'Ornato of the County of Nice between 1832 and 1860 being an exception in the world). In this chapter, we will look at how tourism took on new dimensions during the inter-war period, with public and diplomatic powers investing in it. We will see that France played an important—though not unique—role in this respect, while at the same time having to contend with the difficult balancing act between its ambitions and the reality on the ground.

Before 1919: The First Attempts to Take International Tourism into Account

International tourism was favoured over domestic tourism in the early twentieth century by governments because it generated foreign currency. France looked to its neighbours for inspiration to capture them. In 1910, it imitated the principle of the *Kuretax*, which the Prussian state had been applying since at least 1893 (Montaner 1956), under the name of "cure-taxe". Based on the Austrian model, the same year it founded a National Tourist Office (ONT; Larique 2007). The Office's budget was very modest. It was funded by the Touring-Club de France, an additional tax on tourist tax and a government subsidy (Monferrand and Berthonnet 2012). Its remit was to centralize all matters relating to tourism; liaise with associations; manage tourist transport, travel and accommodation operations; and, from the end of the 1910s, organize advertising abroad for classified resorts (classification introduced by the law of 24 September 1919).

Since 1910, the State has also levied a tourist tax on every foreign vehicle crossing the border (Clinquart 2000). The border was no longer considered a barrier, but rather a point of entry. Passing through customs became the first stage in a tourist's journey, and it was important to put them in the right frame of mind. To avoid upsetting travellers (and giving a bad image of France), the Directorate General of Customs tried to ensure that checks on travellers were not vexatious. However, the strictness of the regulations it intended to apply, as well as the sometimes brutal behaviour of its agents, were incompatible with this objective. The press often reported rough encounters between travellers and customs officers on duty at stations and roadside offices. This is why, to reduce clashes, the Directorate General attached great importance to inform the public by publishing posters in several languages which had to be put up "in a conspicuous and well-lit place" so that travellers could find out about their obligations in good time. Reissued several times, these notices were for a long time the only means of communicating with the public that Customs used (Clinquart 2000).

But just as the flow of international tourists was increasing, the First World War suddenly interrupted this dynamic. While domestic tourism slowly picked up again from the 1915 summer season (Evanno and Vincent 2019), international flows were now interrupted or severely restricted. Paradoxically, the First World War was an opportunity for tourism professionals to think about how to better adapt to international tourists. Some hotels took advantage of the presence of those on leave from the other side of the world to better understand their expectations (United States, Canada…). Yet, the primary focus of hotel owners was to attract a new clientele once the conflict ended. In the 15 March 1918 edition of the newspaper *Ouest-Éclair*, Octave-Louis Aubert, one of the main promoters of tourism in Brittany, advocated "opening our hotels in the most attractive [and] most restful resorts to American leave-holders" so that they could "take advantage of their leave to visit France". A few lines further on, he said: "the soldiers who will be returning in their thousands with their families, will not fail to make the most of their trip to the Eastern Front [of France] by coming to recharge their batteries in a region that they will have found welcoming".

This certainty was shared by both professionals in the field and the French government. The latter was convinced, perhaps as early as 1914, that international tourism would bring in valuable foreign currency when the war ended and tourism flows resumed (Vincent and Evanno 2022). During the war, France financed propaganda missions abroad, led for example by Pierre Chabert in North America (Della-Vedova 2019: 251–261) and by Ludovic Gaurier (1919: 4) in South America. One of the stated aims was to continue promoting tourism outside France to encourage "the peaceful invasion of tourists from all over the world". Ludovic Gaurier summed up his government's ambition perfectly when he revealed that "the longer these travelers stay and travel around our country, the more they will leave behind the gold that the necessities of war have forced us to spend at home." For the moment, there has been no historical study of the effects of these reports. Only Gilles Della-Vedova notes that some of Pierre Chabert's proposals were included in the reorganization of the ONT. The other proposals seem to have remained unimplemented.

Promoting Tourism Abroad

At the end of the war, while the tourist market began to mature, France was also benefiting from providential memorial tourism. All that remained was to attract these international tourists. To encourage this recovery, the first French tourist office was set up in London in 1920 and the Banque de France introduced the traveller's cheque. France's efforts to revive international tourism soon bore fruit, so much so that the practice experienced significant growth, in line with predictions made by professionals and the government during the conflict. As an indication, up to 300,000 Americans (for the year 1929) came to France every year during the 1920s. Admittedly, this figure did not reach the initial targets (i.e. millions of visitors), but the positivc balance on the "Travel" line of the balance of payments exceeded 450 million dollars, i.e. double that of "Transport" or "Capital Income" (Ginier 1969).

Therefore, the French authorities were convinced to pursue their policy in favour of international tourism by allocating funds to promote it abroad. It was time to move on from a form of tourism based on picking and choosing, where visitors come naturally—although efforts had been made since the nineteenth century—to a genuine tourist culture. At the time, France was pursuing a strategy that could be found elsewhere in Europe (for example, for Greece, see Dritsas 2014; see also Vincent and Evanno 2022): it had to make people want to come and visit France. This promotion of tourism required the production of what was then known as "tourism propaganda". This consisted of brochures, promotional films, tourist maps and posters aimed at potential source countries. Unfortunately, sending promotional material across borders was often a lengthy process, even requiring the payment of customs duties. To get around these difficulties, governments tended to open local agencies. In France, the Commissariat Général au Tourisme set up committees of correspondents to develop national advertising. The ambition was even to set up one in the USSR, but the conditions for leaving Soviet territory were difficult for Russians: only 865 passports were issued for France in 1935 (Clinquart 2000). The return on investment did not justify France devoting a budget to it. On the contrary, it was necessary to conduct a targeted policy aimed at countries likely to attract tourists. This policy had to be effective, at the risk of being aggressive in an already highly competitive environment. French spa towns had to be more attractive than their German or Czechoslovak counterparts.

Given that cinema, radio and television were in their infancy, potential travellers had little opportunity to imagine what a destination might look like. In the mid-1920s, Europe was experiencing its first economic recession since the end of the war (excluding the inflationary situation in Germany). In times of crisis, the governments of countries that gave in to the temptation of protectionism were inclined to limit their citizens' travel abroad. France, a major beneficiary of international tourism, had a lot to lose. To overcome this reluctance, in 1924 it invited governments and international tourism NGOs to form the Central Tourist Council. It aimed to coordinate tourism collaboration between governments and NGOs. However, the Council did not invite national tourist organizations (NTOs) and its refusal to admit Germans upset many participants (Bechmann Pedersen 2020). The result was virtually zero. Faced with this initial failure and given the importance of trade for the Netherlands too, Dutch National Tourism Director Willem Treub felt that efforts should be made to stimulate tourist travel as an invisible export, by inviting as many organizations as possible the following year. This time, the meeting was based on national tourist offices. It brought together fourteen countries. An International Union of Official Tourist Propaganda Organizations (IUOTPO) was then created in 1925, with annual congresses starting in 1930. This was an international non-governmental body governed by legislation drawn up in the host country (the Netherlands) and using French for its exchanges. Similar hopes accompanied the birth of the British Holiday Association. At its first meeting in 1929, it named the promotion of international cooperation as one of its aims (Bechmann Pedersen 2020).

Finally, in 1934, the IUOTPO took on a new stature by becoming the International Union of Official Propaganda Bodies, which dealt with statistics, promotion, border formalities, etc., while working in collaboration with the League of Nations. In 1935, its chairman took part in the work of the League's Economic Committee, proof that tourism had once again been identified as a service industry that could help countries to emerge from the recession caused by the 1929 crisis (Shackleford 2020). At the same time, this Economic Commission was advocating the liberalization of trade and the free movement of people within the international arena (Lanfant 2004). The Union embodied the internationalist spirit more than any other intergovernmental forum or NGO at the time. It embraced the Wilsonian principle of national self-determination, but this also made the issue of culture and cultural borders particularly thorny (Manela 2007).

Making It Easier to Cross the Border

The case of potential Russian tourists unable to leave the Soviet Union illustrated another problem of international tourism: the movement of people meant that passports and visas had to be issued and used, whereas before the 1914–1918 war, travel documents were hardly necessary and customs formalities were relatively light. In the aftermath of a war that had pitted European countries against each other head-on, it was the crossing of borders that needed to be made easier. Despite their rivalries, all the European states were pursuing the same goal: to facilitate border crossings, a *sine qua non* for the existence of international tourism. Indeed, as the Economic Committee of the League of Nations confirmed in 1935, tourism had become a major factor in the international economy. Therefore, they had to find "the means of adapting customs regulations to the needs created by the incessant development of automobile locomotion and of unifying the provisions governing the subject in each country".

As a major recipient of foreign currency from international tourism, it was not surprising to see France once again working to improve border crossings. On the initiative of the tourist associations with which French customs had developed a collaboration (from which both parties benefited), an unofficial congress brought together customs experts from 22 countries in Paris in February 1932 (Clinquart 2000). Two years later, in 1934, it was again France that worked to establish an international convention to facilitate border crossings. The convention was to be like the one on postal regulations and the one on the international movement of automobiles. At its general meeting in May, the Central Council for International Tourism adopted a resolution to this effect. Finally, in January 1937, it was once again on the initiative of the French government that a new meeting of Belgian, Dutch, German, Swiss, Italian and French experts representing customs and tourist companies examined a preliminary draft of an international convention on tourism, which was then to be presented to the various governments, but the draft was not completed before the outbreak of war. In the meantime, bilateral conventions resolved the most urgent problems.

At a national level, France also worked to make it easier to cross its border by abolishing the tourist tax on vehicles with the law of 25 June 1920. To make it easier financially, it replaced it with a road tax, the amount of which varied according to the power of the vehicles and the length of stay. When crossing the border for the first time, foreigners had to obtain a *laissez- passer* and pay a fee based on the length of their stay. This could be for a minimum of 48 hours and a maximum of two months. After two months, the tax was payable at the full rate, and users had to contact the indirect taxation authorities. It was not until 1934 that the right of circulation was abolished (Clinquart 2000). In 1935, the government opted for a tax exemption for foreign tourists who claimed the benefit of it because, according to the decree that renewed this system, "it has not escaped the legislator that France does not currently receive the number of visitors to which the natural beauty of its sites and the high level of its culture could legitimately lead it to claim" (decree of 23 February 1936; thanks to Benoît Haberbush for this information).

For the Universal Exhibition in Paris (1937), the government went even further. It tried an experiment to reduce the cost of travel to France for foreign tourists. It was decided to have Customs issue vouchers giving them a discount on the price of petrol. Initially limited to the duration of the Exhibition, the system convinced the authorities, who decided to repeat the experiment in 1938 and 1939 (Clinquart 2000). From 1938 onwards, however, the benefit was limited to foreign motorists who held "tourist travel cards" costing 30 francs, which they obtained from customs offices and which were sold by customs officers on behalf of the Société Nationale des Chemins de Fer (decree of 2 May 1938).

Enhance Reputation and Meet International Customer Requirements

Despite the efforts made by the French authorities, the investments made by the players on the ground were not up to what the French Minister in Canada (i.e. the Minister Plenipotentiary in Canada) thought they should be. In 1936, he told the Ministry of Foreign Affairs that the French were relying too much on their good reputation and the affection they enjoyed. This was not a new criticism, as it had already been voiced in the 1920s. In this sense, the recommendation made by the journalist André de Fouquières was symptomatic. He felt that Dinard (Brittany), which he knew well from 25 years of holidaying there, was not yet at its peak. He encouraged the railway companies and newspapers to advertise the resort nationally rather than abroad, believing that its international reputation had already been achieved ("L'enquête de l'*Ouest-Éclair* sur le tourisme dans la région", *Ouest-Éclair*, 12 August 1924; Vincent 2016).

In fact, France's reputation was not enough to attract foreign tourists. On the contrary, it sometimes discouraged them... In the early 1930s, for example, France was the victim of a differentiated application of the export of capital (e.g. by the Czechoslovakians): States could limit the maximum amount of cash that tourists could take with them, and reciprocity of equivalence was not automatic. Despite the existence of traveller's cheques or similar products (hotel and restaurant vouchers issued by the Thomas Cook agency in 1868 (L'Aulnoit and Alexandre 2018: 169), the American Express traveller's cheque from 1891, traveller's cheques issued by the Banque de France from 1920), tourists sometimes had to take with them all the money they needed to pay their expenses (accommodation, food, transport, extras, etc.).

What's more, France had a bad reputation for being fussy at the border. In the late 1920s, Dutch tourists complained about the indiscreet and brutal searches carried out by French (and apparently Italian) customs officers—unlike in Germany, Belgium and Switzerland. Although multilingual "good behaviour" posters were constantly reissued until the early 1930s, this was not always enough to reassure travellers.

Finally, the reputation of the infrastructure was also tarnished by its lack of comfort, which was similarly singled out by French customers. The massification of tourism throughout the twentieth century had not led to the disappearance of several problems denounced by "small pockets", a denunciation that was the source of other more global issues. According to contemporaries, a "new" consumer was emerging, relatively gregarious and particularly informed about economic aspects rather than cultural ones. José Ortega y Gasset echoed this in his book *La rebelión de las masas*, published in 1930. As early as 1924, the newspaper *Ouest-Éclair* had already identified this expectation after inviting its readers to express their views on aspects of the tourist's daily life, subjects previously considered "vulgar" (in the sense of ordinary, prosaic, lowly, common). Of the 278 arguments developed during the 1924 survey, 209 concerned practical aspects (mainly relating to the road, hygiene and comfort), 48 economic aspects (in particular the high cost of living) and 21 cultural aspects, in the broadest sense (Vincent 2016).

The French government was undoubtedly aware of the situation. At the end of the war, in 1919, it was already regretting that "France [was] losing a wealthy tourist clientele to foreign spa towns because the infrastructure of French resorts is not up to scratch" (law of 24 September 1919, *Journal Officiel* of 26 September 1919 quoted by Jégouzo 2019). It wasn't just the spa towns that were affected. On the coast, resorts had been suffering from the same problems, at least since the beginning of the century, which necessitated the passing of the Cornudet law in 1919 (supplemented in 1924), to require tourist towns to improve their health (Evanno and Vincent 2021). But this was not enough. From then on, France focused its efforts on two sectors in the 1930s: hotels and safety. From this point of view, the Paris Universal Exhibition (1937) had a considerable influence. Firstly, it enabled France to introduce legislation to force hoteliers to comply with international standards (Manfredini 2013: 223–232). The law of 7 June 1937 granted approval from the Haut-Commissariat au tourisme to ensure that the hotel in which the guest was to stay complied with certain rules: displaying prices accurately and, not self-evidently, respecting them. In addition, certification imposed strict standards that would evolve over the years. The government could gradually raise the tolerance thresholds for comfort and hygiene. Thus, according to the criteria defined in 1939, the establishment had to be equipped with at least one shared bathroom (or a shower "*à la rigueur*") and hot and cold running water in most rooms. Although France was keen to modernize its hotel stock, only a small minority of owners complied when the Second World War broke out (Evanno 2016).

Finally, to attract foreign tourists, France had to reassure them about the safety of the country, as they feared being attacked by brigands before arriving, or being the "victim" of a strike in a country where social unrest was rife (several events left their mark: the riots of February 1934, the Font Populaire strikes in 1936...). Today, travel advice mentions this all over the world, and it was already the case in Europe in the 1930s. There is no doubt that we need to work hard on these recommendations, which are always highly political. In July 1936, the newspaper *Cyrano* made much of the turbulent and difficult situation in Europe, as well as "upheavals of all kinds affecting the social order". It praised Monte-Carlo: because of its natural location, Monte-Carlo had never suffered and "will never suffer from external events", "in the greatest calm and perfect tranquility", where tourists benefited from special prices during the summer (edition of 17 July 1936: 18). The French consul in Monaco informed the Minister of Foreign Affairs, deeming it a direct attack on the French resorts on the Côte d'Azur. In June 1936, there had been several incidents involving tourists. Trips were disrupted by strikes, as in the case of 200 Dutch people who arrived in Villefranche by boat but, with no coach available on land, ended up staying in Monte Carlo. There were many similar stories: tourists were held to ransom by strikers, such as the two American travellers who, not speaking the local language, did not understand what was happening to them; motorists from Geneva were forced to pay to use French roads... The following year, in 1937, shortly before the start of the Universal Exhibition, these rumours of motorists being held to ransom resurfaced (sometimes due to a misunderstanding of the petrol vouchers introduced by the government). These rumours were so persistent that they forced the French diplomatic services to intervene with foreign institutions to reassure them. The latter studied the situation before reassuring their citizens, as in the case of the Netherlands, which did not advise against visiting France after enquiries with the Royal Netherlands Tourism Board (ANWB).

Conclusion

The outbreak of the Second World War shattered internationalist hopes for a lasting peace, but the travel industry continued to be seen as having an important role to play. Sune Bechmann Pedersen (2020) has recorded several accounts of this during the war years. In July 1941, for example, The *Times* stated that "when peace comes, [Thomas Cook] will have a great work to do for civilization by helping to reopen the channels of communication between nations" (Brendon 1991: 279). Similarly, the Nazi occupation of Denmark did not prevent the labour movement's travel agency, Dansk Folkeferie, from learning to want to get to know each other better, so that "our children and grandchildren do not [experience] the same Ragnarök [prophetic end of the world in the Nordic world] that our generation had to endure" (Warschawsky 2008: 5).

Such confidence ultimately reflected the fact that the desire to travel abroad had not completely died out with the outbreak of war. In October 1939, the French legate in The Hague told the Minister for Foreign Affairs that he had been very surprised to receive, since the end of the summer, requests from Dutch tourists wishing to visit France during the winter of 1939–1940 rather than Switzerland or Italy. However, these requests came up against drastic restrictions on access to border regions. While domestic tourism continued to be practised, the international dimension (except for members of the armed forces and logisticians) was rather marginal from 1940 until 1944, with the notable exception of excursions organized by German soldiers in France (Evanno and Vincent 2024). Further historical research is still needed to gain a better understanding of this period.

From the start of 1945, even before the end of the fighting in France (German capitulation on 8 May), the hotel industry was a priority for the Provisional Government of the French Republic. A rapid resumption of activity was essential to attract tourists and, above all, "foreign currency". For this reason, few sanctions were taken against hoteliers whose establishments had been requisitioned during the war (Evanno 2016). Although their responsibility was difficult to establish, the authorities wanted them to be able to restart their business immediately. In the winter of 1944–1945, the government asked coastal municipalities to set aside a budget for tourist activities. The American authorities agreed (Endy 2005). On 11 March 1948, in the bilateral Franco-American agreement under which France signed up to the Marshall Plan, tourism was included as an important part of American aid. Introduced by Ralph Owen Brewster of the State of Maine, the plan enabled France to obtain precious dollars to bring its infrastructure into line with the demands of foreign travellers (Evanno and Vincent 2021). As for the European NTOs, in 1947 they re-launched a collaboration like that of the IUOTPO at a congress in The Hague to continue their reflections on facilitating international tourism.

Acknowledgements Special thanks to Emma Le Floch for her help.

References

Bechmann Pedersen S (2020) A passport to peace? Modern tourism and internationalist idealism. Eur Rev 28(3):389–402

Boyer M (2000) Histoire de l'invention du tourisme XVIe–XIXe siècles: origine et développement du tourisme dans le Sud-Est de la France. La Tour-d'Aigues, Edition de l'Aube

Brendon P (1991) Thomas Cook. 150 years of popular tourism. Secker & Warburg, London

Clinquart J (2000) L'administration des douanes française de 1914 à 1940. Institut de la gestion publique et du développement économique, Paris, online https://doi.org/10.4000/books.igpde.4467. Accessed 4 Nov 2023

Cousin S (2008) L'Unesco et la doctrine du tourisme culturel. Civilisations 57. https://doi.org/10.4000/civilisations.1541. Accessed 4 Nov 2023

de L'Aulnoit B, Alexandre P (2018) Thomas Cook, 1808–1892. L'inventeur des voyages. Robert Laffont, Paris

Della-Vedova G (2019) « Du nouveau à l'ouest » Exportation et acclimatation du système touristique nord-américain en France au lendemain de la Première Guerre mondiale. In: Evanno

Y-M, Vincent J (eds.) (2019) Tourisme et Grande Guerre. Voyage(s) sur un front historique méconnu. Ploemeur, Editions Codex, pp 251–261
Dritsas M (ed) (2014) Tourism and crisis in Europe, XIX–XXI centuries. Eco Nomia Publishing, Athens
Endy C (2005) The cold war holidays. American tourism in France. University of North Carolina Press, Chapel Hill
Evanno Y-M (2016) La guerre, aubaine pour le développement hôtelier dans le Morbihan (1940-1945)? In: Andrieux J-Y, Harismendy P (eds) Pension complète. Tourisme et hôtellerie (XVIII -XXee siècle), Rennes, PUR, pp 155–167
Evanno Y-M, Vincent J (eds.) (2019) Tourisme et Grande Guerre. Voyage(s) sur un front historique méconnu. Ploemeur, Éditions Codex
Evanno Y-M, Vincent J (2021) Tourisme et crises sanitaires mondiales dans l'Histoire: véritablement un impensé? Mondes du Tourisme. 20. https://doi.org/10.4000/tourisme.3795. Accessed 4 Nov 2023
Evanno Y-M, Vincent J (2023) Brittany hotel industry and second word war: total crisis, global opportunism (1940–1952). In: Larrinaga C, Strangio D (eds) The development of the hotel and tourism industry in the twentieth century. Comparative perspectives from Western Europe, 1900–1970. Palgrave Macmillan, London, pp 101–117
Evanno Y-M, Vincent J (2024) L'Occupant comme touriste. Représentation des soldats allemands et leurs pratiques dans les images des guides touristiques en France: le cas du guide *Die Vendée* (1940). In: Acola D, Bernard N (eds) Illustrer les guides touristiques imprimés (du 19e siècle à nos jours), Rennes, PUR
Gay J-C Decroly J-M (2018) Les logiques de la diffusion du tourisme dans le monde: une approche géohistorique. L'Espace géographique. 47(2), pp 102–120. https://doi.org/10.3917/eg.472.0102. Accessed 4 Nov 20237
Gaurier L (1919) La Propagande touristique à l'étranger. Bordeaux, impr. de J. Bière
Ginier J (1969) Les touristes étrangers en France pendant l'été. Paris, Éditions Génin
Jeck M (2008) The beginnings of tourism in the Grand Duchy of Luxembourg. Au temps où le Luxembourg était à 6 heures 30 de Paris. Articulo, J Urban Res. https://doi.org/10.4000/articulo.815. Accessed 4 Nov 2023
Jégouzo L (2019) L'évolution de la politique publique du tourisme en France. Mondes du tourisme 15. https://doi.org/10.4000/tourisme.2193. Accessed 4 Nov 2023
Lanfant M-F (2004) L'appel à l'éthique et la référence universaliste dans la doctrine officielle du tourisme international. Revue Tiers Monde 178:364–386
Larique B (2007) Les débuts et déboires de l'organisation officielle du tourisme en France: l'expérience malheureuse de l'Office National du Tourisme (1910–1935). Entreprises et histoire. 47(2), pp 73–92. https://doi.org/10.3917/eh.047.0073. Accessed 4 Nov 2023
Manfredini J (2013) La nation française mise en scène. Les terroirs gastronomiques à l'Exposition internationale de Paris en 1937. In: Andrieux J-Y, Harismendy P (eds) L'assiette du touriste. Une quête de l'authentique. Rennes, PUR, pp 223–232
Manela E (2007) The Wilsonian moment: self-determination and the international origins of anticolonial nationalism. Oxford University Press
Monferrand A, Berthonnet A (2012) Cent ans d'organisation administrative du tourisme (1910 à nos jours). Pour mémoire, special issue, July 2012, 17–27
Montaner A (1956) Zur finanzwissenschaftlichen Problematik der Kurtaxe. Zeitschrift für Nationalökonomie/J Econ 16(1–2):212–224
Shackleford P (2020) A history of the world tourism organization. Emerald Publishing Limited, Bingley
Vincent J (2016) À la recherche de la satisfaction touristique en Bretagne: analyse à partir des enquêtes de presse de 1924 et 1977. En Envor, revue d'histoire contemporaine en Bretagne. https://hal.science/hal-02423928/document. Accessed 4 Nov 2023
Vincent J, Evanno Y-M (2022) Domestic and international tourism, an impossible opposition. Téoros. http://journals.openedition.org/teoros/11123. Accessed 4 Nov 2023

Vincent J, Evanno Y-M (2021) Tourisme et crises sanitaires mondiales dans l'Histoire: véritablement un impensé?, Mondes du tourisme. http://journals.openedition.org/tourisme/37953#citedby. Accessed 12 Nov 2023

Warschawsky A (2008) Folkeferie - ferieformer, ferieindhold og dannelsesidealer 1938–1988. Arbejderhistorie 2:1–16. https://sfah.dk/assets/uploads/tidsskrift/Aargang-2008/nr2/ah08-2-A_Warscharwsky.pdf. Accessed 4 Nov 2023

Johan Vincent is Associate Professor in History at ESTHUA, Institut national de Tourisme of the University of Angers (France), member of the TEMOS laboratory (UMR 9016 CNRS), and associate researcher at the ESO laboratory (UMR 6590 CNRS). He is working on the history of tourism, heritage, risks, and lands issues. With Yves-Marie Evanno, he coordinated notably *Tourisme and Grande Guerre. Voyage(s) sur un front historique méconnu (1914–2019).*

Yves-Marie Evanno is a historian who teaches at the Université catholique de l'Ouest Bretagne Sud, France. His research focuses on the lives of French civilians during the World Wars. For several years, he has collaborated with Johan Vincent on the theme of tourism in times of crisis, co-editing *Tourisme et Grande Guerre: Voyage(s) sur un front historique méconnu, 1914-2019* (Codex Editions, 2019).

Chapter 8
Costa del Sol. Tourism and Business in the Configuration of a Touristic Area in Spain

Marta Luque-Aranda and Víctor M. Heredia-Flores

Abstract During the first third of the twentieth century, before the Spanish Civil War, the Mediterranean coast of Andalusia specialized in tourism. The area around the city of Malaga, known as Costa del Sol, in Spain, evolved from an initial vocation of receiving minority tourism of Anglo-Saxon origin, which sought warm weather, to a clear specialization in mass tourism from Europe and based on the sun and beach segment, which occupied a large part of the active population. This chapter analyzes the stages of this process and the creation of specific infrastructures such as hotels, golf courses, airport and other services.

Introduction

The take-off of tourist activities as one of the bases of Spanish economic prosperity occurred after 1950. However, it is necessary to remember that the origin of this prosperity, fostered by the income generated by the massive arrival of tourists, has its roots at the end of the nineteenth century. It was then that an internal and external demand began to appear that led to the development of a whole network of services allocated to facilitate travel, accommodation, and leisure in the receiving areas. And although tourism activity as a source of foreign currency did not begin to be seriously recognized by governments until after the First World War (Vallejo-Pousada et al. 2016), the private initiative detects the potential of this sector to promote the

PID2021-122476NB-I00 research project, financed by MCIN/AEI /10.13039/501100011033/ and the FEDER/ERDF Una manera de hacer Europa / A way of making Europe.

M. Luque-Aranda · V. M. Heredia-Flores (✉)
Department of Economic Theory and Economic History, University of Malaga, Málaga, Spain
e-mail: martaluque@uma.es; vmheredia@uma.es

C. Larrinaga, D. Strangio (eds.), *Tourism Destinations and Policies in Europe During the 20th Century*, Contributions to Economics,
https://doi.org/10.1007/978-3-031-88447-4_8

economic development of certain areas of Spain since the end of the nineteenth century.

Among the pioneering geographical areas in terms of receiving tourists, is the city of Malaga and its western coast, which will be called Costa del Sol, and which with the passage of time will become almost completely economically dependent on the tourism sector. This geographical area specialized during the first half of the twentieth century in tourist activity, creating a varied offer of accommodation services, transportation and leisure activities.

Initially, the area around the city of Malaga received foreign tourism, mainly of Anglo-Saxon origin, closely linked to the British colony established in the city and on its western coast, and to a lesser extent it received tourists from the interior of Andalusia. Both visitor profiles sought warm weather in winter, either for health reasons, or simply as an ideal complement to rest (Burgos-Madroñero 1974). However, this type of demand ended up evolving toward mass tourism from Europe and based on the sun and beach segment. We can place the turning point during the Spanish Civil War, when tourist activity slowed down, although without disappearing. In the case of the province of Malaga, this gap also meant a change in the tourist epicenter, which will move from the capital to the western coast. Coast that throughout the first half of the twentieth century will be transformed, and now under the internationally known brand Costa del Sol, it will become one of the main tourist destinations worldwide.

In order to achieve a complete vision of the tourism phenomenon, it is necessary to study its origin: the slow but continuous emergence of internal and external demand and the parallel definition of a tourist offer focused on certain points. This, along with some of the business initiatives that made the construction of the Costa del Sol destination possible, will be analyzed in this chapter. Pioneering businessmen who envisioned the possibility of tourist development in Malaga and its western coast and initiatives that led to the outsourcing of the Costa del Sol: improvements in transport infrastructure, which include roads, railways and airport; accommodations; urbanization projects and spa facilities; and sports leisure, such as the construction of the first grass golf course in southern Spain.

Malaga and Tourism as a Way Out at the End of the Century Crisis[1]

At the end of the nineteenth century, the city of Malaga was going through an agrarian and industrial crisis. This motivated the search for alternative sources of income, and it was when it was decided to opt for tourism as a solid alternative for the recovery of the local economy. The city's mild climate, which made it possible to turn it

[1]On the origins of tourism in Malaga, Arcas and García (1980), Pellejero-Martínez (2005) and (Pellejero-Martínez 2016), and Palou and Pellejero (2020).

into a winter season, became its main attraction. But to carry out this project, the city needed to undertake a series of urban reforms that would improve its appearance and its hygienic-sanitary conditions. As well as creating a tourist offer that would provide it with an adequate network of transport, accommodation and leisure activities (Pellejero-Martínez 2005).

In this context, the Propaganda Society for the Climate and Beautification of Malaga was born in 1897. Imitating the initiative unions that already existed in other places, their purpose was to promote urban improvements that would increase the attractions of the city and advertise the goodness of its climate. They were also dedicated to organizing celebrations and cultural activities that served to attract the attention of the elitist tourist trends of the time (Pellejero-Martínez 2016).

It will be in the first decades of the twentieth century when the tourism model experiences its first change. Tourists are beginning to look for places where they can enjoy sunbathing and warm waters, so they will go mainly in spring and summer. An offer of sea bathing facilities then emerged: the La Estrella and Apolo spas, which offered complementary catering services, concerts, dances, or even cinema, and the spa of Baños del Carmen, of singular importance. It was inaugurated in 1918 and promoted a new way of enjoying sea bathing at the same time that it became an authentic recreational park, with sports facilities, dance floors, attractions, and a restaurant (Lara-García 1997).

Starting in the 1920s, the tourism phenomenon in Spain experienced a boom, in which the increase in private investment and greater intervention by public powers were decisive. More specifically, in Malaga there was a renewal and expansion of the hotel and leisure offer, promoting the celebration of the city's most important festivals: Holy Week in spring and the fair in summer. Accessibility by road was also significantly improved and access by air was even inaugurated. According to data from the state body in charge of the sector, the National Tourist Board, in 1929 the city received 12,313 visitors, placing it in fifth place among Spanish tourist destinations. However, despite the increase in demand for summer tourism, the aforementioned organization continued to maintain the advertising of Malaga as an "incomparable winter resort" (Pellejero-Martínez 2016).

During this period the accommodation offer had two important milestones: in 1920 the renovation and expansion of the Hernán Cortés Hotel, which changed its name to Caleta Palace. A building designed expressly for hotel use on the beachfront in the residential area of El Limonar; and in 1926 the inauguration of the luxurious Hotel Príncipe de Asturias, in the residential neighborhood of La Caleta, a grandiose establishment equipped with all kinds of amenities and which had an exclusive pavilion for the Spanish royal family (Heredia-Flores 2000). Along with these two large hotels located on the beach, the hotel offering in Malaga was completed with others located in the most central streets of the city, highlighting among them the Simón and the Niza, on Larios Street, and the luxurious Regina on Puerta del Mar, run by the Swiss Cristian Heierle. At the end of the 1920s, there were 20 hotels in the city with a total capacity of 1505 beds, as well as a series of small hostels run mostly by foreigners, such as the Hacienda Giró by C.H. Faber or the Cooper Pension (Luque-Aranda and Heredia-Flores 2022).

The Movement Toward the Western Coast: The Seed of the Costa del Sol

Since the mid-nineteenth century, many of the wealthy families of the capital of Malaga chose the nearby villages of Torremolinos and Churriana as places of rest to spend time, preferably in summer. Specifically, in the surroundings of the latter, recreational farms linked to agricultural exploitations were built. The case of Torremolinos was similar, although in this village the mere condition of a resting place had more weight. At the end of that century, the journalist Augusto Jerez Perchet wrote that Torremolinos fulfilled its role of welcoming many families from Malaga with hospitality during the summer, despite there being no railway to facilitate communication between both towns, something that he clearly saw necessary (Jerez-Perchet 1884). The construction of summer houses in Torremolinos continued and intensified in the twentieth century, many of them being used for seasonal rental, mainly to families from the cities of Malaga, Cordoba, Antequera, and Granada (Luque-Aranda and Heredia-Flores 2022). Thus, as stated in a guide from the late 1930s, in those years Torremolinos had a multitude of splendid chalets in which families from Malaga and other inland cities spent the summer season enjoying its beach and the goodness of its climate (Enfedaque-Blasco 1940). One of these houses, which today is owned by the City Council and has become a tourist attraction, is "Villa Pepita," known as the house of the Navajas. Neo-Arab style, it stands on a slope in the Bajondillo area. Its construction began in 1925 and was completed four years later.

It was during the first decades of the twentieth century when the west coast of Malaga became the fundamental pillar of the future tourism development of the province. From Torremolinos, a town that was annexed to the municipality of Málaga in 1924, to the border with the province of Cádiz, very close to the Strait and the British colony of Gibraltar, initiatives aimed at attracting international tourists began to take shape. Thus, little by little foreigners were acquiring properties in the area, either to convert them into residences where they could spend time or even to settle permanently, or to dedicate them to hotel operations. We can mention, among others, George Langworthy in Torremolinos, George William Grice-Hutchinson in San Julián, Gerald Brenan, and Gamel Woolsey in Churriana, Reinhold Tschuschke, the Owens, and the Lagunos in Marbella (Luque-Aranda and Heredia-Flores 2022).

The potential of this coastal strip was predicted by the engineer Ramiro Campos Turmo in the 1920s. In several publications he defended the exceptional nature of its climate, the attractiveness of its landscapes and its wide possibilities to become an international tourist center, and even proposed a name for the area: Costabella (Campos-Turmo 1928). Another name that deserves to be taken into account for the work of promoting this coastal area is that of José Zuzuarregui, lawyer and town councillor of Marbella who in 1932 published an article in the Malaga newspaper El Cronista, in which, in addition to praising the benefits of his town, pointed out that it was destined to be one of the first centers of world tourism, but therefore it was necessary to develop a hotel industry (Luque-Aranda and Heredia-Flores 2021).

All of this contributed to the proliferation of different tourist initiatives during the 1920s and 1930s: hotel accommodation, a varied leisure offer, the implementation of more effective advertising and improved means of transportation. An increase in tourism supply that was accompanied by increasing tourism demand.

The First Accommodations for Tourists and the Business People who Started Them

When the twentieth century began, the western coast of Malaga, currently a world tourist destination, did not have a hotel offer capable of accommodating tourists (Luque-Aranda and Heredia-Flores 2021). Although there is evidence of the first hotel establishment that accommodated foreigners in Torremolinos, the inn of Nicolas Parodi, at least ten years before Richard Ford included it in his book of travels through Spain in the mid-nineteenth century, it will be necessary to wait for the twentieth century so that along the coast other establishments will appear able to meet the needs of new tourists and clients with high purchasing power (Luque-Aranda and Heredia-Flores 2022). They will be accommodations scattered along the coast, mostly very modest, small size that will serve a still minority tourism with high purchasing power.

Although the aggregate offer was still very small, starting in the 1920s, two models of hotel establishments were identified on the western coast: the first one, the traditional inns and small urban hotels aimed at business travelers or occasional travelers; and the second one more aimed at the growing clientele of foreign origin, mostly British, and with high purchasing power. Both models were small, family-friendly establishments, but the second type offered some extra amenities. Among the hotel establishments that adapted to the second model we can point out the Fonda de la Cala de Mijas, located on the beach and run by the German Reinhold Tschuschke, or the Orilla del Mar hotel, in Calahonda, which offered minigolf in its own facilities. The British couple Owen, owner of this accommodation, advertised it as an oasis of peace between the pine forests and the sea, next to the road to Gibraltar. These two establishments, located east of Marbella, opened their doors in the early years of the 1930s (Luque-Aranda and Heredia-Flores 2022).

Next to the town center of Marbella, the Hotel Miramar opened its doors in October 1933. In this case it was a Spanish couple formed by José de Lagunano and Agustina Zuzuarregui who started it. The Laguna Zuzuarregui family, who had arrived in Marbella in 1930, acquired the Huerta de San Ramón, a property located between the road and the beach, where they built a large house. The couple's initial idea was to exploit it as an agricultural property, but poor economic results made them look for new uses. Probably influenced by José Zuzuarregui, Agustina's brother, who worked as a promoter of the Marbella coast, they began a new business adventure: the opening of a hotel. After the necessary renovations, the house they had built was transformed into a 12-room accommodation. The press highlighted the ideal location of the accommodation, next to a beach perfect for swimming, and the equipment: a leafy park, a tennis court and parking for clients. In that announcement, the journalist stated that Marbella was still an unknown pearl, but that the opening of this hotel had been a success, since it opened channels for the tourist future of the town. The hotel was registered in the luxury category and its owners carried out an important advertising campaign in Anglo-Saxon media and in Morocco, in which they used the concept of sunny coast, a clear precedent of the name Costa del Sol. Their clients arrived mainly from Gibraltar and of the great hotels in Malaga. One of its main attractions was the restaurant, where an international menu was offered. However, the hopeful future that was presented to Miramar was cut short with the Civil War. During the conflict, mattresses and bedding were requisitioned for a field hospital, and when the hotel reopened at the end of the war, customers were already very scarce. This forced the Lagunos to sell the hotel, thus putting an end to this business adventure (Luque-Aranda and Heredia-Flores 2021).

A few years before the opening of these hotels in Marbella, Torremolinos already had an establishment that fit the model of the previous ones. The Castillo de Santa Clara is considered the first hotel on the Costa del Sol (Valle de Juan and Sánchez-Dehesa 2015; Valle de Juan and Beautell-González 2015). Located in a privileged location known as Punta de Torremolinos, the estate had been acquired in 1905 by the British George Langworthy. The new owner's first intention was to rent the property, but he soon decided to settle there along with his wife, who was in poor health and the climate of Torremolinos would be helpful. Years later, after her death, and due to financial problems, Langworthy decided to use some of the buildings on the estate as a hotel. He leased the management of the business to Mrs. Beautell, who announced it in the English news section of the Malaga newspaper La Unión Mercantil. The aforementioned advertisement stated that an English lady received paying guests, that afternoon tea was served, and that the estate had a tennis court. This advertisement, published on November 6, 1930, is the first reference to the hotel activity in Santa Clara. Prior to this, the Santa Clara farm was considered a tourist attraction. In an article published in the newspaper El Sol, in August 1926, it is described how the owner had known how to take advantage of the decorative elements of nature, with viewpoints, paths between rocks and a boat ladder to access the beach. Royal figures, such as King Alfonso XIII, Queen Victoria Eugenia and the Prince of Asturias, came to see the estate and its surroundings. The Malaga Excursionist Society included among its activities its visit because of the wonderful view of the Malaga marina that could be reached from its viewpoints (Sociedad 1929). Also in a tourist guide from 1929 it was recommended to visit the Castillo de Santa Clara, although it was pointed out that the permission of the estate's gardeners was necessary, who years later would play a fundamental role in the hotel's activity (Koethke 1929). Mrs. Beautell handed over the operation of the hotel to her daughter Nancy and her son-in-law Mark Hawker. The clients of this establishment were mainly British who had arrived from Gibraltar. The hotel was in operation for the following decades, although under different managers. After Hawker, Antonio Campoy López, as representative of the gardeners, who at that time had tacit ownership of the property, leased the operation of the hotel to Frederick Saunders, who would maintain it until 1957. At that time the hotel had with 23 employees (Luque-Aranda and Heredia-Flores 2021).

Another early hotel in terms of opening was the Parador de Montemar. Inaugurated in 1934, its start-up is due to Carlota Alessandri. This businesswoman from Madrid living in Malaga bought a property in Torremolinos in 1933, specifically in the area of La Carihuela. With no possibility of agricultural use due to the ruggedness of the terrain, Alessandri's interest was the construction of a hotel to house tourists traveling along the coastal road that crossed the estate, from which they could admire magnificent sea views. At first she transformed the existing house into a small seven-room hotel where a mostly British clientele came. Years later the establishment underwent renovation and expansion works, and obtained exclusive use of a strip of beach where a social club known as El Remo was installed (Alonso-González and Heredia-Flores 2021). The international prestige enjoyed by the hotel was joined by the national prestige when in 1947 Francisco Franco's wife and daughter stayed there. Carlota Alessandri launched the development of an important residential area around the Parador de Montemar, in which many foreign families built summer homes.

After the parenthesis in terms of creating hotel offerings caused by the Civil War, but before the tourist take-off on the Costa del Sol, the opening of the La Roca hotel in Torremolinos stands out. This establishment was opened in 1942 by its owner, Enrique Bolín Bidwell, brother then of the general director of Tourism, Luis Antonio Bolín. The propaganda launched by this hotel was the first written in Torremolinos: "Torremolinos, the paradise of Spain, permanent spring climate" (Taján et al. 2018).

In that same decade, specifically in 1946, the Rodeo hotel was inaugurated in Marbella. On this occasion its promoter was Ricardo Soriano, one of the most prominent figures in Marbella's tourism development. Next to this hotel, Soriano promoted an urbanization to which he managed to attract entertainment personalities, the aristocracy and politics, this being the seed of elite tourism in Marbella (Nieto 1998).

The Initiatives that Contributed to Designing a Better Transport Offer

It is evident that the development of tourism in a given area necessarily involves having transportation infrastructure that allows the arrival of visitors. Thus, when at the beginning of the twentieth century the automobile was becoming a form of transportation increasingly used by tourists in Spain, the debate on the need to reorganize the country's road network gained strength. As a result, in 1926, the National Circuit of Special Surfaces was approved, which included among the tourist itineraries, a route that crossed Andalusia passing through the main cities of the region and another that ran along the entire Malaga coast. The creation of this road network contributed to directing the incipient tourist trend that made use of the automobile toward radial routes from Madrid to the peninsular periphery, especially toward destinations located along the coast (Gil de Arriba 2019). Specifically, the renovation works of the route that ran along the Malaga coast, which had involved the construction of numerous bridges, the correction of the existing route and extensions of the road, were completed in 1929 (Patronato 1931).

Before these improvement works, two concession companies covered the coastal route. Since 1911, Automovilística Malagueña operated a road transport line for passengers and goods departing from Malaga and stopping in Torremolinos, Benalmadena, Fuengirola, Marbella, San Pedro, and Estepona. A journey that took four hours to complete, and that, as reported in the press of those years, was of utmost importance for the development of tourism, since the towns through which it passed were the most picturesque in Malaga, in addition to allow travelers who disembark in Gibraltar to reach Malaga in a few hours. And already in 1922, Juan de Dios Portillo obtained the concession of the line between Málaga and La Línea de la Concepción, a town on the border with Gibraltar. This concession would be the origin of the Automóviles Portillo company, strongly linked to the development of the Costa del Sol (Luque-Aranda and Heredia-Flores 2022).

The other means of land transportation, the railroad, had experienced an exponential increase in the possibilities of passenger transportation since the mid-nineteenth century. This allowed tourist flows to be directed toward geographical points integrated into the railway network or located a short distance from it (Barquín 2013). In the case of Malaga, the city was connected in 1865 with Cordoba and two years later with Madrid, through a line operated by the Andalusian Railway Company. This allowed, among other things, that the rail trip from England was the shortest way to get to Malaga if it was done directly (Luque-Aranda and Heredia-Flores 2022).

As for a railway line that integrated the Malaga coast, or at least part of it, we would have to wait until the beginning of the twentieth century for construction work to begin. It would be the Malaga-Algeciras-Cádiz Company (MAC), a company linked to the Malaga Suburban Railway Company, in charge of developing and exploiting the Malaga-Fuengirola section, which came into operation in 1916. The rest of the route until Cadiz was never completed (Cuéllar-Villar 2008). The tourist projection that this line was going to have was seen by the president of the board of directors of the operating company, the Duke of San Pedro de Galatino, who had already launched different tourist initiatives in Granada, such as the Alhambra Palace hotel. and the tram to Sierra Nevada (Luque-Aranda and Heredia-Flores 2022).

The arrival of tourists by sea was conditioned by the strong competition exerted by the port of Gibraltar. The British colony was an obligatory stop for ships heading from Great Britain to Egypt or India through the Suez Canal (Esteve-Secall 1998). The easiest, and therefore most used, way to get to Malaga consisted of a boat trip to Gibraltar that lasted three or four days, and from there by car or bus, to travel the 70 miles that separated the British colony from Malaga (Luque-Aranda and Heredia-Flores 2022). Despite this, at the beginning of the 1930s, the port of Malaga, which since the last quarter of the nineteenth century had undergone important expansion and modernization works, received ships from the main international shipping companies, such as Royal Mail, White Star Line, Blue Star Line, Orient Star Line, Cunard, Chargeurs Reunis, and Hamburg Amerika Linie (Pellejero-Martínez 2016).

However, the birth of the Malaga airport will be the most relevant event for the future tourist development of the Costa del Sol. This transport infrastructure, which initially had a very limited usefulness, over time proved essential to be able to manage the mass mobility. The birth of the Malaga aerodrome was to a certain extent coincidental, the result of the need that the nascent aviation had to have spaces to make refueling and provisioning stops. In the case of Malaga, it was the French company Latécoère that chose it as a support station (along with Barcelona and Alicante) on the commercial route that linked Paris with Casablanca. For this purpose, in 1919 the company rented a property located between the capital and Torremolinos, known as El Rompedizo, which would be used regularly for the following years by the planes of the aforementioned French company and its successor, Aéropostale. It was the first company that undertook the work to adapt the property: grading of the land, cleaning of plants, construction of a hangar, installation of a radio station and a beacon system composed of electric light bulbs that marked the flight field, facilitating takeoff and landing operations. The frequency of the flights had been set at two weekly, the first of which took place on September 1st, 1919, and although its main purpose was the transport of mail and merchandise, by the end of 1920 203 passengers had already used them. The increasing number of travelers led the company to acquire a vehicle to offer the transportation of these users to their accommodation in Malaga or other nearby towns (Utrilla-Navarro 1994). In 1926 the British Colony Gazette magazine, published in Malaga, pointed out the air route as the fastest alternative to travel from London to Malaga. This trip would involve going by air to Paris, then by express train to Toulouse, and there taking another airplane to the final destination. It was estimated that the duration of the trip would be 27 hours, and as for luggage, the plane gave the opportunity to carry only ten kilos, so the excess had to be checked in on a steamship (Luque-Aranda and Heredia-Flores 2022).

The correct location of the Rompedizo state was reaffirmed by the Technical Commission of the Superior Council of Aeronautics, an organization created in 1927, by determining that the most suitable location for an airport in Malaga was the property itself. That same year, the government established the bases for the construction and operation of the national airport network, and it included Malaga among the cities that should have an airport of general interest. The carrying out of works and the management of the airports was left in the hands of organizations that would be created specifically, and the one established for the province of Malaga, the Board of the National Airport of Malaga, chaired by Luis Fernández de Villavicencio and composed of authorities and representatives of local and provincial institutions, began the procedures for the purchase of the Rompedizo state and part of the neighboring properties with the aim of expanding it and thus being able to give it civil and military use. The aforementioned purchase materialized in 1932 (Utrilla-Navarro 1994).

It was precisely during the 1930s when the French line that operated at Malaga airport stopped doing so. The reason lies in the growing distrust that the French Compagnie Générale Aéropostale, which in 1927 had absorbed the Latécoère company, aroused in the Spanish government. Aviation was becoming a strategic sector and its control had become vital.

After the acquisition of the aerodrome by the State, works followed to provide it with the basic infrastructure that will allow it to provide service to regular lines. During the Spanish Civil War the airport was converted into an air base and suffered several bombings that caused damage to its facilities. After the occupation of the province by Franco's troops, repair and expansion works were undertaken on both the landing strip and the facilities. Various buildings were built, including the first control tower, inaugurated in 1938, and a passenger station for civil aviation ten years later (Aguado-Pacheco and Utrilla-Navarro 2010). The works on this last infrastructure were carried out by the Malaga City Council. The justification for this work was based on the recognition of being an investment in the future. A municipal document from 1939 stated that a civil airport was necessary not only to strengthen air communications at that time, but also to support the foreseeable increase in them derived from the intensification of tourism. It also added that said increase in tourism would bring "immeasurable benefits for Malaga." That same year, the City Council acquired several pieces of land from neighboring properties, thus producing the second expansion of the aerodrome surface. The works on the new passenger station finished in 1948. In parallel, the flight field was conditioned and in 1946 the Malaga airport was recognized as a customs aerodrome open to international traffic. This measure hardly had immediate effects due to the isolation that the country suffered and consequently due to the limited activity of airline companies in Spain (Utrilla-Navarro 1994).

The first international company that resumed commercial flights was the Italian Ala Littoria, which established routes with Tetouan, Melilla, and Seville, and offered a link from the latter city to Rome (Utrilla-Navarro 1999). After the disappearance of the Italian company in 1945, the passenger terminal was only used by Iberia, which maintained air connections with Madrid, Melilla, Tetouan, and Seville. From 1947 and until 1949, the Compañía Auxiliar de Navegación Aérea (CANA) was authorized to operate non-scheduled flights. This had two nine-seater aircraft and flew the Tetouan-Melilla-Malaga-Granada-Malaga-Tetouan route. Despite the limited capacity of the devices, this route enjoyed high demand. Starting in 1948, it was Aviaco that made flights to Seville and Barcelona, and for three months in 1950 Gibraltar Airways established lines between the colony and Tetouan, Seville, and Malaga (Utrilla-Navarro 1994).

Gibraltar airport, built during the Second World War, was initially used by British tourists who accessed Andalusia by air, but since the late 1950s, when charter flights linking the Costa del Sol with northern Europe began to operate, Malaga airport became a fundamental piece in the development of mass tourism on the Costa del Sol. (Utrilla-Navarro 1999). The key to this is its location: halfway between Malaga and Torremolinos, next to the main road and next to the suburban railway line. A location that provides numerous advantages in terms of the mobility generated around the airport.

The First Complementary Offer: The Birth of the Costa del Golf

Between Malaga and Torremolinos, very close to the airport, another infrastructure came to light that would prove essential in the development of tourism on the Costa del Sol: the first golf course. However, its training period was long, and its results on tourist demand were evident years later.

It was in the mid-1920s when a group of personalities from Malaga, linked to the Malaga Initiatives Union, defended that the construction of a golf course was essential to attract outsiders (Luque-Aranda 2015). With this purpose, the Malaga Golf Club sports association was established on March 9, 1926. Chaired by the then mayor of the city, José Gálvez Ginachero, its regulations stated that the purpose of the society was to fill a void to turn Malaga into an attractive winter resort, by allowing winter residents to practice this sport. The partners contacted Queen Victoria Eugenie and her mother, Princess Beatrice of Battenberg, to inform them of the project. Both were interested in it and became linked to it. The queen managed the participation of the British Harry Colt in the design of the future field (Zarca 1998).

To put the project into practice two years later, the company acquired a land located between Malaga and Torremolinos. The Malaga City Council and the National Tourist Board (Patronato Nacional de Turismo, PNT) contributed financially to both the purchase of the land and the start-up of the course and the construction of the clubhouse. The economic contribution of the state tourism agency, influenced by the agency's delegate in Andalusia, Luis Antonio Bolín from Malaga, was based on the extraordinary tourist interest of the project (Rodríguez-Pérez 2021).

In 1931 the works were practically completed, but the political change slowed them down, as the PNT paralyzed the delivery of the pending amounts committed. In order to reactivate them, the society transferred ownership of the field to the public body. The PNT took possession in November 1932 and the works were resumed immediately, which allowed the inauguration of the field in July 1934. From that moment on, they began to hold competitions in which local fans and tourists participated, which thanks to the climate of the province they could enjoy the practice of this sport throughout the year (Luque-Aranda and Heredia-Flores 2021).

Torremolinos, Sociedad Anónima: The Most Ambitious Project that Could Have Been and Was Not[2]

The projection of the tourism sector, and particularly its development on the western coast of Malaga, was divined by a group of investors from Malaga who chose Torremolinos as the ideal place to turn it into an important tourist center in the image of some cities in the Atlantic and the European Mediterranean. The climatic conditions of this small town in Malaga were similar, if not better, to those of the French Riviera, where winter resorts such as Cannes, Nice, or San Remo had proliferated. Furthermore, the fashion born in the early years of the twentieth century for sunbathing and the taste for bathing in warm seas allowed the arrival of tourists to expand throughout the year.

The initiative that this group of investors launched was the first of many others that sought to provide the province of Malaga with a robust tourism structure. It was an extremely complete and ambitious project. The promoter was the Madrid-based architect Gonzalo Iglesias, who in 1926 presented a report in which the exceptional conditions enjoyed by Torremolinos were recorded to qualify as an important tourist center, particularly as a winter resort. He also pointed out that the existing deficiencies could be corrected easily and quickly, but that it had to be done urgently. To achieve this, he proposed an intense and intelligent action that simultaneously developed all the improvements in urban planning, hygiene, supplies, accommodation, and leisure.

In the opinion of the promoter, the difficulty of the project was that the improvements necessary to achieve the transformation of the city were not going to have economic compensation in the works themselves, so it could be difficult to attract the necessary capital. But for this he established compensation for the investment in the increase in the value of the property, especially the land. To launch the project, a public limited company would be established, called Torremolinos S.A., with a share capital of one million pesetas, of which half would be contributed by the promoters, and the other half would be issued with 6% amortizable bonds in twenty-five years. The premature death of Iglesias meant that this first urban development project in Torremolinos did not materialize.

Years later, the main partner that Iglesias had counted on, the Malaga lawyer Enrique Ramos Puente, rescued the idea of urban development in Torremolinos, but on this occasion focused on the construction of a spa and an entire tourist center around it. Thus, in May 1934 he presented a document under the title "Report on the Construction Project of a Spa in Torremolinos," in which the exceptional conditions of this village were once again praised, and that even without encouragement or propaganda, these had been sufficient to attract an increasing flow of visitors, especially foreigners, who settled there despite the lack of suitable accommodation. The aforementioned report also stated that until then the only thing that had been done

[2] Information obtained from the primary documentation deposited in the Antequera Municipal Historic Archive, belonging to the Ramos Archive, included in the Family Archives Fund.

to promote this tourist trend had been the road that crossed the village and the golf course, but that the rest of the attractions continued to be their natural conditions, since little or nothing had been done to complete them with improvements in comfort or leisure options. In Ramos' opinion, the time had come to act, since there was a magnificent opportunity and there would be no excuse for not taking advantage of it.

The business he proposed would begin with the construction of a spa on El Bajondillo beach, for which there was the option to purchase two neighboring properties. At the time the company was established, the concession of the strip of land that existed between the boundaries of these properties and the sea would be requested: 70 m of a beach of fine, clean sand. Of the lands on which there was a purchase option, a part would be destined for the construction of the spa and its access, and the rest could be used to start any business related to the spa or simply parcel them out and sell them to a price that would double the purchase price, thus amortizing a large part of the capital invested. Based on what was stated in the report, an initial capital of 125,000 pesetas was established, distributed as follows: acquisition of land, 60,000 pesetas; construction of roads and plantations, 20,000 pesetas; initial construction of the spa, 25,000 pesetas; other management expenses, 20,000 pesetas. The decision was made to establish a public limited company that would adopt the name Torremolinos S.A., rescuing the initial idea of Gonzalo Iglesias.

On January 16, 1935, said company was established with its founding partners, Antonio Navajas Ruiz, Enrique Ramos Puente, Juan Fazio Cárdenas and Manuel Luque Lavado. The deed of incorporation stated that its purpose was to build and operate a spa on the beaches of Torremolinos and develop businesses and industries that favor and increase tourism: pensions, hotels, restaurants, entertainment venues, sports, and other similar establishments. In addition, the acquisition, urbanization, subdivision of land and construction of buildings, either to sell or to rent, were added as another corporate purpose. Two of the founding partners, Antonio Navajas and Manuel Luque, contributed to the company those properties that the initial report proposed as a purchase option. The first Board of Directors was made up of Antonio Navajas, as president, Juan Fazio, as secretary and Enrique Ramos as managing director.

The first actions carried out were fencing, preparation, and beautification of the land. For the latter, trees purchased from a Valencian nursery were planted. In parallel, the efforts for the construction of the spa began, and as a prerequisite, the Malaga City Council was requested to fix the existing road that would link with the central mall of the spa project, as well as the construction of two other roads from different points of the village to the aforementioned mall.

The political context did not facilitate the development of the project, and with the outbreak of the Civil War in 1936, the ongoing actions were paralyzed. From that moment on, the company entered into a lethargy that would last until 1941, the year in which a General Shareholders' Meeting was held again. It reported the unfavorable circumstances that had accumulated and the desire to resume activity. It was also reported that the land, which constituted the corporate asset, had not depreciated, so the interests of the shareholders had not been diminished. Furthermore, it was expected that positive results would be obtained in the following year. This hope was based on the efforts made before the Malaga City Council and the agreements that had been reached with the City Council's Expansion Commission. Through these agreements, they agreed to give up the land necessary for the construction of the road to the beach, as well as to grant financial aid that would become effective upon completion of the spa work.

In 1942 the situation was more favorable, since the City Council had already approved the project for the road to the beach, which would make it possible to begin work on the spa, since without this access its construction was useless. In addition, the resumption of the railway that linked Malaga with Torremolinos had been announced, another of the essential needs for the development of the resort. Activity was therefore reactivated, and in 1944 the works on the avenue to the beach, the Tajo road, the planting of trees, the construction of a water tank, and two houses had already been carried out. Starting in 1945, construction tasks stagnated due to the lack of productive means, and the company's activity was reduced to renting homes and selling land. The situation was aggravated with the approval in 1950 of a new Urban Planning Plan, as a result of which the lands on which some initiative could still be developed were seriously affected by the construction of the promenade. This was the end of the company, which ended up liquidating its assets in 1956 and dissolving in 1957.

1950: The Decade Before Takeoff

With the arrival of the 1950s, the global tourism industry began a period of splendor. There is a change in the paradigm of leisure travel: it stops being a minority activity and becomes a mass phenomenon, in which the sun and beach model becomes the most in demand. Model for which Malaga and its coast had a clear advantage, as these elements were its great tourist assets. It will also be in this decade when the Costa del Sol tourism brand is consolidated, and sumptuous, comfortable, and modern hotels begin to rise among the fishermen's houses.

Tourist demand, both national and international, was increasing, and it became necessary to provide the destination with the necessary infrastructure to accommodate it. The hotel offer is going to expand significantly, leaving behind those first establishments with limited capacity. Despite the initial difficulties derived from the shortage of construction materials, between 1952 and 1959 the number of hotels increased by 71% (Zambrana Pineda et al. 2002).

In this decade, emblematic hotels such as the Marbella Club or El Fuerte emerged, both in Marbella. The Marbella Club was born at the hands of Alfonso de Hohenlohe, who, like his uncle Ricardo Soriano, became one of the great promoters of the Costa del Sol (Mata-Lara 2005). Hohenlohe had arrived in Marbella in 1946, and immediately saw its tourist potential. In 1953 he converted the farmhouse on his estate and a strip of land down to the beach into a social club. A year later he transformed the club into a hotel, thus creating one of the most iconic establishments on the Costa del Sol (Nieto 1998; Rodríguez-Feijóo 2011). As for the El Fuerte hotel, opened in 1957, this was the first large hotel located in the urban area of Marbella. Its promoter, José Luque, had bought two years earlier a property on which an old flour factory was built and after a major renovation, a large three-story building was inaugurated (Prieto-Borrego 2011).

But it will be in 1959 when the first large five-star hotel on the Costa del Sol opens, specifically in Torremolinos. The Pez Espada hotel soon achieved international fame, and it will be after its opening that the Costa del Sol reaches its greatest splendor. Its design, on the beach itself, is an example of the architecture of relaxation and opened an interesting debate. There were those who were against it, considering that it broke with the predominant Andalusian aesthetic that had attracted the first tourists. But of course it had defenders who argued that this new hotel model was necessary to be able to compete internationally. Its clientele, who generally enjoyed high purchasing power, could enjoy luxury services at relatively low prices thanks to the price control policy established by the Franco regime.

References

Alonso-González F, Heredia-Flores VM (2021) Málaga a la sombra de la historia. Ediciones del Genal, Málaga

Aguado-Pacheco M, Utrilla-Navarro L (2010) La arquitectura aeroportuaria malagueña. Eugénesis, estética y funcionalidad del nuevo edificio terminal del Aeropuerto de Málaga, Plan Málaga. Un Aeropuerto para el Futuro. Madrid

Arcas-Cubero F, García-Sánchez A (1980) Los orígenes del turismo malagueño: La Sociedad Propagandística del Clima y Embellecimiento de Málaga. Jábega 32:42–50

Barquín R (2013) El turismo y los primeros ferrocarriles españoles (1855-1900). TST 24:110–136

Burgos-Madroñero M (1974) Málaga siglo XVIII-XIX: Los extranjeros. Jábega 7:49–52

Campos-Turmo R (1928) Costabella (La Riviera española). Notas para la implantación de una ruta de turismo. Málaga

Cuéllar-Villar D (2008) Los ferrocarriles de vía estrecha en Andalucía. In: Cuéllar Villar D, Sánchez Picón A (dirs) 150 años de ferrocarril en Andalucía: Un balance, Sevilla, Consejería de Obras Públicas y Transportes, pp 241–305

Enfedaque-Blasco V (1940) Guía de Málaga y de la provincia 1939–1940. Málaga

Esteve Secall R (1998) El puerto y el ferrocarril: las puertas de entrada. In: Historia de la Costa del Sol, Málaga, Diario Sur, pp 25–32

Gil de Arriba C (2019) "Geografías turísticas": moda y modos de viajar en la España de la primera mitad del siglo XX. Ayer 114:147–174

Heredia-Flores VM (2000) La arquitectura del turismo. Los orígenes de la oferta hotelera en Málaga. Jábega 86:3–20

Jerez-Perchet A (1884) Málaga contemporánea. Estudios y paisajes de la capital y la provincia. Málaga

Koethke F (1929) *Guía del Turista Andalucía*, s.e., Málaga

Lara García MP (1997) La cultura del agua: Los baños públicos en Málaga. Editorial Sarriá, Málaga

Luque Aranda M (2015) El desarrollo del sector turístico durante la Segunda República y el Primer Franquismo: La Federación Española de Sindicatos de Iniciativa y Turismo. Universidad de Málaga, unpublished doctoral thesis

Luque Aranda M, Heredia Flores VM (2021) Pioneering projects in the tourism development of the Costa del Sol (Spain). In: Battilani P, Larrinaga C (eds) Coastal tourism in southern Europe in the XXth century. New economy and material culture. Peter Lang, Berlín, pp 115–131
Luque Aranda M, Heredia Flores VM (2022) El origen de la Costa del Sol. Infraestructuras y servicios para el desarrollo turístico de Torremolinos en la primera mitad del siglo XX. In: Larrinaga C, Strangio D (eds) El turismo en España e Italia antes del boom turístico. Silex, Madrid, pp 147–170
Mata-Lara AM (2005) Un hombre para una ciudad. Marbella, Ricardo Soriano
Nieto M (1998) El despegue de la Costa: Marbella atrae a la aristocracia y grandes fortunas. In: Mellado VM, Granados Cabezas V (coord) Historia de la Costa del Sol, Málaga, Prensa Malagueña, S.A., pp 89–96
Palou-Rubio S, Pellejero-Martínez C (2020) Promoción turística y desarrollo geoeconómico, 1900-1936: Málaga y Barcelona. Ayer 117:189–220
Patronato del Circuito Nacional de Firmes Especiales (1931) Memoria de los trabajos efectuados desde la creación del Circuito en febrero de 1926, al 31 de diciembre de 1930. Obras que se proyecta ejecutar en 1931 y liquidación del último ejercicio económico. Madrid
Pellejero-Martínez C (2005) Turismo y economía en la Málaga del siglo XX. Revista de Historia Industrial 29:87–114
Pellejero-Martínez C (2016) De incomparable station d'hiver a Costa del Sol: Málaga, 1875-1973. Revista de la Historia de la Economía y de la Empresa X:253–283
Prieto-Borrego L (2011) José Luque Manzano (1916–1984). In: Parejo A (coord) Cien empresarios andaluces. Lid, Madrid, 628–634
Rodríguez-Feijóo A (2011) Alfonso Hohenlohe Iturbe (1924–2004). In: Parejo A (coord) Cien empresarios andaluces. Lid, Madrid, pp 644–651
Rodríguez-Pérez MJ (2021) La dinámica de Luis A. Bolín en el Patronato Nacional de Turismo (1928-1931). Promoción turística e inmobiliaria. In: Larrinaga C (ed) Luis Bolín y el turismo en España entre 1928 y 1952. Marcial Pons, Madrid, pp 17–50
Sociedad (1929) Sociedad Excursionista de Málaga. Resumen de su labor cultural durante el año 1928 a 1929. Málaga
Utrilla Navarro L (1994) Historia del Aeropuerto de Málaga. AENA, Málaga
Utrilla Navarro L (1999) El Aeropuerto de Málaga. Ocho décadas de historia del transporte aéreo, Málaga, AENA
Valle de Juan MA, Beautell-González C (2015) El Hotel Santa Clara y Mistress Beautell. La verdadera pionera del turismo en la Costa del Sol, Málaga, Ediciones del Genal
Valle de Juan MA, Sánchez-Dehesa R (2015) La Punta de Torremolinos y la Finca de Santa Clara. In: Comunidad de Propietarios La Cornisa de Santa Clara Torremolinos: El Castillo de Santa Clara. Un lugar emblemático, Málaga, Ediciones del Genal, pp 17–100
Taján A et al (2018) Torremolinos, de pueblo a mito. Torremolinos, Litoral
Vallejo-Pousada R, Lindoso-Tato E, Vilar-Rodríguez M (2016) Los antecedentes del turismo de masas en España, 1900-1936. Revista de la Historia de la Economía y de la Empresa, X: 137–188
Zambrana Pineda JF et al (2002) Estadísticas del siglo XX en Andalucía, Sevilla, Instituto de Estadística de Andalucía
Zarca A (1998) Del Club de Campo a la Costa del Golf. In: Historia de la Costa del Sol, Málaga, Diario Sur, pp 81–88

Marta Luque-Aranda is a PhD in Economics and Lecturer in Economic History, University of Málaga. Research interests: economic history of Spain, economic history of tourism, and the labour market from a gender perspective. She has co-edited with Carmelo Pellejero *Inter- and Post-war Tourism in Western Europe*, 1916–1960, Palgrave Macmillan, London

Víctor M. Heredia-Flores is Associate Lecturer in Economic History and holds a degree in Contemporary History and a PhD in Economics, University of Málaga. Research interests: history of public services, industrial history, and history of education.

Chapter 9
Implementation of the Yugoslav Socialist Accommodation Sector Model in the Municipality of Piran-Pirano

Metod Šuligoj and Petra Kavrečič Božeglav

Abstract Šuligoj and Kavrečič Božeglav have formulated an innovative model of the accommodation sector shaped and implemented by socialist Yugoslavia in the Upper Adriatic Municipality of Piran-Pirano. The model illuminates the internal incongruities within the Yugoslav socialist framework. Accommodations were provided to the privileged political and economic elite as well as less price-sensitive, discerning international tourists (e.g. good hotels, private second homes, campsites in the Adriatic/Mediterranean environment). Simultaneously, accommodation was offered to the domestic working class, offering holiday options despite their lower economic status and disadvantages (e.g. holiday homes, cheap campsites). Employing a modelling technique often overlooked in tourism history studies, the research illustrates a unique amalgamation of Western and socialist holidaying (accommodating) practices and provides a narrative elucidation of this phenomenon.

Introduction

In addition to the fall of the Axis Powers and the liberation, the year 1945 divided Europe into two separate blocs. On the other side of Churchill's Iron Curtain, the Communist Parties of the individual countries took power under the strategic influence of the Soviet Union. This resulted in significant changes in social, political and economic life, which also affected the development of the tourism industry (Gorsuch 2003). The Soviet Union saw tourism as a way to strengthen and promote its national identity and the only correct regime. The regime therefore encouraged the tourism activities of loyal citizens. However, in the early post-war years, this philosophy was applied in a rather selective and non-egalitarian way (Gorsuch 2003: 761, 769). Other Eastern Bloc countries have followed these lines, although not fully. Bulgaria

M. Šuligoj (✉) · P. Kavrečič Božeglav
University of Primorska, Koper/Capodistria, Slovenia
e-mail: Metod.Suligoj@fts.upr.si; petra.kavrecic@fhs.upr.si

C. Larrinaga, D. Strangio (eds.), *Tourism Destinations and Policies in Europe During the 20th Century*, Contributions to Economics,
https://doi.org/10.1007/978-3-031-88447-4_9

(Ivanov 2009), Czechoslovakia (Mücke 2021), Romania (Stefan 2023), and the German Democratic Republic (Moranda 2005), for example, have all gradually become more welcoming to international tourists. These countries presented their natural and cultural-historical attractions as well as achievements of the Communist Party and loyal toilers, to domestic and international tourists (see also Webster and Ivanov (2016)). Integration into international tourism flows ensured the inflow of foreign currency into countries that were otherwise lagging behind in economic development compared to the more developed West. However, the Soviet Union (Gorsuch 2003) and Albania (Hall 1984) maintained rather closed borders, especially for Westerners, and their tourism was therefore mainly based on domestic tourists. All these different orientations have influenced the development of tourism, including the accommodation sector.

In socio-economic terms was socialist Yugoslavia slightly different (Banaszkiewicz et al. 2017). Initially, it copied the Soviet model of development, but as it has distanced itself from the Soviet Union from 1948 onwards, it became at least partly more open, more liberal and more developed, although still undemocratic and without a free market. Especially after 1955, the socialist authorities began to put more emphasis on the service sector, including tourism (Prinčič 1997: 5, 7–11; Repe 1996: 160), the importance of which was both economic and ideological (Hall 1984; Šuligoj and Kavrečič 2023; Tchoukarine 2010, 2015). This also affected the more developed and well-known Yugoslav destinations on the Upper Adriatic (Kavrečič and Šuligoj 2021), which formally became part of the state in 1954.[1] The new regime and social order have had a significant impact on tourism, although tourism was not specifically addressed immediately after the end of the World War II. What was new, however, was the initial strong focus on domestic social tourism—as in most other socialist European countries—and later (after 1955) on inbound tourism (Kavrečič and Šuligoj 2021; Šuligoj and Kavrečič 2023). One of the consequences of this dynamic was the investment in heterogeneous accommodation facilities aimed at different target groups, both nationally and in terms of social status. The present historical study focuses on the Municipality of Piran-Pirano, one of the internationally recognised tourist destinations already in the Habsburg period. This provided good preconditions for the further development of tourist infrastructure and superstructure, also within the framework of the new (socialist) socio-economic order. Accordingly, the aim of this study is to shed light on the model of the accommodation sector that was shaped and implemented by the socialist Yugoslav authorities. A model that reflects the heterogeneity and inconsistency of a social order that was supposed to strive for egalitarianism and inclusiveness at its core (Šuligoj and Kavrečič 2023), including workers' right to holidays. On the other hand, it also supported tourism for domestic elites and inbound/international tourists who could afford more and better, which is characteristic of stratification in Western societies. In this research, we combine these two contrasts, which have not yet been explained in terms of tourism (Kavrečič and Šuligoj 2021: 166). The present research thus complements previous research on the

[1] More can be found in Verginella (2010).

development of tourism and the accommodation sector in the geographical area where tourism was/is a traditional economic activity, e.g. Kavrečič and Šuligoj (2021), Brezovec (2015), Brezovec and Brezovec (2021), Vrtačnik (2005), Rogoznica (2005, 2008).

In this chapter, the main methodological approach is the analysis of archival material, including the tourist press, as well as other historical references. The emphasis is on a particular case study, the Municipality of Piran-Pirano and its tourist development in the years following the end of the World War II. This study recognises that tourism is an interdisciplinary field and as such should be considered in the context of historical studies. Accordingly, we address here the business and related social aspects within the multidimensional history of tourism. They are explained through narrative analysis, which is a well-established approach in historiography, including business historiography, see Hansen (2012: 693), and Mordhorst and Schwarzkopf (2017). While the history of tourism in socialist Yugoslavia has been addressed by historians and other scholars (e.g. Patterson 2001; Duda n.d., Tchoukarine 2010, 2015; Repe 2006a, b) the studies have focused more on the macro level than on specific localities; for the area of the Upper Adriatic, research has been carried out, for example by Balažič (2010), Rogoznica (2009), Šuligoj and Kavrečič (2021, 2023), Brezovec (2015). This allows for the study of smaller areas, such as tourist areas (destinations) and tourism businesses within the accommodation industry, in specific socio-economic and socio-political settings that are not well described. Furthermore, this study uses a modelling technique that has been overlooked in the historiography (Norkus 2012) to illustrate the relationship between target groups of tourists and types of accommodation services. According to Norkus (2012), the model is designed to represent a real or nearly real social construct, structural relationships that are not necessarily easily visible. Geovisualisation has only been used to a limited extent to show the spatial distribution of supply.

Socialist Accommodation Sector Model in the Municipality of Piran-Pirano

The incremental growth of tourism in the Upper Adriatic received a significant boost from the establishment of the Vienna–Trieste rail link and other transport connections by air, land, and sea (Šuligoj and Sinkovič 2018). This surge created a demand for additional accommodations. A pivotal moment in the Piran-Pirano region was marked by the inauguration of the opulent 176-room Palace Hotel in 1908, a crucial lodging facility that continued to play a key role during the eras of Italian fascism and Yugoslav socialism (Brezovec 2015). Already in the early socialist period, existing accommodation facilities, like most other economic subjects and facilities, were nationalised (Brezovec 2015; Rogoznica 2005, 2014). The limited exceptions included small providers, such as food and beverage outlets (Kukanja 2015), lessors. However, the large socialist companies, linked to the ruling political elites, were the main operators of accommodation facilities. In terms of promotion and sales, they were present on the domestic and later (especially after 1955) on the international market. They targeted national as well as status-mixed target groups, who also demanded better services and were therefore willing to pay more. Together with small private accommodation providers (Balažič 2010), by also targeting the wealthy and foreigners, they deviated from the initial guidelines of providing quality holidays for all Yugoslav citizens, with a special emphasis on workers. A similar departure from the basic socialist philosophy occurred with the private second homes afforded to the wealthier and more powerful/influential Yugoslav citizens.[2] The Upper Adriatic area was a popular tourist destination for private investment in second homes (Jeršič 1968; Opačić and Koderman 2019), which were also used for personal purposes and therefore cannot be unconditionally placed in the accommodation sector (in terms of economic activity). The owners, however, benefited from all the facilities and services of the destination for locals and tourists. Patterson (2001) describes the owners as a "new class" who, because of their political connections and contributions (to the creation and promotion of the state, the state regime and the Communist Party), lived a very Western lifestyle in a socialist "egalitarian" system with an average standard of living lower than in the West.

The complete opposite were the (union) holiday homes of socialist companies and public sector employers, which were placed in so-called social tourism. They were intended for the loyal domestic working class who, due to lower incomes, could not afford more expensive accommodation. This was also the practice in other European socialist countries (Rosenbaum 2015; Šuligoj and Kavrečič 2023) or in other autocratic regimes, such as fascism (Kavrečič 2020). In summary, the Yugoslav system was socially responsible and did not discriminate against vulnerable social groups, such as pensioners, the disabled and the unemployed (Šuligoj and Kavrečič 2023), but at the same time it created domestic privileged groups with better opportunities to spend their leisure time.

The previous description clearly shows the inconsistencies in the Yugoslav tourism development policy, which were also reflected in the structure of accommodation facilities in the destination Piran-Pirano (and elsewhere in the country). This is clearly illustrated by the 3 × 2 matrix in Fig. 9.1. It presents a matrix model of tourist accommodation that includes economic and non-economic domains, which are additionally discussed in the following sub-sections.

Accommodations for Mixed Target Groups

The post-World War II socialist authorities placed Yugoslavia in the space between the Western and Eastern blocs, with more porous borders, which also had an impact on tourism. With the Yugoslav-Soviet split, known as the *Informbiro*, in 1948, the Eastern Bloc regimes, such as Czechoslovak and Hungarian, did not allow their

[2] Foreign citizens were not allowed to own property.

		Ownership	
		Public	Private
Target group	Mixed	*Hotel* *Inn* *Campsite*	*Private room* *Inn*
	Domestic tourists*	*(Union) holiday homes*	
	Influential owners		*Second homes*

* particularly from working class

Fig. 9.1 Matrix of accommodation structure by target group and ownership

citizens to visit Yugoslavia. Apparently, the market had shifted in favour of the Western countries. However, the situation was not so black and white, and socialist Yugoslavia continued to attract tourists from both sides (Tchoukarine 2010: 109). The undemocratic communist authorities realised the importance of foreign consumption in tourism, which naturally encouraged the authorities to implement a more "liberal" economic and tourism-friendly environment (Repe 2006a; Šuligoj and Kavrečič 2023; Duda n.d.). The importance of tourism was stressed at the 1949 plenum of the Communist League of Yugoslavia, where Yugoslav Foreign Minister Edvard Kardelj "emphasised the importance of international tourists for Yugoslavia" and "declared that the interest of foreigners in the country was increasing and helping to spread the knowledge of the Yugoslav struggle abroad" (Tchoukarine 2010: 116).[3] In practice, this was reflected in investments in accommodation and other tourism and leisure infrastructure, as well as in promotional activities abroad. Tourism during the socialist period is thus considered to be a strong driver of consumption (Perović et al. 2017), both domestic and international, especially in the already internationally recognised Adriatic coastal areas. Moreover, for the coastal Municipality of Piran-Pirano, part of the disputed border area,[4] tourism also offered the possibility of socio-economic development after the World War II, despite many practical legal conundrums, such as ownership of facilities (Rogoznica 2005: 397–398).

The available data show that in the case of the Municipality of Piran-Pirano, the pre-war accommodation facilities were not operational after 1945 or were used for other purposes. The Yugoslav army "occupied" 13 hotels, 21 guesthouses and villas with a capacity of 1400 beds. Of these, the army "occupied" the large, upscale hotels such as the Palace and the Riviera. Another 36 villas were used by Yugoslav army officers and their families. Cultural, social and health institutions also used other tourist facilities. In 1947, the military government left some facilities to be used for tourist marketing (Rogoznica 2005: 397). In the same year the first

[3] Indeed, this differs little from the views of other democracies and non-democracies (Kavrečič 2020).

[4] Also resolved with temporary international agreements, such as the establishment of the Free Territory of Trieste (1947–1954).

accommodation for commercial tourism was arranged: 36 beds in Hotel Central (Portorož-Portorose), 44 beds in Rotonda (Piran Pirano) and 14 beds in Vila Nazinala in Strunjan-Strugnano (*Dokumentacija k Družbenemu Planu Gospodarskega Razvoja Okraja Koper Za Razdobje Od 1957. Do* 1961. *Year 1958*: 50). In 1951 the hotel Palace added another 340 beds (Trebše-Štolfa 1996: 14), which was the main accommodation for international tourists. Despite these initiatives, the attitude towards tourism followed the new model of the planned economy, as Rogoznica (2005: 402) mentions that only few international tourists came during this period. Promotional activities outside the area were mainly aimed at the inhabitants of Trieste-Trst, which was under international administration after the war and then ceded to Italy. The modest offering was particularly evident in the early post-war years until 1954. This can be seen in Table 9.1, where only the abovementioned hotel beds were available for tourists. The situation improved at the beginning of the 1950s, when more facilities were available. Table 9.1 compares the accommodation capacities in the entire coastal area that today belongs to Slovenia, and at the same time shows that most of these capacities were located in the Municipality of Piran-Pirano (Piran-Pirano, Portorož-Portorose, Strunjan-Strugnano), which was already then the most tourism-oriented part of Slovenia. Accordingly, Portorož-Portorose was the most well-established tourist centre not only in the municipality but also in the wider socio-geographical area, see Pucer (1985), Vrtačnik (2005), Šuligoj (2015).

Table 9.1 Beds in hotels and other facilities in the coastal part of the District of Koper-Capodistria from 1947 to 1953

		Year						
Accomodation facility	Area	1947	1948	1949	1950	1951	1952	1953[a]
Hotel Palace	Portorož-Portorose	/	/	/	/	340	410	421
Hotel Central	Portorož-Portorose	36	36	36	36	36	40	240
Hotel Helios-Bristol	Portorož-Portorose	/	67	67	67	67	67	/
Hotel Partizan	Portorož-Portorose	/	/	/	35	35	40	/
Hotel Metropol	Piran-Pirano	/	/	/	44	44	44	40
Hotel Rotonda	Piran-Pirano	44	44	44	44	44	44	50
Jezero Fiesa facilities	Piran-Pirano	/	/	/	/	/	/	180
Vila Nazinala	Strunjan- Strugnano	14	14	14	14	14	18	/
Triglav	[b]	/	/	/	/	72	72	93
Turist	Ankaran-Ancarano	/	/	75	119	119	119	123
Inn/lodging	Koper-Capodistria	/	/	/	18	18	/	/
Holiday Homes[c]	/	/	/	210	831	503	503	295
Total		94	161	446	1208	1292	1357	1442

[a] In the source the year 1952 is followed by 1954. It is possible that there is a mistake and the data are for 1953. In Table 9.2 the data for 1954 are different from here

[b] The municipality is not specified. It could be the Hotel Triglav in Koper-Capodistria, which was opened at the end of 1951 (Brezovec 2015: 121)

[c] Specific accommodation is discussed in the next section. Oscillations in the data are not explained

Source: *Dokumentacija k Družbenemu Planu Gospodarskega Razvoja Okraja Koper Za Razdobje Od 1957. do 1961. Year 1958*: 50–51

From 1954 onwards, the most important Yugoslav urban planners, in particular the architect Edo Mihevc, assigned specific roles to the Upper Adriatic towns that had been assigned to Yugoslavia after the resolution of the border dispute with Italy. Koper-Capodistria was designated as "an administrative and industrial centre," the town of Izola-Isola as "an industrial and fishing centre" and Piran-Pirano and Portorož-Portorose as "a tourist centre" (Čebron Lipovec 2019: 207). The idea was that Piran-Pirano would be preserved as a "historical pearl", as a tourist attraction whose accommodation infrastructure would be and has been built in Portorož-Portorose (Čebron Lipovec 2012: 223). The main architect also planned and constructed tourist resorts (accommodation complexes) in Ankaran-Ancarano, Strunjan-Strugnano and Lucija-Santa Lucia (Čebron Lipovec 2012: 226), which complemented the coastal tourist supply of the Yugoslav Upper Adriatic (District of Koper-Capodistria). This part of the county had a total of 1445 beds after 1954, which represented 12.7% of Slovenia's accommodation capacity, otherwise estimated at around 10,000 beds. The more important tourist accommodation and other facilities were transferred to the state administration and state-owned companies already at the end of the 1940s on the basis of the so-called forced-ownership measures (Rogoznica 2014: 77). Nevertheless, according to Kukanja (2015: 219), private guesthouses were still mostly owned by Italians in the immediate post-war period. Similarly, inns were still privately owned in 1949 (*Dokumentacija k Družbenemu Planu Gospodarskega Razvoja Okraja Koper Za Razdobje Od 1957. Do 1961. Year 1958*). Due to the complicated situation of the Italian population in the District, the owners did not invest in infrastructure, which consequently led to their rapid decline. The new political authorities revoked many of their licences (Kukanja 2015: 219). According to the social plan, there was a positive turn of events after 1949: "Since the emigration of the Italians, the inns were left without owners. For this reason, it was possible to organise the state hospitality company in such a way as to merge several guesthouses. This created the basis for a socialist hospitality industry" (*Dokumentacija k Družbenemu Planu Gospodarskega Razvoja Okraja Koper Za Razdobje Od 1957. do 1961. Year* 1958: 51).

In 1954, after the end of the strict centrally planned state economy, private inns were reintroduced: by 1956 there were 20 of them (*Dokumentacija k Družbenemu Planu Gospodarskega Razvoja Okraja Koper Za Razdobje Od 1957. do 1961. Year* 1958: 51–52, 53). However, of all types of tourist accommodation, hotels were able to accommodate the largest number of tourists (international and domestic), see Table 9.2. These data also confirm the continued dominance of the Municipality of Piran-Pirano in the district (see the top four hotels in Table 9.2).

According to the data in Table 9.2, we can see that the number of beds in hotels increased slowly. The most significant increase in number can be seen in the Palace and Central hotels and in Ankaran-Ancarano. In almost all hotel facilities, we can see the major increase in 1955, which can be attributed to the signing of the Duino—Devin bilateral agreement between Yugoslavia and Italy, which facilitated the border crossings.

Especially Portorož-Portorose attracted various groups of tourists. Tourists from the domestic political and economic elite were observed, as well as foreigners

Table 9.2 Beds in hotels and other facilities in the coastal part of the District of Koper-Capodistria from 1954 to 1956

		Year		
Accomodation facility	Area	1954	1955	1956
Hotel Palace	Portorož-Portorose	433	433	463
Hotel Central	Portorož-Portorose	170	215	240
Hotel Helios	Portorož-Portorose	112	148	148
Hotel Metropol	Piran-Pirano	140	164	164
Hotel Triglav	Koper-Capodistria	98	98	98
Hotel Galeb	Koper-Capodistria	/	/	13
Dom Ljudske milice[a]	Koper-Capodistria	27	27	27
Gostinsko podjetje Turist	Ankaran-Ancarano	123	204	204
Hotel Riba	Izola-Isola	/	/	33
Gostišče »Jadran«	Izola-Isola	6	6	12
Holiday Homes[a]	[b]	374	374	1524
Camping pitches	[b]	/	/	170
Total		1483	1669	3096

[a] Specific accommodation facility discussed in the next section
[b] The Municipality is not specified
Source: *Dokumentacija k Družbenemu Planu Gospodarskega Razvoja Okraja Koper Za Razdobje Od 1957. do 1961. Year 1958*: 53–54

Table 9.3 Number and share of domestic and international tourists from 1954 to 1956 for District of Koper-Capodistria

Year	Domestic tourists	Domestic tourists (%)	International tourists	International tourists (%)	Total
1954	43,693	81.55	9883	18.45	53,576
1955	47,287	75.37	15,454	24.63	62,741
1956	39,616	79.10	10,466	20.90	50,082

Source: *Dokumentacija k Družbenemu Planu Gospodarskega Razvoja Okraja Koper Za Razdobje Od 1957. do 1961. Year 1958*: 59

looking for quality tourist accommodation. Although Šuligoj and Kavrečič (2023) found a marginal share of international tourists in local holiday homes and provided a brief general explanation, this cannot be considered as their systematic focus on a heterogeneous clientele (see the bottom of Table 9.1). Due to the lower price sensitivity of international tourists and the large inflow of tourists from France, Germany and Austria in 1956, the authorities raised the prices of food and other tourist services. However, this has proved to be an extremely bad decision, with a drastic fall in tourist arrivals, both domestic and international (see Table 9.3). Nevertheless, some accommodation facilities have managed to cope with this situation. For example, the "Gostinsko podjetje Hotel Central" in Portorož-Portorose managed to avoid the crisis thanks to Czech tourists who came to the hotel through the ČEDOK travel company and with the help of the Yugoslav travel company Putnik. These tourists were provided with a solid board in the hotel and did not spend additional money

Table 9.4 International tourists and overnight stays in the coastal part of the District of Koper-Capodistria from 1955 to 1956

	1955		1956	
Country	Tourists (%)	Overnight stays (%)	Tourists (%)	Overnight stays (%)
Austria	31.4	45.8	17.6	23.9
West Germany (FRG)	28.8	26.3	19.4	29.9
Italy	12.8	4.6	25.8	9.8
France	4.3	3.1	7.5	4.5
Sweden	2.1	2.1	2	2.8
Switzerland	4	3.4	2.8	3.1
England	3.4	4.4	5.6	7.5
East Germany (GDR)	/	/	2	0.5
Belgium	1	0.4	1.9	1.3
Other countries (USA, CZ, Poland etc.)	12.2	9.1	15.4	22.7

Source: *Dokumentacija k Družbenemu Planu Gospodarskega Razvoja Okraja Koper Za Razdobje Od 1957. do 1961. Year 1958*: 59

outside the facility (Guštin 2010: 25–26), which is probably to be expected given their lower economic standard. Otherwise, the majority of international tourists came from Germany and Austria (Trebše-Štolfa 1996: 15), not to overestimate the more distant Swedish and Dutch markets (Guštin 2010: 29)—see also Table 9.4. The Yugoslav authorities also tried to increase the income of international tourists also through promotional activities at tourist fairs, focusing their advertising on sea and sun, relaxing holidays and affordable prices (Guštin 2010: 27). In 1947 there were only 3% (6720) of non-domestic tourists and in 1953 the number increased to 11% (16,425) (Kavrečič and Šuligoj 2021). However, it is not possible to make a coherent and convincing comparison for the post-war years up to 1954, when the area under study was assigned to Yugoslavia, as the available data do not indicate whether this area was included in the Yugoslav tourist statistics. The number of international tourists can be more precisely followed after 1954. The data for the years 1954 to 1956 (Table 9.3) show an unstable development with significant fluctuations in the number of tourists.

The beginning of the next decade (1960s) brought changes in tourism trends. In 1961 and 1962 the number of domestic and international tourists in the District of Koper-Capodistria increased significantly, see Table 9.5. It should not be neglected that accommodation providers were strongly oriented towards the summer season, with unsold capacities outside the season. Domestic tourists with higher purchasing power (e.g. managers, political representatives) and, in particular, international tourists, all of which are relevant to this section, thus remained a partially realised potential.[5]

[5]The data in Tables 9.3 and 9.5 should be interpreted with caution, as international tourists were accommodated in hotels, inns and campsites (Fig. 9.1), while a significant proportion of domestic tourists also stayed in holiday homes, which are discussed in the next section.

Table 9.5 Number of overnight stays in the District of Koper-Capodistria in 1961 and 1962

	Year	
Number of overnight stays	1961	1962
Domestic tourists	357,734	489,275
International tourists	169,900	300,637
Total	527,634	789,912

Source: *Dokumentacija k Družbenemu Planu Gospodarskega Razvoja Okraja Koper Za Razdobje Od 1957. do 1961. Year 1958*: 71; Trebše-Štolfa 1996: 16

In 1962, the percentage of international tourists in the District represented almost half of all international tourist overnight stays in the then People's Republic of Slovenia (one of the six republics of socialist Yugoslavia). This is a sign of the importance of international tourism in the region, the supply of which is based on sea-related content. The increase in international tourist income is evident when compared with the figures for the first few years after the war. In the following decades the tourist infrastructure, especially in Portorož-Portorose, changed drastically. In the period from 1960 to 1980 it was transformed into a fashionable tourist centre with significant investments in hotel infrastructure. The hitherto non-touristic area called Bernardin-Bernardino has been designated for tourism purposes and a new hotel resort has been built there. The aforementioned architect Edo Mihevc supervised the construction. As a result of the extensive investment programme, the number of hotel beds in Portorož-Portorose increased from 3000 in 1964 to more than 7000 in 1976. Before the break-up of Yugoslavia, tourism in the region was dominated by nine large companies. In Portorož-Portorose there were four hotel companies: Bernardin Hotels, Riviera Hotels, Palace Hotels and Metropol Hotels. In Piran-Pirano, the main company was Piran Hotels. In Strunjan-Strugnano there was a recognisable health resort (Brezovec 2015: 122–124). It should be noted that international tourists were mostly accommodated in hotels and similar facilities such as inns. Camping sites should not be overlooked. This type of accommodation became increasingly popular in the post-war period. After the end of the World War II, the development of transport infrastructure and means of transport, as well as the development of mass tourism, favoured the differentiation of the supply, also in the direction of outdoor accommodation (camping). In this context, the Yugoslavian Eastern Adriatic coast was also known for its naturist camps, which were a complement to conventional campsites. Campsites represented not only a form of "spending time in nature", but also a more affordable, cheaper accommodation (Cvelić Bonifačić 2011). Camping tourism initially attracted tourists from the lower classes of the socialist countries, but from the early 1970s it also attracted tourists from the middle and upper classes (Repe 2006a: 71). In the District of Koper-Capodistria, the first campsite was established in Ankaran-Ancarano (Nikolaj) in 1955 (*Dokumentacija k Družbenemu Planu Gospodarskega Razvoja Okraja Koper Za Razdobje Od 1957. Do 1961. Year* 1958: 58). The investment in camping accommodation in the area was slower due to inadequate municipal infrastructure, e.g., in Piran-Pirano (Trebše-Štolfa 1996: 16); Trebše-Štolfa (1996: 14) recorded the first camping sites in the District of Koper-Capodistria in 1956, when there were 170 camping pitches. This delay in development is also visible in Table 9.2.[6] The development of camping tourism in the District has also not been in the direction of naturism, which is different from the practice a little further south on the Istrian peninsula.

Accommodations for Domestic Working Class

From an ideological perspective, it is clear that the Yugoslav communist authorities strongly supported tourism for the domestic working class. The most important accommodation facility became the holiday homes built and intended for the leisure/holidays of workers and young people (Rogoznica 2014; Šuligoj and Kavrečič 2023; Kavrečič and Šuligoj 2021), the number of which increased in the District after 1954 (Kavrečič and Šuligoj 2021).

The aim of the Yugoslav authorities was to introduce the socialist model into tourism, focusing on domestic tourists. The main focus was on the working class. The trade unions organised trips to the sea for workers and young people. The slogan of the authorities was "tourism to the working people" (Rogoznica 2005: 399). With the introduction of a paid holiday allowance in 1946, the government made it possible for workers to go on holiday. In fact, in Yugoslavia this activity was considered a necessary ritual of the population, "an essential part of the standard of living and the right of the entire population". Most workers and their families stayed in the holiday homes of their employers. Their summer holidays were based on the following idea (Duda n.d.):

> Workers' holiday homes are cheaper and make you feel more relaxed because around here there are mostly your friends and acquaintances. It is more comfortable than being with unknown people. In addition, everything is organised, so that you do not have to think about anything. So you can spend comfortable and really carefree holidays.

This type of domestic tourist accommodation was also built or arranged in the territory of the Municipality of Piran-Pirano. Slovenian and other Yugoslav (domestic) tourists, who came to Portorož-Portorose within the framework of the trade union organisation and were given special discounts, were usually accommodated in holiday homes. Employers in the public, cooperative and state-owned sectors invested in these holiday facilities (Table 9.6) and also paid holiday allowances to workers. In the 1950s, for example, 36 holiday homes in the District were given to companies and institutions of the People's Republic of Slovenia to provide accommodation for workers during their summer holidays. After 1954, the Yugoslav authorities encouraged the further development of domestic social tourism for

[6] The Documentation for the Social Plan for the Economic Development of the Koper District for the Period from 1957 to 1961, Volume 5, Trade, Catering and Tourism, 1958 (in Slovenian: Dokumentacija k družbenemu planu gospodarskega razvoja okraja Koper za razdobje od 1957. do 1961. leta, peti zvezek, Trgovina, gostinstvo in turizem 1958), offers some camping-related empirical data with poor interpretation, therefore we do not particularly consider this here.

Table 9.6 Holiday homes by sectors in District of Koper-Capodistria from 1954 to 1956

	Year		
Sector	1954	1955	1956
Public sector	81	87	91
Cooperative sector	41	42	45
Private sector	119	92	90
Total	241	221	226

Source: *Dokumentacija k Družbenemu Planu Gospodarskega Razvoja Okraja Koper Za Razdobje Od 1957. do 1961. Year 1958*: 52

working people. Thus, in 1954 there were 9 holiday homes in the Municipality of Piran-Pirano, in 1955 there were 12 and in 1956 there were 56 (Kavrečič and Šuligoj 2021). Other municipalities in the District were less tourism-oriented. However, employers there also invested in holiday homes (Table 9.6); relevant data showing the growth trend are also presented in Tables 9.1 and 9.2.[7]

Investments continued in the following years until the dissolution of socialist Yugoslavia in the 1990s. As in previous years, investors came from the same sectors as mentioned above (SI PAK PI). In 1958, there were 68 holiday homes in the Municipality of Piran-Pirano, in 1962 there were already 110 (Kavrečič and Šuligoj 2021); until the dissolution of the state, there were more than 7100 beds in holiday homes and youth holiday camps on the Slovenian coast (Brezovec 2015: 122). Figure 9.2 shows their spatial distribution in the years of growth in the most touristic part of the Municipality of Piran-Pirano.

As a specific type of accommodation, holiday homes were not classified according to quality standards. The facilities and services offered were not uniform and depended, of course, on the companies to which they belonged. The investor/owner was responsible for the management and maintenance of the holiday accommodation. Workers arranged their holiday dates with the union, which in practice acted as a booking service. The investors, in agreement with the union, also employed a caretaker to organise the work during the operation of the home, e.g. maintenance work, keeping records of tourists and property, serving food and drink (if offered) and the like (Kavrečič and Šuligoj 2021). This means that the management of these holiday homes has not followed the management practices of the hospitality industry, particularly the western hospitality industry. This can be described as amateur/intuitive management. Accordingly, it is clear that this type of accommodation was very different from "traditional" hotels and inns. The holiday homes were intended for domestic workers and, in a certain manner, represented an extension of the working environment in order to maintain and

[7]A number of inconsistencies can be found in the Documentation for the Social Plan for the Economic Development of the Koper District for the Period from 1957 to 1961, Volume 5, Trade, Catering and Tourism, 1958. Although it is an official document of the District authorities, it should be interpreted with caution.

Fig. 9.2 Distribution of holiday homes in the coastal part of the Municipality of Piran in 1962 (Cartography: Rubin geoinformatika d.o.o.; Base layer: Beltram, 1969; elaborated by the authors)

emphasise the connection with the place of work. As such, they also helped to develop loyalty, as the working environment played a positive role in the lives of hard-working men and women. This type of social tourism, with services at more affordable prices, enabled the population with lower purchasing power to have a well-deserved holiday and increased loyalty not only to the workplace and employer, but also to the regime/state. However, Šuligoj and Kavrečič (2023) described it as both innovative and socially responsible, as it involved workers and disadvantaged social groups (unemployed, disabled, pensioners). In doing so, the state has also contributed to the rise of mass tourism.

Second Homes or "Vikendica" for the Domestic Elite

Yugoslav society had another specific housing practice that we have identified (Fig. 9.1): second homes (or weekend houses, commonly called "vikendica" in Slovenian) represent an interesting and yet atypical type of accommodation in a socialist state. This is also pointed out by researcher Karin Taylor (2010) in her chapter "My Own Vikendica, Holiday Cottages as Idyll and Investment", in which she begins with the consideration that "Josip Broz Tito had a holiday home, so did the mechanic Tonči". This quote shows not only that second homes were a popular form of holiday accommodation, but also that they were by no means uniform. Yugoslavia's communist president Tito enjoyed his luxurious second home on the Brioni Islands in the Upper Adriatic, while the mechanic might have had a more modest hillside cottage (Taylor 2010: 171). But the underlying question is whether every mechanic could really afford a second home. Yugoslav society was by no means uniform, and the authoritarian regime in fact generated a very diverse socialist society. This was also reflected in domestic tourism. Although mass tourism was the most common and popular form of tourism in the post-war period, there were people who were looking for higher quality, alternatives, peace and quiet. This was provided in particular by privately owned second homes, often located in rural areas, but also by the Adriatic Sea. This phenomenon began in the early 1960s.

Owners of second homes by the sea perceived them as non-touristic. This distinction is very clearly expressed in the following words (Taylor 2010: 171): "We have 'ours' here, it is simply different to being a tourist. It's a totally different feeling, a different relationship. You're comfortable, free [...] In your own property you live your own life."

The Slovenian geographer Matjaž Jeršič (1968) provides some data on private second homes in the Upper Adriatic region of the People's Republic of Slovenia and partly in the People's Republic of Croatia, namely on the Western Istrian peninsula. The homes were built entirely for this purpose or with the reorganisation or reuse of the existing facility (previously used for other purposes). They were built especially to satisfy the need for recreation and relaxation, to escape from everyday work and from the urban and industrial environment. It was also a fashion that developed in post-war societies. Several factors have influenced this development, in particular the acquired right to paid holidays, the greater separation of work and leisure time, the improved economic standard and purchasing power, and similar items. This also allowed the population to benefit from the tourist services in the tourist destinations and to participate in this new trend: it reached the lower social classes to a limited extent. The class distinction is clear in this type of accommodation, which could only be afforded by those with a higher personal income. As Jeršič's (1968) research shows, education was also a factor, since according to the data collected in 1967, 43% of second home owners had a higher level of education. Those who could actually afford to own a second (holiday) home were the most prominent party leaders, high-ranking functionaries and similar influencers. It is significant, however, that in line with political ideology, the former houses and villas in tourist areas that had belonged to the upper classes in the pre-socialist period were mostly assigned to public use, including providing accommodation for workers on holiday. The socialist elite of the time generally preferred to build their own properties (Taylor 2010: 176). In addition to their own recreational use, there was also a desire to invest in real estate and the possibility of financial gain from renting out property to tourists (Jeršič 1968: 58–59).

In the area of the Municipality of Piran-Pirano, the number of old houses that have been converted into secondary holiday homes were: 135 in the town of Piran-Pirano and 44 in Portorož-Portorose. The purchase or short-term (tourist) rental of old houses for holiday purposes was most intensive in the period from 1953 to 1961. At that time, the local authorities were interested in selling houses that were uninhabited and in a state of disrepair tourists (Jeršič 1968: 62). This was the result of the emigration (exodus) of most of the Italian-speaking population from this area after the World War II. According to Jeršič (1968: 57), in 1967 there were 57 private second homes in Portorož-Portorose, 38 in Fiesa-Fiesso and 142 in Piran-Pirano. The Municipality of Piran-Pirano was thus the most attractive in this specific segment compared to other coastal parts of the District. As a consequence, at the beginning of the 1970s, in 1971, there were 381 second homes on the territory of the Municipality of Piran-Pirano, and in 1981 the number increased to 778 (Koderman 2014: 128).

Conclusion

Since the previous studies have directly or indirectly shed light on various aspects of tourism and leisure in socialist Yugoslavia (e.g. Patterson 2001; Duda n. d., Tchoukarine 2010, 2015; Repe 2006a, b), Šuligoj and Kavrečič (2021, 2023), this study develops on this basis a (matrix) model of the accommodation sector that the socialist Yugoslav authorities shaped and implemented in the coastal Municipality of Piran-Pirano. The model merely mirrors the incongruities of a Yugoslav socialist social order with tourist accommodation for different target groups (social groups). The Municipality of Piran-Pirano provided accommodation for the domestic socialist elites (political and economic), e.g. quality hotels and private second homes. This is in line with previous study by Rosenbaum (2015), which, however, did not focus on this case. Thus, Yugoslavia exhibited thoroughly Western characteristics that were inconsistent with the public expression of socialist ideas such as inclusiveness and egalitarianism. They were enacted within a domestic social tourism dedicated to the working class, as previously described by Duda (n.d.), Šuligoj and Kavrečič (2021, 2023). This socially homogeneous target group benefited from much cheaper accommodation, such as holiday homes and campsites. This study complements Šuligoj and Kavrečič (2023), underscoring the significance of responsible tourism encompassing socially disadvantaged groups. In contrast, international tourists engaged in conventional commercial tourism were primarily housed in upscale accommodations and campsites within the Adriatic/Mediterranean context. Representing a segment of the mixed tourist target group, they play an integral role in the illustrated (matrix) model (Fig. 9.1), exemplifying a distinctive coexistence.

This study pioneers the examination of socialist social order intricacies within the accommodation sector of a renowned tourist destination. Employing a methodological approach often overlooked in historiography, modelling complements the narrative analysis prevalent among historians. This work aims to encourage the integration of modelling techniques in the study of complex historical issues within tourism history. Additionally, it underscores the challenge of insufficient/inconsistent historical sources, emphasising the imperative for extensive archival research, including on-site visits to various archives. This not only facilitates in-depth comparative studies with other Eastern Adriatic destinations during the socialist period but also opens avenues for comparisons among competing destinations in the Adriatic under different socio-political orders in post-World War II Yugoslavia and Italy. Accessible records also allow for more complex quantitative analysis, which has largely been neglected.

References

SI PAK PI 36. Skupščina občine Piran s predhodniki. Počitniški domovi 1962-1965 (odločbe). Knjige gostov počitniških domov OBLO Piran. Pokrajinski arhiv Koper/Archivio Regionale di Capodistria

Balažič G (2010) Turizem Kot Dejavnik Socialnogeografskega Razvoja v Občini Piran v Obdobju Socializma. Geografski Obzornik 57(1):13–18

Banaszkiewicz M, Graburn N, Owsianowska S (2017) Tourism in (Post)Socialist Eastern Europe. J Tour Cult Chang 15(2):109–121. https://doi.org/10.1080/14766825.2016.1260089

Brezovec T (2015) Razvoj hotelske ponudbe na slovenski obali. In: Šuligoj M (ed) Retrospektiva turizma Istre. Založba Univerze na Primorskem, Koper - Capodistria, pp 111–142

Brezovec T, Brezovec A (2021) Yugoslavia awaits you: post WW2 tourism promotion of the Yugoslav Coast. In: Battilani P, Larrinaga C (eds) Coastal tourism in Southern Europe in the XXth century: new economy and material culture. Peter Lang, Berlin, pp 171–186

Čebron Lipovec N (2012) Arhitekturni Pomniki Izgradnje Kopra Po Drugi Svetovni Vojni. Annales 22(1):211–232

Čebron Lipovec N (2019) Post-War Urbanism along the contested border: some observations on Koper/Capodistria and Trieste/Trst. Dve Domovini 49:199–220

Cvelić Bonifačić J (2011) Kamping: Osnove Hrvatskog i Europskog Kamping Turizma. KUH, Poreč

Dokumentacija k Družbenemu Planu Gospodarskega Razvoja Okraja Koper Za Razdobje Od 1957. Do 1961. Leta. 1958. Koper: Okrajni ljudski odbor, Zavod za planiranje

Duda I (n.d.) Everyday life in both Yugoslavias: catching up with Europe. Yu Historija. Accessed 8 Dec 2023. https://www.yuhistorija.com/society_txt01c.html

Gorsuch AE (2003) "There's no place like home": Soviet Tourism in Late Stalinism. Slav Rev 62(4):760–785. https://doi.org/10.2307/3185654

Guštin M (2010) Identiteta - Dediščina Kot Temelj Razvoja Portoroškega Turizma. In: Brezovec A, Mikolič V (eds) Turizem kot medkulturni dialog. Fakulteta za turistične študije - Turistica, Portorož, pp 21–35

Hall DR (1984) Foreign tourism under socialism the Albanian "Stalinist" model. Ann Tour Res 11(4):539–555. https://doi.org/10.1016/0160-7383(84)90047-1

Hansen PH (2012) Business history: a cultural and narrative approach. Bus Hist Rev 86(4):693–717

Ivanov SH (2009) Opportunities for developing Communist heritage tourism in Bulgaria. Tourism 57(2):177–192

Jeršič M (1968) Sekundarna počitniška bivališča v Sloveniji in zahodni Istri. Geografski vestnik 40(1):53–65

Kavrečič P (2020) Tourism and fascism. Tourism development on the East Italian Border. Contributions to Contemporary Hist 60(2):99–119. https://doi.org/10.51663/pnz.60.2.05

Kavrečič P, Metod Š (2021) Socialist-style tourist accomodation. In: Battilani P, Larrinaga C (eds) Coastal tourism in Southern Europe in the XXth century: new economy and material culture. Peter Lang, Berlin, pp 155–170

Koderman M (2014) Spatial analysis of second homes in the municipality of Piran. Acadca Turistica 7(2):179–191

Kukanja M (2015) Razvoj prehrambnega gostinstva na obalnem območju slovenske Istre: zgodovinski pregled. In: Šuligoj M (ed) Retrospektiva turizma Istre. Založba Univerze na Primorskem, Koper - Capodistria, pp 201–256

Moranda S (2005) The dream of a therapeutic regime: nature tourism in the German Democratic Republic, 1945-1978, Ph.D. The University of Wisconsin – Madison, Wisconsin. https://www.proquest.com/docview/305374270/abstract/5749F061FCCA4BC2PQ/1

Mordhorst M, Schwarzkopf S (2017) Theorising narrative in business history. Bus Hist 59(8):1155–1175. https://doi.org/10.1080/00076791.2017.1357697

Mücke P (2021) Hidden, yet visible workers of Czechoslovak international tourism. Macro and micro-historical views of ČEDOK's branches abroad and tour guides during the period of Late Socialism (1968-1989). J Tour Hist 13(1):75–94. https://doi.org/10.1080/1755182X.2020.1854353

Norkus Z (2012) Modeling in historical research practice and methodology: contributions from Poland. Hist Theor 51(2):292–304. https://doi.org/10.1111/j.1468-2303.2012.00627.x

Opačić VT, Koderman M (2019) Interrelations between spatial distribution of tourism and the second homes in Croatia and Slovenia. Geografski Vestnik 91(1):49–79. https://doi.org/10.3986/GV91103

Patterson PH (2001) The new class: consumer culture under socialism and the unmaking of the Yugoslav Dream, 1945-1991. Ph.D., United States - Michigan: University of Michigan

Perović L, Roksandić D, Velikonja M, Höpken W, Bieber F, Helsinki Committee for Human Rights in Serbia (eds) (2017) Yugoslavia from a historical perspective. Helsinki Committee for Human Rights in Serbia, Belgrade

Prinčič J (1997) Slovensko Gospodarstvo v Drugi Jugoslaviji. Modrijan, Ljubljana

Pucer A (1985) Portorož - 100 Let Organiziranega Turizma. Sprehod Skozi Čas. Katalog k Razstavi Pokrajinskega Arhiva Koper. Pokrajinski arhiv, Koper

Repe B (1996) Turizma Ni Mogoče Zavreti, Čeprav Bi Ga Prepovedali z Zakonom. In: Rozman F, Lazarević Ž (eds) Razvoj turizma v Sloveniji, 28. zborovanje slovenskih zgodovinarjev. Zbornik referatov. Zveza zgodovinskih društev Slovenije, Ljubljana, pp 157–164

Repe B (2006a) Oris razvoja turizma v Sloveniji po drugi svetovni vojni. In: Jerše S, Mihelič D (eds) Med srednjo Evropo in Sredozemljem: Vojetov zbornik. Založba ZRC, ZRC SAZU, Ljubljana, pp 705–715

Repe B (2006b) Turistična Zveza in Razvoj Turizma v Sloveniji Po Drugi Svetovni Vojni. In: Šajn S (ed) Turizem Smo Ljudje: Zbornik Ob 100-Letnici Ustanovitve Deželne Zveze Za Pospeševanje Prometa Tujcev Na Kranjskem, Turistične Zveze Slovenije in Organiziranega Turizma v Sloveniji. Turistična zveza Slovenije, Ljubljana, pp 61–99

Rogoznica D (2005) Obnova in Razvoj Turizma Na Območju Cone B Svobodnega Tržaškega Ozemlja (s Posebnim Poudarkom Na Okraju Koper). Acta Histriae 13(2):395–422

Rogoznica D (2008) La ricostruzione dell'industria alberghiera e lo sviluppo del settore turistico nell'area capodistriana (1945-1956). Quaderni XIX(1):377–388

Rogoznica D (2014) Aplikacija in uveljavitev modela socialističnega turizma na slovenski obali (1947-1990). Arhivi: glasilo arhivskega društva in arhivov Slovenije 37(2):73–84

Rosenbaum AT (2015) Leisure travel and real existing socialism: new research on tourism in the Soviet Union and Communist Eastern Europe. J Tour Hist 7(1–2):157–176. https://doi.org/10.1080/1755182X.2015.1062055
Stefan A (2023) Unpacking tourism in the Cold War: international tourism and commercialism in Socialist Romania, 1960s–1980s. Contemp Eur Hist 32(3):365–384. https://doi.org/10.1017/S0960777321000540
Šuligoj M (ed) (2015) Retrospektiva turizma Istre. Koper - Capodistria: Založba Univerze na Primorskem
Šuligoj M, Kavrečič P (2023) Characterization of workers' specific summer holiday practices in the Yugoslav Socialist socio-economic context. Southeast Eur Black Sea Stud 0(0):0. https://doi.org/10.1080/14683857.2023.2231677
Šuligoj M, Sinkovič L (2018) "Ladies and gentelmen, all aboard!" Travelling in the Northern Adriatic until the Second World War. Historicky Časopis 66(4):629–648
Taylor K (2010) My own Vikendica: Holiday Cottages as Idyll and investment. In: Grandits H, Taylor K (eds) Yugoslavia's sunny side. A history of tourism in socialism (1950s–1980s). Central European University Press, Budapest, pp 171–210. https://doi.org/10.1515/9786155211874-008
Tchoukarine I (2010) The Yugoslav road to international tourism. Opening, decentralization, and propaganda in the early 1950s. In: Grandits H, Taylor K (eds) Yugoslavia's sunny side. A history of tourism in socialism (1950s–1980s). Central european University Press, Budapest, pp 107–138
Tchoukarine I (2015) Yugoslavia's open-door policy and global tourism in the 1950s and 1960s. East Eur Polit Soc 29(1):168–188. https://doi.org/10.1177/0888325414551167
Trebše-Štolfa M (1996) Razvoj Turizma Na Območju Pokrajinskega Arhiva Koper Do Ukinitve Koprskega Okraja v Luči Upravno-Teritorialnih Sprememb. In: Bonin Z, Radulovič B (eds) . Arhivsko društvo Slovenije, Ljubljana, pp 12–18
Verginella M (2010) Zgodovinjenje slovensko-italijanske meje in obmejnega prostora. Acta Histriae 18(1/2):207–216
Vrtačnik K (2005) Tourism cycle(s) of portorož - portorose. Ann Series Hist Sociol 15(1):39–54
Webster C, Ivanov S (2016) Political ideologies as shapers of future tourism development. J Tour Fut 2(2):109–124. https://doi.org/10.1108/JTF-05-2015-0029

Metod Šuligoj is Full Professor in the Faculty of Tourism Studies—Turistica at the University of Primorska, Slovenia. His cross-disciplinary research interests include management in the tourism industry, the history of tourism, and special interest tourism, especially dark tourism.

Petra Kavrečič Božeglav is Associate Professor in the Faculty of Humanities at the University of Primorska, Slovenia. Her study field is focused on the history of tourism, history of everyday life, and regional history.

Concluding Remarks

A concluding chapter should present and reflect the results of the book's research interest and include a section on how the results contribute to the field. Therefore, with regard to this volume, tourism policy, like any other sectoral policy, is strongly influenced as much by the socio-economic configuration of the national community and its cultural values as by the institutional system within which it is formulated.

Sectoral policies can be considered the product of a complex and comprehensive set of factors, such as the political environment, values, ideologies, distribution of power, institutional structures, and the process leading to their definition.

In particular, in order to examine tourism policies, it is necessary to study the institutional structures that help shape them and the mechanisms of interaction that are established between the various actors that take part in this shaping process, not only public but also private actors.

The study of tourism policies must take into account both the causes and the consequences of political action, consisting of a series of actions that directly or indirectly influence all the various elements of tourism. Policymaking is part of a broader process that takes place in a larger and evolving political and territorial system, which influences policy choices and is in turn influenced by them, in a relationship of interaction and reciprocity that tends to repeat itself over time. We can undoubtedly say that the analysis of the evolution of the configuration of certain tourist destinations (Butler 1980), the subject of this volume, enriches the history of tourism in Europe.

The individual contents of the case studies offer new research perspectives thanks to the way in which states (in this book: France, Switzerland, Italy, Spain, and Yugoslavia) dealt with moments of economic and social crisis or rupture (such as wars and financial shortages) and how these represented a turning point for strengthening the improvement of a tourist destination.

The analysis of the individual case studies highlighted how localities or regions and businesses were able to change or 'invent a tourism destination' through

C. Larrinaga, D. Strangio (eds.), *Tourism Destinations and Policies in Europe During the 20th Century*, Contributions to Economics,
https://doi.org/10.1007/978-3-031-88447-4

tourism destination policies, adapting or showing resilience to the transformations of time.

Impact analyses of the tourism sector have often focused exclusively on the economic-financial impact, understood as an assessment of the financial costs and benefits deriving from the development and enjoyment of tourist goods and services and therefore included in operators' budgets. Tourism is in fact recognised as an economic activity that produces a strong induced effect and therefore contributes to local development: it is a transversal activity that covers vast areas, creates income and employment, and increases tax revenue. For example, tourism also increases the local capacity to attract investment in sectors other than tourism (Lankford and Howard 1994). For this impact assessment, the literature identifies input-output analyses as the best methodologies (Archer 1996). But the economic-financial aspect is one of the impact dimensions. The performance of tourism activities brings with it the creation of numerous externalities on the environment (Baumol and Oates 1975), on physical resources, and on the socio-economic system of the area in which it operates, which is also the subject of this volume.

Thus, the role of the state emerges as organiser and 'inspirer' in order to strengthen the tourism industry and thus the private sector, albeit in alternating phases and with varying degrees of intensity.

Tourism and the tourism industry are strongly linked to the territory and places, but they are also part of a general vision, which focuses on regional autonomy while moving in a unified context.

References

Archer B (1996) Economic impact analysis. Ann Tour Res 23(3):704–707

Baumol WJ, Oates WE (1975) The theory of environmental policy. Englewood Cliffs, Prentice-Halt

Butler R (1980) The concept of a tourism area cycle of evolution: Implications for management of resources. Canadian Geographer 24:5–12

Lankford SV, Howard DR (1994) Developing a tourism attitude impact scale. Ann Tour Res 24(1):121–139

The manufacturer's authorised representative in the EU is Springer Nature Customer Service Centre GmbH, Europaplatz 3, 69115 Heidelberg, Germany. If you have any concerns regarding our products, please contact ProductSafety@springernature.com

Printed and bound by CPI Group (UK) Ltd, Croydon, CR0 4YY
05/10/2026
02228153-0003